PSYCHOLOGY AND RELIGION

'*Psychology and Religion* is an authoritative survey of what we know about the psychology of religion. It is very clear and readable, and reflects Michael Argyle's considerable reputation and experience.'

Fraser Watts, University of Cambridge

Should psychology try to explain religion or try to understand it? Pioneers in psychology like Sigmund Freud and William James took opposing views on the matter, and it has been a hot debate ever since. Interestingly, though in the past psychology was used to attack religion, recent findings in the area have been more sympathetic to religion. How should we understand their relationship today?

Michael Argyle's new book introduces the psychology of religion. One of the world's most famous social psychologists, Argyle ranges over the whole of psychology to look at the results of psychology's study of religion, including those of his own important studies. It is full of fascinating and surprising insights into people and their religious worlds, and his belief in both the empirical value of psychology and the spiritual value of religion is evident in this comprehensive and accessible survey of what psychologists know about religion – and what they don't.

Michael Argyle is Emeritus Professor of Psychology, Oxford Brookes University. He is the best-selling author of over twenty books, including *The Psychology of Money* (with Adrian Furnham), *The Psychology of Religious Behaviour, Belief and Experience* (with Benjamin Beit-Hallahmi), *The Psychology of Happiness, Bodily Communication, The Psychology of Social Class*, and *The Social Psychology of Everyday Life* (all available from Routledge).

Michael Argyle
Psychology and Religion
An Introduction

London and New York

First published 2000
by Routledge
2 Park Square, Milton Park, Abingdon, Oxon, OX14 4RN

Simultaneously published in the USA and Canada
by Routledge
270 Madison Ave, New York NY 10016

Routledge is an imprint of the Taylor & Francis Group

Transferred to Digital Printing 2006

© 2000 Michael Argyle

Typeset in Adobe Garamond by RefineCatch Limited, Bungay, Suffolk

British Library Cataloguing in Publication Data
A catalogue record for this book is available from the British Library

Library of Congress Cataloging in Publication Data
Argyle, Michael.
    Psychology and religion : an introduction / Michael Argyle.
        p.   cm.
    Includes bibliographical references and indexes.
    ISBN 0-415-18906-3 (hardcover). – ISBN 0-415-18907-1 (pbk.)
    1. Psychology and religion. 2. Psychology. Religious. I. Title.
    BF51.A73   1999
    200'.1'9 – dc21   99-16956
                                                            CIP

ISBN 0-415-18906-3 (hbk)
ISBN 0-415-18907-1 (pbk)

Publisher's Note
The publisher has gone to great lengths to ensure the quality of this reprint
but points out that some imperfections in the original may be apparent

Printed and bound by CPI Antony Rowe, Eastbourne

CONTENTS

LIST OF TABLES

LIST OF FIGURES

PREFACE

This is a rather unusual book on the psychology of religion. As usual I try my very best to set down what is empirically true in the light of what is now extensive evidence on this subject. But I also take a sympathetic view of religion – I have faith in both enterprises, psychology and religion, and believe that in the end they can be harmonised. And this will not be achieved by psychology's explaining religion away. I have not solved this problem yet, but I have greatly enjoyed myself trying to. And I do not think that there is one-way traffic here where only the psychologists have access to the truth; some of it goes the other way, too. Religion is a very important part of human life and experience, and psychologists have something to learn from it.

So I hope that this book will be of value to psychologists, and also to those taking courses in religious studies, or psychology of religion for theology, or those who are just keen to understand religion further.

I have drawn in places from an earlier book, with Benny Beit–Hallahmi, *The Psychology of Religious Behaviour, Belief and Experience*. Harriet Harris, Anne Lee, Nick Emler and Fraser Watts have been very helpful in reading and commenting on chapters for me. I learnt about Korean mega-churches from Young-Gi Hong. I have also learnt a lot from members and discussion groups of the Oxford University Church to whom I have presented some of these materials, particularly to Brian Mountford and Marjorie Reeves. Also to Laurie Brown, Leslie Francis and other members of the Alister Hardy Society. Several of my colleagues in the Oxford Department of Experimental Psychology have provided valuable inputs: Gordon Claridge, Paul Harris, Mansur Lalljee.

Several of the Oxford libraries have been very helpful as always, particularly the Radcliffe Science Library, the Theology Faculty Library, the Lower Camera, and the PPE Room of the Bodleian.

Michael Argyle
Easter 1999

ACKNOWLEDGEMENTS

While the publisher has made every effort to contact all copyright holders, if any have been inadvertently omitted the publisher will be pleased to make the necessary arrangments at the first opportunity.

1

THE RELATION BETWEEN PSYCHOLOGY AND RELIGION

Classic conflicts between science and religion

In the 'scientific revolution' of the sixteenth century early scientists like Francis Bacon saw no conflict between science and religion, and were prepared for science to be subordinated to theology. In the seventeenth century, Newton and Boyle thought that the laws that they were discovering, such as the law of gravity, were God's laws, that they were celebrating God's craftsmanship in designing the universe. They looked on the universe as a giant clockwork system which had been wound up by God; Newton thought that God was still actively sustaining the natural world. These scientists were religious men themselves, and their work was welcomed by theologians.

But the seeds of the first trouble were sown in the sixteenth century with Copernicus' theory that the earth is not the centre of everything, but goes round the sun, and that the earth moves, and rotates. He argued that this could explain the known movements of the sun, moon and planets better than theories of spheres and epicycles, but this was felt by many to be in conflict with the Bible. The theory was gradually accepted by other astronomers, such as the Italian Galileo, who was made to appear before the Grand Inquisitor and spent the last eight years of his life under house arrest in Florence for believing and teaching the Copernican doctrine. It was mainly Protestant scientists in England and Holland who carried on Copernicus' work, and the Germans, led by Kepler. Protestant theologians were quite accepting: Calvin declared himself in favour of scientific work and said that not everything in scripture need be taken literally. Luther said that the moon was a symbol of divine care for him but he also recognised that its light came from the sun. He referred to the universe as a 'theatre of the glory of God' (McGrath, 1997). Twelve hundred years earlier, Augustine had accepted that there was a natural order and was quite happy for the creation story of Genesis to be reinterpreted in a less literal way. Historians have suggested that Protestantism was more receptive to science than Catholicism, but in fact the situation was more variable than this (Brooke, 1991). However, to this day, as we shall see later, very few successful scientists are Catholics, though many are Protestants, and even more are agnostics.

The Bible does not state the date of the creation, but literal interpretations of Genesis have been used for centuries to produce theories about the age and history of the earth. In 1650 James Ussher, Archbishop of Armagh, calculated its age from those of biblical characters and concluded that it was created in 4004 BC on Saturday 22 October at 8 a.m. This view was not shared by geologists; some of them held a party in 1996 to celebrate the earth's '6,000th birthday'. In the nineteenth century Lord Kelvin put the age of the earth at 400 million years, a very different figure. Curiously this discrepancy does not seem to have worried religious people much, quite unlike the disputes over the solar system and the later trouble over evolution. There was some friction, however; in 1833 Charles Lyell resigned his chair of geology at King's College, London, partly because of trouble with Bishop Copleston over Lyell's refusal to believe in the Flood, though Copleston said that any conflicts with geology could be accommodated by some biblical reinterpretation (Brooke, 1991).

One of the greatest conflicts between science and religion has been over evolution. There had been happy co-operation between science and religion in the early nineteenth century in Britain, but after Darwin things changed. In 1859 he produced his *Origin of Species*, which offered an account of the origins of mankind that appeared totally at odds with that in the book of Genesis. According to Darwin man developed from monkeys and simpler creatures, by chance; there was no design or purpose behind it, and no special creation. The situation was made more acute in Britain by his colleague T. H. Huxley having a lot of fun about our proposed monkey origins. The theory is not directly verifiable, and there are problems about the lack of intermediate species in the fossil record, but it has been very widely accepted. In 1860, at a meeting of the British Association in Oxford, T. H. Huxley had his famous debate, which he won, with the Bishop of Oxford, Samuel Wilberforce. When asked if he would prefer to be descended from an ape on his grandmother's or his grandfather's side Huxley replied that he would rather be descended from an ape than from a bishop (Brooke, 1991). In 1925 William Jennings Bryan, in the Scopes 'monkey trial' in the USA, tried to prevent evolution's being taught in American schools. He lost but there are still several states where fundamentalists have prevented evolution's being taught, or where it must be presented as a hypothesis along with others. Evolution can be seen as God's way of carrying out his job of creation, so there is no need to assume it is in conflict with religion.

Socio-biology is the application of biological principles, particularly of evolution and survival value, to human behaviour. This has had some success in understanding human emotional expression, family relationships, and also altruism. The problem is that we do not know in these cases how much is due to innate biological factors and how much to socialisation, learning from the culture. Some altruistic behaviour can be explained by the selfish gene and related hypotheses, by saying that genes will survive better if individuals help their close kin for example. Studies of birds have found that they do indeed help close kin, and that when this happens more of the young survive. However, we do not yet know how far these principles work for humans. Altruism could also be explained by the close bonds formed with kin, or by social expectations that we should care for our relatives, and is affected by religious and other ideas in people's heads. In any case this hypothesis does not explain altruism to those outside the immediate circle of family and friends, or the complex forms of moral thinking in which people engage, which are very unlike the mechanical responses which animal models suggest. This is discussed further in Chapter 13.

Dawkins (1991) has taken an atheistic position claiming that evolution can explain all, including religion. So the existence of religious beliefs and institutions would be explained entirely in terms of their survival value. But any ideas, whether religious or scientific, would be discredited and have no claim to any kind of truth, if they are simply the result of blind evolutionary processes. Others argue that religion is more a matter of social evolution, of the gradual discovery of religious ideas (Campbell, 1975). There is certainly some continuity since the earliest times in religious practice, experience and beliefs, and there has been almost continuous debate and trial and error.

In 1996 there was another debate at Oxford, this time in the University Church, between the ethologist Richard Dawkins and Keith Ward, the Regius Professor of Theology. Dawkins demanded that religious propositions, such as the existence of God, should be treated in the same way as scientific ones, and that they should be capable of being confirmed or disconfirmed in the same way. However, Ward (1996) argued that they are not like this at all: 'its importance [i.e. the concept of God] lies in the fact that it is essential to the rational practice of worship and prayer' (p. 104), it is about seeking personal transformation, and the human concern with truth, beauty and goodness.

As many have pointed out, evolution has not been able to explain human consciousness, or our concern with rationality, beauty or morals. To the reductionist materialist, consciousness is an irrelevant extra, unless it can be shown to enhance survival. The truth of mathematical principles does not depend on their being good for our health or enabling us to have more children.

Resolving the conflicts between science and religion

We have seen that the usual way in which these conflicts have been dealt with has been to say that science and religion have different spheres of operation. Calvin, Luther, Augustine and many other divines have been prepared to say that the book of Genesis, for example, need not be interpreted literally, that matters of physical fact are for the physical sciences to decide. As Wittgenstein was to say later, they are different language games, both of them legitimate. Not all will accept this solution: for example, biblical fundamentalists and scientific materialists.

However, religion has an interest in some factual matters, such as the resurrection, miracles, and the after-life (a fact only verifiable later). And it could be argued that religion does take account of other facts such as the experience of God, the nature of ritual, the history of religion, and the effects of religion, including the possible efficacy of prayer.

There are problems with the boundaries of science too. Physics is no longer about clockwork universes and billiard balls, but is far more abstract and mysterious. Cosmology, for example, deals with such matters as the beginning and end of time, and the limits of the universe, taking us very close to theological matters. Particle physics has produced a new view of the material world; it doesn't say anything about God or salvation, but it is much less 'materialistic' than nineteenth-century physics had been. Eddington said that religion first became possible for a reasonable scientific man in about 1927. Heisenberg, Bohr and Einstein had shown that (1) light behaves both like a particle and like a wave, and it is possible to hold two quite different models of it at the same time, (2) the act of measuring, for example, the position of an electron alters what the scientist is trying to measure (this is very obvious in the case of observing human behaviour), (3) one physical state gives rise to the next, but only in terms of probability, there is no precise determination, at the level of particles, (4) the smallest particles, quarks, seem like ultimate building-blocks of matter, but they lose their identity when absorbed into atoms, which work as a whole. At the level of particle physics, determinism, reductionism and the independent existence of the material world fail, and it is necessary to entertain contradictory models of it simultaneously (Brooke, 1991).

Peacocke (1993), in his Gifford Lectures, developed a way of finding co-operation between science and religion, using science to interpret theology. He sees the whole process of the emergence of life and the evolution of mankind as part of the process of creation, so that physics and biology can illuminate how this was done. It ends with the appearance of consciousness and human personality: we are conscious not only of the outside world, but also of ourselves, we can control our own behaviour and make choices, which are rational, in taking account of the consequences, using abstract ideas and language. We also have further yearnings, beyond the satisfaction of biological needs, to understand life and death and to fulfil ourselves.

He thinks that all this can be partly explained by lower-order processes like evolution, but that some of it can be interpreted only as deliberate design. This is supported by the discovery of the 'anthropic principle'. It has been realised that the constants of the physical universe are exactly right for the emergence of the substance carbon, and other features necessary for the evolution of life (Barrow and Tipler, 1986). Another line of thinking points to the parallels between religion and mathematics. Penrose (1994) pointed out that the laws and principles of mathematics are not just ideas in our minds, but 'inhabit an actual world of their own that is timeless and without physical location'. They are not created by us but are discovered and are found to apply to the physical world. In all these ways they have some similarities to religion.

Recent thinking about science and religion, as seen in successive sets of Gifford Lectures, has realised that the two language games here are not entirely distinct (Barbour, 1990). Under the influence of logical positivism it was thought for a time that scientific propositions had to be verifiable or falsifiable to have meaning. It was soon realised that some propositions were meaningful whether they were falsifiable or not, and that scientific theories were often linked rather indirectly to the data, which were themselves theory-laden. Kuhn (1970) pointed out that scientific theories were not just intellectual theories, but involved commitment to a whole style of thinking and research, assumptions and research methods, which he called 'paradigms'. Findings were meaningful only within the paradigm; adopting the paradigm was a partly irrational process. Paradigms were like social movements, and were influenced by social, political and economic factors. This view has been criticised on the grounds that scientific changes are less sudden and less irrational, but the main point has been widely accepted. So scientific paradigms were in some ways rather like religions.

Another version of this doctrine was due to Lakatos (cited in Peterson et al., 1998), who argued that groups of scientists are committed to 'research programmes' which have a hard core of ideas that are not open to falsification, together with auxiliary hypotheses that could be modified or rejected. It has been suggested that theology can be seen as a research programme of this kind too (Peterson et al., 1998).

Religion, seen as a research programme, can be said to have its data and its core theory. The data may be thought to be sacred writings, or religious phenomena and experiences. We shall suggest later that the psychology of religion may be able to provide some of these data. On the other hand, science may be a poor model for religion, in that in science there is no direct knowledge, less emotionality, and little commitment to behaviour.

New conflicts between psychology and religion

We have seen that the main way of resolving the conflict between religion and the physical sciences is to say that science deals with the physical world and religion with the inner world. But psychology deals with the inner world too, and tries to do so in a scientific way, so how do we resolve this conflict? There are further problems. Psychology even attacks consciousness, in discovering where it is located and what it does. It has had considerable success in discovering laws from which human behaviour can be predicted. Explanations can even be given for why individuals hold beliefs. There are experiments on the production of unusual states of consciousness – by the influence of drugs, for example. Moral behaviour and beliefs can be studied similarly. And there is a lot of research that explains how human personality develops and functions. So all the spheres of human activity and experience which have been regarded as the special sphere of religion have also been studied by psychologists in a quite different, and scientific, way. We will look at some of these issues more carefully and see how different varieties of psychology have tackled them.

Behaviourism

There are no behaviourists any more; they are extinct. Pavlov, Skinner and other early psychologists studied very simple forms of learning, mainly in animals, and they discounted or ignored conscious experience in humans; reports of it were sometimes referred to as 'verbal behaviour'. No reference was made to feelings, thinking, or other kinds of subjective activity. This approach had some success with humans in the practice of certain kinds of behaviour therapy, especially for phobias. Some behaviourists attacked religion, saying that they could explain it in terms of learning processes – it might be due to those involved having simply been rewarded for their religious behaviour. The brain was seen as a 'black box', and there were models of how it worked; it was sometimes seen as a kind of telephone switchboard, later as a computer.

Behaviourism was abandoned during the 'cognitive revolution' in psychology, which recognised not only consciousness but also its contents – plans, rules, values, theories and explanations, and whole worlds of experience, such as morals, mathematics, and the study of science. It was found that even animals have some cognitive activity; for example, rats have 'mental maps' of the mazes they have learnt. An important part of the human inner world is language, giving us words for referring to and categorising events and experiences, and for communicating with one another.

Consciousness, now accepted by all, in some cases reluctantly, has come to be regarded as the greatest unsolved scientific problem, the 'ultimate mystery'. Psychologists, philosophers, neurologists and workers in machine intelligence have been trying to understand and explain it (Marcel and Bisiach, 1988). It is generally assumed that consciousness depends on the presence of higher levels of neural process, which have evolved, though how they produce conscious experience is the ultimate mystery, which seems to be insoluble.

Conscious experiences do more than reflect the outside world; they have 'qualia', that is, awareness of the quality of the colours, such as red, as well as the feeling of emotions and motivations. Pleasure is the subjective state corresponding to reinforcement (Rolls, 1997). To be conscious is to be able to manipulate items in thought and imagery, together with the associated emotional imagery (Weiskrantz, 1997). These neural events which have a conscious side are able to take a causal role in directing behaviour, and can take account of reasons, values and long-term plans, as well as imagining the likely outcomes. Neural events and the corresponding conscious experiences may be two sides of the same thing, two models that operate at the same time, just as light can be waves or particles, and as a piece of wood can be described in terms of molecules, or in terms of its hardness, strength and colour (Searle, 1984). Patterns of causation can occur at the higher level of analysis: for example, of volition, choice, initiation and monitoring of behaviour.

The biological advantage given by consciousness might be (1) the capacity to solve new problems, or deal with new situations, by being able to manipulate images of acts and events, (2) being able to imagine the consequences of several different possible acts, or (3) a superior power to deal with other people through being able to imagine their point of view, to build up models of them so that their behaviour can be predicted better. It has been suggested that the reason the human brain became so large was to deal with the complexity of social life in large groups of primates (Humphrey, 1983). There is a close connection between consciousness and language, and it has been suggested that conscious thoughts are often like imagined verbal communications to others (Barlow, 1987).

The modern equivalent of behaviourism is the use of computer models of the brain. Computer programs can model cognitive processes very well, indeed, they can perform them better, as with chess-playing machines.

Such machines can 'try out in imagination' thousands of alternative moves, but it does not follow that they are 'thinking'. Searle (1984) argued that a person locked in a 'Chinese room' equipped only with a rule book, and who could send and receive messages, could give the impression of speaking Chinese though he had no knowledge of the language or the messages being received and answered. The person inside the room did not understand the messages, and the same is true of machines that simulate mental processes – to understand it is necessary to be conscious. There are some other differences between brains and computers: computers can use only the programs that have been put in, and they cannot solve new problems. Machine intelligence experts are no longer prepared to say that machines which can play chess or mimic other kinds of thinking are 'conscious' (Michie, personal communication). Penrose (1994) said that consciousness depends on brain-functions which are non-computable; they are not machine-like operations, but depend on some new kind of organisation in the brain.

Psychoanalysis

Psychoanalysis poses a quite different challenge to religion from that of behaviourism. Freud offered explanations of some of the main religious phenomena; for example, that God is a projected father-figure, and ritual an obsessional neurosis. Furthermore these 'explanations' of religion suggest that religion is an infantile, neurotic and irrational activity. Freud himself thought that religion was an illusion and would fade away as science became more influential. It is generally recognised that finding a possible psychological origin for a belief does not imply that the belief is false, if there are grounds for holding it, but it may weaken the beliefs of those who accept the explanation. In fact the father-projection theory has received some modest support, the neurotic theory of ritual has not, and the further theory of the societal origins of religion is simply untestable, as well as very implausible, as we explain in Chapter 7.

Psychoanalysis is unlike most of the rest of contemporary psychology in making less claim to be a branch of normal science, and as a result is not taken very seriously by most academic or research psychologists. Parts of it have been subject to rigorous research, and Freud's ideas about the psychology of religion have been investigated in this way. Jung's ideas are more compatible with religion than Freud's but are even more difficult to test, perhaps impossible. As we shall see, they are closer to religion in some ways, but even more difficult to verify in a scientific way.

Theologians, however, have been very interested in psychoanalysis, and have found it more sympathetic to their outlook than more scientific varieties of psychology. It appears to deal with some of the same topics as religion – the search for salvation, close relationships, moral decisions and guilt feelings, for example. A number of theologians have looked for parallels between the two systems. Undertaking a course of psychoanalysis is similar to religious instruction and conversion. In both cases you have to adopt a new style of thinking, follow daily and weekly rituals, and hope to be changed. In becoming a Christian, for example, you have to believe in the Father, the Son and the Holy Spirit; in being psychoanalysed, to believe in the Ego, the Super-ego and the Id (Robert Thouless, personal communication). And there is evidence that both kinds of activity are good for you. We explore later the similarity between getting married and making a leap of faith in religious conversion. Many more parallels can be dreamt up with little difficulty. Psychoanalytic ideas can be used to inter-pret the meaning of Bible stories, like that of Adam and Eve, in terms of sexual symbolism (see p. 102).

The religious life and the pursuit of religious truth have something in common with psychoanalysis. Watts and Williams (1988) suggest that the knowledge of and insights into oneself which psychotherapy may give provide a good model of religion. Both in religion and in psychotherapy people are seeking salvation, trying to solve their problems and find out how to live a better life. And both activities are quite different from the physical sciences.

However, there seems to be no way of deciding which, if any, of the parallels and interpretations suggested by Freudian theory are correct – and this is why psychoanalysis has not been accepted by most mainstream psychologists. Furthermore there are many religious phenomena for which Freudian theory does not seem to have an explanation. God as a father-figure, yes, but not the Holy Spirit or similar entities. Worship perhaps, but not sacrifice. Not religious experience. The theory of ritual has not worked.

The conclusion is that we must turn to more rigorously scientific kinds of psychology, if we can do so while retaining an interest in the topics relevant to religion.

Social and related areas of mainstream psychology

Social and related areas of psychology are broad fields, covering social behaviour and beliefs, as well as research into well-being and social relationships. They include most aspects of the psychology of religion. They are more rigorous than psychoanalysis, but less reductive than behaviourism. They include some biological topics, such as the origins of facial expressions, and some aspects of linguistics, since most human social behaviour involves speech. They overlap with parts of sociology. And they take note of the historical and cultural setting of behaviour, and make use of ideas from anthropology and sociology. We may note that the founders of sociology assumed that religion was the result of deprivation and would probably fade away through secularisation. Sociology certainly studies behaviour, but it takes account of the meaning of the behaviour to those who produce it and those who respond to it. These are varied topics, but they have in common a commitment to rigorous experimental or statistical methods of research.

Personality psychology also takes account of individual differences in personality, but does so in an empirical manner, to find the origins of personalities and how they function in different situations; this is rather different from the treatment of the topic of personality by philosophers.

We look for laws of social behaviour, in the form of regularities of causality or correlation, the causes and effects of behaviour. This has been successful in locating such regularities, and they are often found to be replicated in many later studies. This makes possible some degree of prediction, though this is a matter of probability rather than prediction of individual behaviour. In the case of language, the aim has never been to predict what someone will say, but only the rules that he or she will follow when saying it.

There are 'softer' approaches to social psychology, which say that experiments are inappropriate, since they treat people like machines, or that there are no laws, as Kenneth Gergen (1982) has argued. The answer to this is that many laws have been found, by the use of experiments and other methods. Harre and Secord (1972) argued similarly that we should not do experiments, but should try to understand behaviour by asking those involved for 'accounts' which explain why they acted as they did. However, this does not lead to a body of empirical laws which could be used for practical purposes, or to a body of theory to explain social phenomena in general.

Social psychology usually adopts a 'non-ontological' approach to questions of religion or politics; that is, it avoids taking any position on whether beliefs are true or not. It may be possible to have a double vision here, the external view of psychology and the internal view of those who have the beliefs or experiences. This is different from the idea of keeping religion and science separate; it is saying that the two points of view can operate simultaneously. In the case of politics, psephologists seem to have no difficulty in understanding why other people vote as they do, and then on occasion voting themselves. In the case of music something similar happens: music students may have to take courses in the physics of musical sounds; this does not persuade them that Beethoven is bunk, but merely explains some of the principles of sound production. The horticulturalist grows roses, and can advise on the use of manure or fertilisers, but to re-create the beauty of the rose requires an artist or a poet. Again, the same person can play both roles. Creative writing and art can be studied by psychologists, but no one could predict what is going to be created without creating it themselves. In all these cases the object of study, e.g. art or music, mathematics or politics, is taken seriously, and accepted as valid, not seen as an illusion to be explained away by psychology.

This means that we can accept the findings of social and related branches of psychology without anxiety that they will debunk religion. They may help us to understand how religion works, as physics does for music. They may be able to provide new data about religion which were not previously available. This book presents materials of this kind. They may provide us with a wealth of data about religion; for example, about the nature of religious experience, the basic phenomenon of religion. And psychological research can provide crucial data on the effects of religion, whether it is good for us and, if so, from which kinds of religion we can benefit.

A number of research methods have been used in the psychology of religion. (1) *Social surveys* have been widely used to find the extent of religious activity in a population, how it varies with age, gender, class and other factors, and historical changes. More sophisticated designs have used statistics to find the independent influence of separate variables, and the causal sequence of events leading to healing, for example. Research on the effect of religion on health, mental health and happiness is done in a similar way, using self-report, or objective measures of well-being. (2) *Experiments* have the great advantage of making clear which the direction of causation is, and of holding unwanted variables constant. However, few experiments have been done in this field, the main ones being on the triggers for religious experience and the effects of religion on helping and other good works. Some of these experiments have been designed to test alternative theories about the causes of events. (3) *Field experiments* are where the study is carried out in a real-life setting, e.g. giving people different drugs in church. (4) *Quasi-experimental designs* are where use is made of naturally occurring phenomena, without the investigator's having to make any interventions. Studies of the effects of conversion, or of joining sects, are examples. Some of these involve longitudinal methods, assessing people at two or more points in time. (5) *Individual differences* are studied by correlational methods, and by comparing contrasted groups. Statistical methods are used to find the dimensions of religiosity, and how they relate to other personality traits. Some studies use physiological measures, e.g. of brain activity.

What follows

Chapters 2–3 describe the development of religion in children, the phenomenon of conversion and other changes with age, and whether religion is associated with any particular kind of personality.

Chapters 4–5 report research into religious experience: how far is it universal? what are the effects on those who undergo it? what are the worldly conditions that produce it?

Chapters 6–7 deal with religious beliefs, what people believe, what is meant by holding religious beliefs, whether they are literal or metaphorical, theories of symbolism due to Freud and Jung.

Chapters 8–9 describe the main forms of religious ritual, such as worship, healing and sacrifice, using ideas from anthropology to explain how they work, and psychological research to find out if, for example, healing works.

Chapters 10–11 ask whether religion is good for us, in terms of happiness, health, mental health, and other benefits, and whether there are any costs.

Chapters 12–13 look at the links between religion and morals and whether there are benefits for the community in the form of better moral and pro-social behaviour.

Chapters 14–15 document whether there has been a decline of religion in modern society and a growth of secularisation. It examines the rise of new churches and sects, in the West but also in the East and the Third World.

Conclusions

1 Astronomy, geology and evolutionary theory have produced major conflicts between science and religion. One solution is to say that science deals with the physical world, religion with the inner world. However, psychology claims to study and explain subjective phenomena too.

2 Behaviourism was quite incompatible with religion, but is now extinct, and conscious experiences are no longer ignored. They are the most immediate evidence for a non-material world. Psychoanalysis claimed to explain religion away, but there is little empirical support for its claims, or for its argument that psychological explanation for beliefs implies that the beliefs are false.

3 Mainstream psychology deals with some occurrences regarded as part of the phenomena of religion, such as moral behaviour, personality, attitude change, and beliefs. However, a non-ontological approach makes it possible to study these things while making no judgement on their reality.

4 A final step can be made, to take seriously the objects of experience and belief, as in the cases of mathematics and music. The same could be done for religion. The role of psychology now is to help to understand rather than to undermine.

2

SOCIALISATION

Introduction

In all human communities the religious beliefs and practices of the society are passed on to children by various kinds of instruction. The same applies to many other aspects of the culture; all are aspects of the shared way of life. Children brought up in Israel, Italy or Kyoto are likely to have religious views which are similar to those of most other people in these places. There is evidently a strong effect of the surrounding culture on religious beliefs and behaviour. This is brought about by social learning in the family, and by religious education in churches, Sunday schools and religious schools. The effects of these influences are powerful but not always successful as we shall see. We shall see in this book that in many ways religion is a social phenomenon, so it is no surprise that individuals have to learn about it from society. But is religion *only* something that has been learnt from society? Is this a complete explanation of why there is religion?

Social influence of the family

The family is in a strong position to influence the religious beliefs and activities of the children. For several years children are not aware that there is any other view than that of their parents, and are happy to accept the parental religious views uncritically.

Many studies have found that the religious behaviour and beliefs of children resemble those of their parents. When the children are of student age, for example, the correlations with parents are between .50 and .60, highest for church attendance, rather lower for prayer. Furthermore the similarity between parents and children for religious behaviour is closer than that for political, sporting or other areas of behaviour (Cavalli-Sforza et al., 1982).

However, this parent–child similarity is not all due to parents influencing their children. It may be partly due to similarity of personality, in turn due to genetic factors. It may be partly due to having the same environment, including the same religious environment. And there may be reciprocal influence of children on parents – it is not unknown for children to convert their parents. Nevertheless parents clearly do influence their children. There is another way of tackling this problem, asking people to rate the importance of different influences on their religious development. Hunsberger found that mothers were rated as the most important influence, fathers a little less and friends a lot less (Hood et al., 1996).

Parental influence is greatest, as shown by parent–child similarity, under certain conditions. These are:

- close relationships between parents and children
- children still living at home
- the marked effect of the mother's beliefs (mothers have more effect than fathers, though this may change now that more mothers are going out to work)
- parents holding the same religious beliefs.

Fundamentalist Protestants and to some extent Catholics have a very strong desire to keep their children in the faith; they demand more obedience, in religious matters and others, and use coercion and corporal punishment to enforce it (Ellison and Sherkat, 1993; Danso et al., 1997).

How exactly do parents exert all this influence? Erickson (1992) studied 900 16- to 18-year-olds, and by using statistical modelling found that the greatest factor was adolescents taking part in religious activity in the home; for example, taking part in prayers and Bible reading. Parents often take their children to church with them; 68 per cent of conservative Protestant parents did so, but only 27 per cent of mainstream Protestants

(Bibby, 1978). This all involves two kinds of social learning: modelling the parents, and behavioural participation which is reinforced. Parents also influence their children's religion by talking to them a lot about religion, which has more effect on girls than on boys for some reason (Hoge, Petrillo et al., 1982). Boston (1988) describes a remarkable example of a brother and sister aged 5 and 6 who preached hellfire to other children as they arrived at school; their father had been arrested for similar roadside preaching.

During adolescence there are often shifts towards greater or lesser religiosity, indeed, there is evidence of both, that is, there is conversion and deconversion. Ozarak (1989) followed up several hundred teenagers and found that those from the most religious homes became more religious while those from the least religious homes became less so, at an average age of 14.5. Their family background limited the amount of change in religiosity. Peers had an effect, but this was limited by the fact that the teenagers chose friends who were similar already.

There has been much study of 'apostasy', which refers to those who were brought up in a family that belonged to a church but who later have no such attachment. Hunsberger and Brown (1984) studied 836 Australian psychology students; there was an apostasy rate of 36 per cent, which is higher than the 10–20 per cent found with North American students. The ones most likely to leave their church came from families where religious emphasis, especially from the mother, was weak, and were individuals who had an intellectual orientation towards religion, that is they had early doubts, and liked arguing about religion with their friends. They went through a great deal of intellectual activity before deciding to leave. Wilson and Sherkat (1994) followed up 1,562 American high school pupils from their final year over sixteen years. Those with strong ties to family were less likely to leave the family religion and more likely to return if they did; early marriage and parenthood had the same effect, but only for males. Those involved in the counter-culture of the 1960s were less likely to return. Does all this apostasy show a failure of socialisation processes? Not really, since it is partly due to weaker family influence, and to stronger peer-group influence. And apostasy is often temporary, those involved returning to the faith of their family and childhood later, sometimes when in their thirties.

As well as apostates, there are also 'amazing believers', who believe despite not having been brought up as members of a church. Hunsberger and Altemeyer (1995, cited in Hood et al., 1996) studied some of these by screening large numbers of students; they are quite rare. They had experienced a little early religious training after all, and they had been converted while trying to cope with some crisis. When we discuss conversion later in the chapter we shall show the importance of peer-group pressure, and this is one explanation of these amazing believers.

The peer group is a second source of childhood socialisation, in matters of religion and everything else. From about 13 children are working out their religious beliefs, with the co-operation of their friends, leading to the crystallisation of their beliefs by about 15, often changing their minds at about $14\frac{1}{2}$. However, the similarity with friends is less than that with parents on religious attitudes, .20 v. .60 in one study (Cavalli-Sforza et al., 1982). Peers have more influence than parents on matters of sport and other leisure pursuits. And children rate friends below parents and church as sources of influence on religion (Hood et al., 1996). However, after children leave school friends become more important than parents: at college, for example (Ozarak, 1989). There is also some reverse causation here, in that children may choose as friends those who agree with them over religion.

Friends are, however, important as a source of religious conversion, as we shall see; powerful social support is a major factor in attracting people to sects (p. 225). And churches are very cohesive bodies, in that many people say that their best friends belong to their church (p. 152).

Religious education

In all communities the young are instructed in matters of religion or doctrine. This may be because it is thought necessary for the survival of society, or for the good of their souls. It is done by the study of sacred books (for example, learning Bible stories), instruction in myths and theology, and taking part in rituals. It may be carried out by priests or special experts. Pratt (1950) believed that for later religious life it was essential to be immersed during childhood in a religious community, in order to learn the symbols of religion and their emotional associations; he thought that childhood was a critical period for the acquisition of religion. But as we shall see shortly, children cannot really understand religion in any but a literal sense until some time in adolescence, so that what they are taught has to be related to what they can understand.

Educational methods are very successful in all the many topics which are taught in school, but the effects of Sunday schools and church schools have been found to be quite weak. Those who go or have been may be more religious, but this is mainly due to the influence of their parents, and when this has been allowed for very little impact of religious education (RE) can be found. Francis (1987) studied 5,000 English 11-year-olds, and found that going to a Catholic school had a small positive effect on attitudes to Christianity, but that going to a Church of England school actually had a small negative effect. This is a rather surprising result, whose explanation is not clear. Francis replicated this result with 15–16-year-olds, and the prediction of church attendance and attitudes to prayer (Francis and Brown, 1991). Parental church attendance was a more important predictor.

American studies have found much the same. They, too, found that parental attitudes or church attendance were the more important factor (Hoge et al., 1982), and that the most positive effect was for Catholic schools (Hyde, 1990). Hood et al. (1996) conclude: 'The bulk of the evidence suggests that church-related school attendance has little direct effect on adolescent religiousness per se' (p. 85). It has been found, however, that knowledge about religion can be taught, and of course it is taught in regular schools. In order to influence religious behaviour, however, taking part in church services where there is a lot of participation in the ritual is more effective (Garrison, 1976). And the effect on behaviour and attitudes may be not through education but through ordinary processes of social influence such as conformity to group norms, and attachment to the group and its leaders.

Conversion

By conversion is meant a change towards more religious belief, behaviour and commitment. In the 'classical paradigm' of conversion research it was assumed that conversions were sudden, such as those produced by early revivalism, and that those concerned were 'born again', with a radical change in the self, on the model of St Paul. The conversions studied by William James from biographical and other literary sources were mostly 'spontaneous', which perhaps means that the causal factors were not known or not mentioned. Research on conversion has taken a new impetus with the rise of sects and cults, the 'new religious movements' (NRMs) which have converted a lot of young people since the 1960s.

However, Clark (1929) studied 2,174 conversions and found that only 33 per cent were sudden, the rest being 'gradual', that is, they took place over a period of time. In many cases there is really 'intensification' of an existing state of faith, or 'switching' to a quite similar denomination. Conversions to some of the new sects and cults may be different, because special methods of persuasion, which have been compared to brainwashing, are used (see p. 226).

Most conversions happen to adolescents. Johnson (1959) combined five American surveys, with altogether 15,000 respondents, and found an average age of 15.2, with quite a narrow range above and below. Similar studies in the USA and elsewhere have found average ages of 15 and 16, and this has remained the same over the forty years since such studies began (Hood et al., 1996). There is a gender difference here: girls are converted one to two years earlier than boys. Some individuals are converted later, and it is quite common in students. However, conversions are rare after the age of 30, though a few are born again, or have 'mystical conversions', both being cases of intensification. Bucke (1901) described forty-three cases of famous historical saints and mystics, who had a mystical conversion at the age of 33, or very close to it. However, Kose (1996) studied seventy British converts to Islam and found that conversion had happened at an average age of 30.

Some theories of conversion

Social psychology
Conversions may in one sense be due to God, but the phenomena can also be explained by familiar principles of social psychology.

This view of religious conversion is very straightforward. Attitudes and beliefs are being changed all the time by politicians, advertisers and others, and the conditions under which this happens are now well known. It is the result of the skills of orators and other communicators, their relationship with those being influenced, the personalities of the recipients, and the relations with groups holding the old and the new beliefs. There can be sudden changes of beliefs, for example, after particularly persuasive or noisy public meetings, or after getting to know and being accepted by members of a new group. The age of 15 can also be explained – this is the time when identity-formation is taking place very actively. Attachment to new groups is an important part of the process of becoming independent of the parents. Joining a new group, sometimes a deviant group, sometimes temporarily, is a way of showing one's independence of one's parents, sometimes of rebelling against them.

There is evidence that these principles apply to conversion. It is found, for example, that converts have had weaker relations with their fathers than matched unconverted individuals (Ullman, 1982). Converts are also found to have been more socially isolated. The personal influence of members of the new religious group is an important cause of conversion, and there is often attachment to these individuals. Whitam (1968) followed up 3,000 Billy Graham converts: acquisition of new friends was said to be the main factor.

Evangelical, revivalist or charismatic meetings are an important source of conversion, and again familiar principles of social psychology apply. These principles are used by the organisers. The Billy Graham meetings, for example, used a large choir singing emotional hymns; an emotional address reminded people of their mortality; they were asked to make public decisions, and there was a follow-up meeting with a minister from a local church to form a permanent link with them. These meetings were most successful when they were very large, when 5.3 per cent of those present came forward to make decisions.

What we have not yet fully explained by the social psychological approach is the occurrence of sudden conversions, and the intense emotions often attached to these events. Jacobs (1987) noted the similarity between conversion and falling in love, in particular in charismatic groups. Curiously, religious conversion has been used as a model to explain falling in love. In both cases there is a sudden attachment to a new person, a leap of faith, which is irrational in being based on incomplete evidence, but which can cause great joy.

Batson's theory

William James (1902) thought that those who are converted had been experiencing a profound personal crisis beforehand. Batson et al. (1993) developed this idea and proposed that conversion is a case of creative problem-solving, producing a new way of looking at things and interpreting events, on the model of the figure–ground reversal in perception – this is where a diagram of a cube, for example, can be seen in two quite different ways. The stimulus for such a change is discontent, especially with the self, an 'existential crisis', i.e. loss of meaning in life. Although others may influence the outcome, the individual works over the problem, like the 'incubation' of a problem needing a creative solution.

The belief of James and Batson that there is always a personal crisis before conversion has received some empirical support. For example, Ullman (1982), in the study described above, found that her converts said that they had been under personal stress for two years. However, all of the studies of crisis have been on new sects or Orthodox Jews, not on mainstream churches. In religious bodies where it is normal for everyone to be converted, it seems unlikely that all of them have been in a state of crisis. Joining a new sect is one thing, joining a large mainstream church is quite different. In any case only certain kinds of stress are likely to work. We know that unemployment doesn't. We shall see that people can be helped by prayer or religious coping when very ill or faced by death, but neither of these has been reported to cause conversion.

Freudian theories

Stanley Hall (1882), one of the earliest investigators of conversion, noted that conversions took place at a similar time as sexual maturation in puberty, and thought that conversion was like sexual love in some way. Psychoanalytic thinking on this subject is a little different: it is said that the father has been internalised as a love object, and that if the father becomes absent or there is a lot of conflict with him, an attachment to a new love object is formed; sudden conversion is like falling in love at this point. When young people join deviant groups, of which their parents disapprove, this is in addition an act of rebellion against them and their authority (Salzman, 1953).

Kirkpatrick and Shaver (1990) proposed a relationship theory of religious belief and conversion. They found that forty-four per cent of individuals who were insecurely attached to their parents were likely to have experienced sudden conversions, and that sudden conversions after the age of 30 were often preceded by divorce or other marital problems. This looks like the opposite of the finding reviewed earlier, that closer relations with the parents produced more religious children – if the parents had been pro-religious. Granqvist (1998) also found that insecure attachment to irreligious parents led to a greater likelihood of adult conversion, and to freely reported themes of compensation for these individuals. For securely attached children of religious parents, however, the parental influences survived. This suggests that God can act as a parent or spouse substitute, and can replace parents. A person that I know who was converted at age 15 shortly after her father had left home said to herself, 'God is my father now.' In Chapter 6 we shall look at images of God and shall see that God is seen as similar to both parents.

Different kinds of conversion

Conversion can take place in more ways than one. The Batson account describes a cognitive response to crisis, the Freudian account fits the absence of a father, the social psychological story is about joining a new group or being influenced by propaganda. Sometimes the change of belief comes first, as the result of persuasion, and religious behaviour second. It can be the other way round, and joining a group leads to taking part in the ritual or other behaviour of the group, which then results in changes of perception and belief. Social psychologists would say that this is to reduce the dissonance of beliefs and behaviour being in conflict, but it may be because religious attitudes are changed by taking part in the ritual. Balch (1980) reports how behaviour can precede beliefs in cases of cult conversion.

Personality factors

Some kinds of personality are more likely to be converted than others. Early American investigations found evidence that converts had been in a state of guilt, shame, self-doubt and unworthiness (Pratt, 1924). In the early part of the twentieth century guilt feelings about sex were common, and fundamentalist preaching was intended to heighten and then relieve these feelings. More recent studies have also found evidence of depression and low self-esteem in converts. Ullman (1982) found that her converts, mainly to new religious movements (NRMs), had less happy childhoods, and in adolescence had more anger and fear than the control group. Beit-Hallahmi and Nevo (1987) found that eighty-seven converts to Orthodox Judaism had less self-esteem than the controls.

Converts to new religious movements show stronger differences in personality than converts to mainstream churches. Anxiety and depression are found in many of them, and a high proportion have been more seriously disturbed (see Chapter 15).

Many of those who were brought up in the turbulent 1960s were attracted into NRMs, seen as radical alternatives to the mainstream of society. In the USA many of them left mainstream religion, but returned to it when they got married and had children (Roof, 1993). 'Whereas religious denominations tend to be at ease with the dominant culture, religious sects and cults are at tension with at least some aspects of this culture' (Hood et al., 1996: 293).

The effects of conversion

Converts may be in a state of guilt or depression before conversion, but they often feel much better afterwards. The main effect is that they have a stronger sense of meaning and purpose in life, as was found by Paloutzian (1981) in a before-and-after study with controls. Joining some communities acts as a 'safe haven' for those who are emotionally disturbed. Many who join NRMs have been on drugs, in some cases 100 per cent of new members. These movements have been very successful in making their new members abandon drugs, e.g. in the case of Hare Krishna (Judah, 1974). This is a considerable achievement since it is so difficult to cure such addictions. It has been achieved by a combination of very strong social support and authoritarian discipline in a closed community.

Conversion may be followed by deconversion, and in the case of the NRMs this is very common, and is likely to happen eighteen months to two years after conversion. Like conversion it may be gradual or sudden, and like conversion it is partly a function of the strength of social ties with other people inside and outside the group. Jacobs (1989) studied forty who deconverted from charismatic groups, Christian, Buddhist and Hindu. He found that deconversion involved breaking the ties with the leader and with the group, and that often there had been trouble with the leader or disillusion with the social life of the group (see Table 2.1).

Sudden conversions to evangelical churches are quite often temporary. Billy Graham's meetings in London and Glasgow in the 1950s could be said to have been amazingly successful in terms of the thousands who came forward to make decisions. However, it was found that many of them were already church-goers – they were not being converted at all,

TABLE 2.1   Reasons for leaving sects given by forty deconverters

Source	%
Disillusionment with a charismatic leader and his actions	
Physical abuse	31
Psychological abuse	60
Emotional rejection	45
Spiritual betrayal	33
Social disillusionment	
Social life	75
Spiritual life	50
Status/position	35
Prescribed sex roles	45

Source Adapted from Jacobs, 1989: 43, 92. Copyright © 1989 by Indiana University Press. Adapted by permission.

merely taking part in an enjoyable religious event. Follow-up studies of those who had not been going to church before found that half of them were still going a year later, in other words half of them had deconverted (Highet, 1957).

Religion at different ages

Religion takes a different form at different stages in the life-cycle.

Children: 4–12 years

Children readily take to religion, and accept whatever they are told without difficulty.

When Petrovic (1988) tested sixty 4-year-olds and asked them who made natural objects like the sky, ground and rocks, 68 per cent thought the sky was made by God, 53 per cent that the rocks were. She asked them what God was like, and 41 per cent said 'a real man', 25 per cent 'a man without a body'.

A number of studies have used informal methods like conversations with children, others have used drawings, interviews and essays on religious topics. All of them have found clear evidence of religious ideas and experiences in young children, though they take very varied forms. They seem to come to a peak between 10 and 12 and then decline (Hay and Nye, 1998). At first children think of God as like giants and dragons;

later as like a real person, like a father (Harms, 1944). Goldman (1964) interviewed 200 children between 6 and 15+, about how they saw various biblical episodes like Moses and the burning bush. Up to age 9 they gave material and literal explanations; for example, that the bush was lit by a torch. After 13–14 they were able to make more abstract and symbolic interpretations, such as that God was appearing in the fire, or it was a fire of love. Fowler (1981) interviewed subjects from age 4 to 84. The older children 7–12 he found thought literally about religion, and understood it in terms of story, drama and myth.

Vergote (1969), in Catholic Belgium, found that the idea of God was closely based on parents. Children began to distinguish between parents and God at 5–7, and by 12 God was seen as invisible and everywhere. Children pray from an early age if taught to do so. They may pray for toys, and young ones think that prayer works in a magical way. They also have a kind of primitive religious experience. Tamminen (1994) questioned 3,000 Finnish children between 6 and 20, mostly brought up as Lutherans. Of the youngest children 95 per cent said 'Yes' to the question 'Have you at times felt that God was close to you?', though this fell off with age. Similar numbers felt that God was guiding or directing their lives, especially when they were afraid or in trouble. This finding about the pervasiveness of very early religious experience has also been noted in American and European studies.

Adolescents and youth: 13–23
The adolescent phase of the religious career starts at 12–14 with a high level of church attendance and beliefs. During the next few years there is an overall decline in religious activity, but a great deal is happening. There is more questioning and doubt, especially among the more intelligent, many drop out at 15–16 from the church in which they were brought up, and many are converted to a new faith, typically at or around age 15. This is an age of both conversion and deconversion. Simplistic beliefs are abandoned by many, as shown in Table 2.2. But, though naïve beliefs are abandoned, those of central importance are not.

Several investigators claim to have discovered a series of stages which people go through. The best-known of these is that of Fowler (1981) who found a loose relation between age during adulthood and the later stages of his developmental scheme. Many stay at his stage 3, 'synthetic-conventional', which is typical of adolescents. There is conformity to the

TABLE 2.2 Percentages of adolescents holding traditional beliefs

Belief	Age		
	12 (%)	15 (%)	18 (%)
Only good people go to heaven.	72	45	33
Every word in the Bible is true.	(79)	(51)	(34)
People who go to church are better than people who do not go to church.	46	26	15
It is sinful to doubt the Bible.	(62)	(42)	(27)
I know there is a God.	94	80	79
There is a heaven.	(82)	(78)	(74)

Source Kuhlen and Arnold, 1944

views of others, but also the emergence of a personal myth, including one's own identity.

There are pressures to join new social groups and a desire to become independent of the parents; this is connected with identity-formation, and decisions about religion play a central part in this (Slugoski et al., 1984). Reich (1991) has found that young people face the contradictions and paradoxes of religion and work out increasingly complex rationalisations to deal with them. Those in their last years at school or their early years at university may spend hours arguing about the existence of God. Conversion may be primarily emotional and a matter of joining a new religious group, not always for religious reasons, but the cognitive side is also very important at this age.

Adults: 23–60

Surveys can show quite large age differences which are really due to historical changes. For example, if there has been a gradual decline in religion, older people are found to be more religious, but not because anyone has changed. In a rare follow-up study over forty years, Shand (1990) found very little change, i.e. a high level of stability, in a group of graduates. There was some decline, however, in beliefs in hell, heaven and resurrection. This continues the move away from fundamentalism shown for adolescents in Table 2.2. In some studies over shorter time-periods a small low point at age 25 or 30 has been found (Ploch and Hastings, 1994).

Comparing individuals of different ages finds that the older ones score higher on Intrinsic religiosity (r = .29, Watson, Howard et al., 1988), while Quest declines with age (r = −.30, Acklin, 1985).

Most of Fowler's stage 4 people were over 40; this he called 'individuative-reflective faith'. Here there is some demythologising and critical reflection on faith, and a desire for deeper understanding. The description of this stage has been criticised as putting too much emphasis on male abstract thinking and not enough on female styles of knowing by feeling and connectedness (Reich, 1997). Few reach Fowler's stage 5, 'conjunctive faith'; here symbols, myths and rituals regain their symbolic power and there is openness to other faiths. The evidence for this and other stage theories is not very strong, and in view of the stability reported earlier the changes are not very great. These investigators all find, however, that there is a trend with age to a more critical, more liberal and less literal faith, like the 'symbolic realism' to be described in Chapter 6.

There is another change with age, and that is that middle-aged people take a more active part in their church, both in its administration and in taking part in services.

Old age: 60 onwards

There is some fall in church attendance after 70 because of physical disability and other illness. However, old people watch religious TV services and listen to radio services more. Thun (1963) tried to trace the later development of religion in the elderly, by interviewing sixty-five of them. There was no uniform trajectory in this group: some had had an unbroken faith since childhood, some had been converted to a different faith, some had abandoned religion altogether. It is sometimes believed that the elderly possess some deep wisdom and dignity. From common observation of the very old this is obviously not always the case.

Belief in the after-life is more widespread in the old; in one American survey 100 per cent of those over 90 believed in it (Cavan et al., 1949). Fear of death can be a problem for those who are closer to it, but, as we shall see later, fear of death is very low in religious individuals (p. 145). Other benefits of religion are also strongest for the elderly – in producing greater happiness, less depression, less loneliness and lower suicide rates. Taking part in the shared ritual and receiving the social support of the church community is a major factor here. In addition religious coping, as part of prayer, is often turned to by the elderly who are ill or bereaved, and this is very successful. These findings are all expounded in later chapters.

Conclusions and discussion

1 A background of parental and other influences is important in producing religious attitudes, beliefs and behaviour. Many lapse from the family faith but the majority return. There may be conversions and deconversions, some of them sudden.

2 This process is only partly successful, since many move away from the religion of their home. Some make a radical move and join a new religious movement, and the emergence of gurus and their followers is separate from and often in opposition to the effects of socialisation.

3 Conversion, especially sudden conversion, is a most interesting phenomenon, and distinctive of religious attitudes and beliefs. It is partly due to the influence of social groups and religious leaders, and occurs at a time in adolescence when identity-formation is taking place. It can also be precipitated by a period of distress, especially loss of meaning and purpose, and take the form of rapid problem-solving. It is more common in those with weak parental attachments, who may be seeking a compensatory attachment.

4 Young children may accept parental ideas about religion, but adolescent ones want to make up their own minds; deciding about religion is connected with identity-formation. Later changes are mainly that religious ideas become more complex, with more acceptance of paradoxes and contradictions, and are less fundamentalist.

3

THE EFFECT OF PERSONALITY

Introduction

This chapter contains more about the traditional solid core of the psychology of religion – variations with gender, and the effects of personality. This is about more than just quantitative differences, it enables us to understand how religion takes on a different form and gives different experiences for different groups of people. This in turn gives us enhanced understanding of what religion is about, from a human point of view at least.

Personality and religion

Do religious individuals have a special kind of personality? In one sense they do, since being religious is part of personality, and the term could be used to describe someone's personality. The more interesting question is whether being religious relates to other aspects of personality, in particular to those stable dimensions or traits measurable and understood by psychologists. If so, this could be regarded as part of the explanation of why some people are religious – and why others are not.

Measures of religiosity

The basic method of research here is to see if there is any correlation between measures of religiosity and different personality variables. A number of different measures of individual religiosity have been so studied.

Attitudes to religion

A lasting contribution of Gordon Allport (1950) to the study of religion was his distinction between what he called 'Intrinsic' and 'Extrinsic' religiosity. Intrinsics are real believers and take their religion seriously. Extrinsics see it more as a means to other ends.

Examples of items measuring Intrinsic religiosity are:

'It is important for me to spend periods of time in private religious thought and meditation.'
'My religious beliefs are what really lie behind my whole approach to life.'

Examples of Extrinsic religiosity are:

'One reason for my being a church member is that such membership helps to establish a person in the community.'
'The primary purpose of prayer is to gain relief and protection.'

These two scales have been widely used in research, and we shall be citing some of it. However, they have been criticised on the grounds that the Intrinsic measures uncritical orthodoxy, while the Extrinsic splits into more than one dimension.

Batson et al. (1993) were seeking a more mature aspect of religiosity and proposed a third dimension, which they called Quest, intended to be more open-ended than the Intrinsic, and which emphasised complexity, doubt and tentativeness. The Quest scale is shown in Table 6.6 (p. 88). This too has been criticised, in that it seems to measure doubt and questioning, rather than commitment to a religious life. Young people have higher scores, and it may be typical of student thinking, perhaps an antecedent of Intrinsic.

Another pair of scales has been devised by Ryan et al. (1993). Their 'identification' refers to a complete assimilation and internalisation of beliefs, their 'introjection' to a lesser degree of assimilation where individuals are religious partly to gain the approval of others, partly because they think they ought to be. The scales are given in Table 3.1. These authors found that identification was positively related to health, mental health and self-esteem, whereas introjection was if anything negatively related.

Beliefs

Beliefs in particular matters, such as the existence of God, can be obtained. There are longer scales for Orthodoxy and Fundamentalism. There are also scales for measuring whether people believe literally or symbolically; all this will be described in Chapter 6.

Religious behaviour

One of the most widely used measures of religiosity is frequency of church attendance, and this correlates well with other measures and also with the effects of religion. Another aspect of religious behaviour is frequency of saying prayers, and this can measure deeper degrees of involvement, and is high for some working-class people who have a low frequency of church attendance.

Religious experience

Religious experience can be assessed by a single question or by a whole scale. If the latter is done, separate measures for transcendent and

TABLE 3.1 Measures of identification and introjection

Identification
Pray because I enjoy it
Turn to God because it is satisfying
Turn to God because I enjoy spending time with Him
Share my faith because God is important to me and I'd like others to know Him too
Pray because I find it satisfying
Attend church because by going I learn new things

Introjection
Share my faith because I want other Christians to approve of me
Attend church because others would disapprove if I didn't
Turn to God because I'd feel guilty if I didn't
Pray because God will disapprove if I don't
Attend church because one is supposed to go
Actively share my faith because I'd feel bad about myself if I didn't

---

Source Ryan et al., 1993

immanent experiences are usually found, as we explain in Chapter 4. Another kind of intense experience is conversion, as was described in the last chapter. And there may be personality differences between those converted to mainstream churches and to small sects.

It can be seen that there may be a range of answers concerning the relation of religion to personality, depending which aspects of religion are studied.

Relation to general personality traits

Is being religious in some sense innate? This can be studied by comparing identical and fraternal twins. The largest twin study of religion was by Truett et al. (1992) who found that religious attitudes were more similar between identical than between fraternal twins, and concluded that 16 per cent of the variability in religious attitudes was due to heredity. This is probably because these attitudes are related to personality traits with some biological basis, which are themselves partly innate.

Research in the Eysenck tradition has used the dimensions Extraversion, Neuroticism, Psychoticism and a Lie scale (Eysenck and Eysenck, 1975). Large-scale studies of religion in relation to these dimensions have consistently found that there is no relation between religion and the two main factors here, Extraversion or Neuroticism.

However, Psychoticism has consistently been found to be negatively related. Francis (1992) with 1,347 14–16-year-olds found this for both church attendance and religious attitudes; Argyle and Hills (in press) with 233 adults found the same for a religious affect score, and for church membership; similar results have been obtained in several other studies. The effect is stronger for males than females. It should be explained that 'Psychoticism' here does not mean what it says: it is really a measure of tough-mindedness and lack of concern for other people. The same studies have also consistently found that religious individuals score higher on the Lie scale. This too needs to be explained. The scale is not regarded as a measure of dishonesty, but more of acquiescence, obedience and conformity.

Sometimes mentally disturbed individuals are drawn to religion. We discuss sects and cults in Chapter 15 where we shall see that many of those who join some of them such as the Moonies were already mentally ill and in some cases had been hospitalised. The same applies to those who join enclosed orders of nuns, who have a high rate of schizophrenia. And those who found new sects and cults have often been through a period of mental disturbance (p. 223). On the other hand, joining these sects and cults is often good for people (see Chapter 11).

A second scheme of major personality dimensions is the so-called 'big five' of McCrae and Costa (1985). Two of the big five are similar to Extraversion and Neuroticism, the third and fourth are 'Agreeableness' and 'Conscientiousness', but the fifth, 'Openness to Experience', has some links with religion. In Chapter 5 we report the somewhat similar dimension of 'schizotypy', which has been found to be related to having religious experiences.

The general finding here is that religion is not much related to the general personality variables known to psychologists. However, there are some interesting links between more specialised areas of personality and particular aspects of religiosity, and to these we now turn.

Authoritarianism

Authoritarianism describes individuals who are submissive to authority, are conventional, and reject deviates and outsiders of all kinds. Adorno et al. (1950) found that church members, especially Catholics, in the USA were more authoritarian than those with no religion, and that like other authoritarians they were more likely to be racially prejudiced. Later Kahoe (1977) found that only eleven items of the 30-item Authoritarianism scale were related to intrinsic religiosity, but that more of the authoritarian items correlated with extrinsic religiosity. One explanation of the authoritarianism of some church members is that authoritarians are less educated ($r = -.50$ to $-.60$), and this could explain the authoritarianism of American Catholics and other less well-educated groups. The most authoritarian denominations in recent studies have been found to be fundamentalists; Altemeyer and Hunsberger (1992) found a correlation of .68 with fundamentalism. And this is true of Hindus, Muslims and Jews as well as Christian fundamentalists. This may be because fundamentalists encourage obedience to authority, conventionalism, self-righteousness and feelings of superiority – all aspects of authoritarianism (Altemeyer, 1988). Or it could be because both Catholics and fundamentalist Protestants demand more obedience in children, take a punitive attitude to sinners, and favour corporal punishment, if this is thought necessary to keep them in the faith (Danso et al., 1997).

While fundamentalism correlates strongly with authoritarianism, other aspects of religiosity do not. Leak and Randall (1995) found with students that Altemeyer's Right-Wing Authoritarianism scale has different correlations with measures of sophisticated, and non-literal, forms of religiosity such as Quest, and the later stages found by Fowler (see p. 28), as shown in Table 3.2.

It can be seen that both Quest and Fowler stage 5 had strong negative correlations with authoritarianism.

Dogmatism

Rokeach (1960) located another dimension of personality, really a style of thinking, which he called dogmatism or the 'closed mind'. This described individuals who are rigid in their thinking, intolerant of ambiguity and unable to deal with new information. American Catholics and Southern Baptists had the highest scores, non-believers the lowest. He found that members of all churches tended to reject members of other churches, and rejected them more if their beliefs were very dissimilar to their own. By rejection here was meant unwillingness to marry or make friends with a member of the other group, for example. Figure 3.1 shows the degree of rejection of members of other churches by (a) Catholics and (b) Methodists, the most and least prejudiced in this study.

Other investigators have taken up the question of whether religious individuals have closed minds. This has been done by seeing how well they can finish paragraphs where opposite points of view have been expressed, or interviewing them about religious dilemmas; they are then given scores on the complexity of their religious thinking. Fundamentalists have lower scores, but so too do those with high scores on orthodoxy or intrinsic religiosity. Those with high scores on Quest come out as more cognitively complex in this sense, but that is almost the definition of quest. Older

TABLE 3.2 Correlations of religiosity with right-wing authoritarianism

Christian orthodoxy	.52	Fowler faith stage	−.57
Church attendance	.29	Quest	−.40
Frequency of prayer	.35		
Percentage of church's beliefs accepted	.45		

Source Leak and Randall, 1995

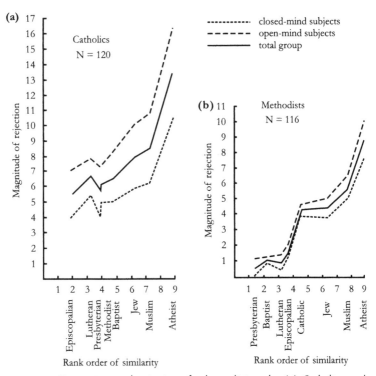

FIGURE 3.1 Dogmatism and rejection of other religions by (a) Catholics and (b) Methodists

Source Rokeach, 1960

people score lower in cognitive complexity (r = −.47, Pratt et al., 1992). Young people may like confronting and discussing interesting religious paradoxes, but older people are getting on with their religious life. And we saw earlier that it may be the essence of religion to make a commitment – which quests have not done, and there are areas of life where cognitive complexity may not be best. It has been found that orthodox believers, as well as fundamentalists, think more simply about a particular kind of religious issue – 'existential' ones: that is, concerning our own death, why we are alive, what is the meaning and purpose of life (Hunsberger, Pratt et al., 1994).

Suggestibility

Suggestibility is a minor, that is, a narrow, personality trait, about how far individuals respond to suggestions, particularly in their bodily behaviour. It is usually measured by response to hypnotism, or tests in which subjects while blindfolded are told they are falling over. In an early study Coe (1916) found that out of fourteen people who had experienced dramatic conversions, thirteen could be easily hypnotised; while out of twelve who had expected to be converted but were not, nine could not be hypnotised. Gibbons and de Jarnette (1972) obtained similar results with 185 individuals assessed for hypnotic susceptibility.

There is also a link with having religious experiences. Spanos and Moretti (1988) found quite strong correlations between Hood's Mysticism scale, as high as $r = .53$ with a measure of hypnotisability. We shall see that religious experiences are partly a matter of expectation and being in the right environmental setting. It is likely that religious healing is partly due to suggestibility: Lasagna et al. (1954) found that hospital patients who were church-goers responded more positively to placebo treatment, and this has been replicated several times.

Suggestibility may have been important at earlier periods of religious history. In traditional cultures it was common for shamans to go into states of possession, for example, to have skewers passed through them or endure other ordeals. This may have been because they were hysterical personalities, who are able to dissociate readily, go into trances and not feel pain (Ward and Kemp, 1991). Experience of the stigmata may have a similar explanation (Thurston, 1951).

Self-actualisers

Maslow (1970) proposed that when lower needs, like safety, physiological needs, and social and esteem needs, had been satisfied some individuals advanced to a need for self-actualisation. Among other features of these people Maslow proposed that they tended to have peak experiences, which included religious experiences. In one of the main studies inspired by these ideas Wuthnow (1978) conducted a survey of 1,000 people in the San Francisco area. Half of them reported having had a feeling of contact with something holy or sacred, 39 per cent reported having had a feeling of harmony with the universe. Those who had peak experiences said that they thought a lot about the purpose of life, found life very meaningful, and were very self-assured. We report in Chapter 12 how they also have generous and idealistic social attitudes.

Another line of Maslow-inspired research has been with the Personal Orientation Inventory (POI), which was intended to measure self-actualising tendencies. However, it is biased against traditional religion, as shown by the finding that Catholic priests score below the test norms, experience of meditation or encounter groups increases POI scores, and high scorers have religious experiences which are triggered by sex or drugs rather than by religion or nature. The personality of high scorers is being assertive, happy-go-lucky and venturesome, which is not at all the same as self-actualising (Wulff, 1997).

The search for meaning

Frankl (1975) proposed that there is a human desire for understanding, of the self and of the purpose of life. This can be discovered through the conscience, which he believed was given transcendentally, and consists usually of concern for others. Those who have failed to find it feel that life is empty and futile, and this may lead to despair and suicide. Frankl is famous for surviving Auschwitz and for helping others to survive and not commit suicide there – by finding a purpose in life, for example, looking forward to meeting again a loved one who needs you, or to being able to finish a book or other piece of work. The future must not be hopeless. He later called this 'logotherapy'; he reports how he helped a mother who had tried to commit suicide by suggesting that she devoted herself to looking after a handicapped son; this gave her a meaning in her life (1962). Another way of finding meaning in life is through religion; as one church notice said, 'Tired of money, sex and power? Check in with God' (Pargament, 1997).

A line of research inspired by Frankl's ideas uses the Purpose in Life (PIL) test (Crumbaugh and Maholick, 1964). This test has been found to be positively correlated with Rokeach's value Salvation, and also with Intrinsic religiosity (Crandall and Rasmussen, 1975), but negatively related with some of Rokeach's other values – Pleasure, an Exciting Life, and a Comfortable Life. There has been some interest in the PIL test in those doing happiness research, since it is a measure of higher, non-hedonistic aspects of happiness.

Jung's psychological types

The part of Jung's ideas which has led to most empirical research is his theory of psychological types. Most of this research has used a test known as the Myers-Briggs Type Indicator (MBTI; Myers and McCaulley, 1985), which places people into the Jungian psychological types. Although this test has been ignored by research psychologists it has been widely used in religious and management circles. I will show how shortly.

The MBTI has been given to thousands of religious people and others, and it has been found that *feeling* rather than *thinking* is typical of the religious. In addition the religious are more likely to be *intuitive* rather than *sensing*, though this is more true of liberal than of conservative church members. *Sensers* perceive physical stimuli directly and concretely, while *intuitors* see them as part of a larger picture and symbolically. There is no particular difference on *extraversion–introversion* (Oswald and Kroeger, 1988).

Other studies have compared the religious life of the different types of personality, and here we can see why the MBTI has become so popular. Ross et al. (1996) classified 195 religious people on the MBTI and gave them another 100 items. The results are interesting.

Sensers and intuitives: intuitives saw God as more of a mystery, and had more tolerance for doubt, complexity and symbolism; sensers wanted definite beliefs and rules.

Thinking and feeling: those in the feeling type (who, as we have just seen, are more common among the religious) are disturbed by inter-personal conflict, think their faith has implications for human relation-ships, find it easier to pray, like narrative forms of communication and personal stories in sermons; those in the thinking type find it difficult to pray, prefer reasoned sermons and rigorous texts.

Extraverts and introverts: there are not many differences here, but extra-verts find fellowship spiritually refreshing, and do not like being alone for long.

Perceivers and judgers: there are few differences here, but judgers like to have a set routine, of prayer, for example, and religion gives them a sense of security.

The MBTI is much used at weekends at convents, for example, where it is used to advise on how individuals can conduct their religious life. Michael and Norrisey (1984) followed up 457 individuals who were advised in this way; nearly all reported a year later that this had been helpful. More hard-headed psychologists would not be impressed by this finding.

However, the baffling thing about all this is that it apparently has no relation at all to the better-known parts of Jung's ideas, about archetypes, which we shall discuss in Chapter 7. It does have some similarity with more familiar personality tests. Extraversion–introversion is well-known to psychologists, sensing–intuition may be the same as openness to experience, one of the big five, and thinking–feeling to agreeableness, another of them (McCrae and Costa, 1989).

Gender differences in religion

Male and female religiosity

Men and women are religious in slightly different ways. Women are on average more religious in every way, starting with feeling God's nearness and guidance at age 9 and 10 (76 per cent of girls, 61 per cent of boys) (Tamminen, 1994). In adolescence and after, women have more guilt feelings, and this may explain the higher proportion of females in more fundamentalist churches, which emphasise guilt and sin more. Women's image of God is more as loving, comforting, forgiving and healing, while men see God as powerful, planning and controlling (D. Wright and Cox, 1967). More women see God as neither male nor female, while many men see God as male (Yeamen, 1987). In some American evangelical churches a 'women's enclave' has developed – this is a part of the chapel for women's services and other activities. The women have a special kind of religious experience which is tied to those settings, where they have authority. Here they have 'regenerative' experiences empowering them to renew their lives (Brasher, 1997).

Psychoanalysts and feminists have speculated on the possible effect of biological differences between the sexes on their religious experience. Erikson, for example, in his book on *Young Man Luther* (1958), argued that where men are outgoing and active, and find a transcendent God, women find an immanent God inside their own bodily experience by passive surrender to him. Erikson regarded the female mode as the more fundamental to religion, and thought that Luther's religious development included discovering a passive, receptive attitude to God (Zock, 1997).

There is no objective evidence for this, but the measures which we describe in Chapter 4 for the study of religious experience could be used to do this.

It is found that femininity, as measured by the Bem Sex Role Inventory, is a better predictor of religiosity than is gender itself. Women value the social more than the individual aspects of religion. They see God as caring, intimate and forgiving. And they value the greater scope in new religious movements for women to explore a wider range of adult roles (Reich, 1997).

There is one respect in which men have been more active in religion, for centuries, indeed millennia, and that is in functioning as priests. Nearly all religious leaders throughout history, from Shamanism onwards, and including present-day leaders of new religious movements, have been men. However, a few have been women, including some of the leaders of Third World movements today, in India, Africa and Brazil (Clarke, 1993). During the twentieth century the situation has changed, and most Christian Protestant churches now ordain women, despite massive resistance in some of them, especially the Church of England and American Baptists. This has not spread to the Roman Catholic Church or to the Jews yet, and shows no signs of doing so. Meanwhile half the ordinands in some theological colleges are now women, and the face of the clergy in many churches has already changed.

Female clergy are a little different. They start when they are older, after being mothers or doing other jobs first, and they have been found to be less neurotic and more extraverted than the population norms, which is not the case for male clergy (Francis, 1991). A survey of 1,239 British women clergy in the Church of England found that most of them thought they had something different to offer from male clergy, especially in being good with women's groups and children, and in running the parish democratically (Robbins et al., 1997). Women clergy have been discriminated against in their churches for promotion, and in the USA many have been sexually abused or harassed by male clergy (Fortune and Poling, 1994).

The extent of gender differences

There is extensive statistical material on gender differences in religion, and these were reviewed by Beit-Hallahmi and Argyle (1997). The differences in beliefs and in weekly church attendance are typical. In Britain, 50 per cent more women go to church or hold basic beliefs than men. In the USA, the percentage is more like 20 per cent, since the absolute numbers are much greater. For example, 44 per cent of American men and 55 per cent of American women go to church (25 per cent more). In Britain the corresponding figures are 12 per cent and 18 per cent (50 per cent more).

The ratios are a little different for different aspects of religiosity. The gender difference is greater for more intense or involving aspects of religion, such as going to confession (93 per cent more for women), being converted by Billy Graham (80 per cent more), saying prayers daily (87 per cent), and going into a trance during charismatic services.

Gender difference varies between denominations. It is almost zero for Catholics, quite high for the Church of England, and often even higher for Protestant sects and NRMs, as high as 4:1 women to men in some (B. R. Wilson, 1961).

The explanation of religious gender differences

The fact that women are more active in religion than men has been known for a long time, though the details are new. However, there is no agreed explanation of this difference, and all we can do is to look at the most likely ones.

Personality differences between men and women

There are substantial personality differences between men and women, and these could account for their differences in religiosity. Some personality differences may be innate, though environmental factors are probably more important. Males are found to be more aggressive and dominant in all species of mammals and in all human cultures; this is found in human children at the pre-school stage. In childhood boys are found to be more competitive and aggressive, girls to be more sociable and helpful and to enjoy social contact for its own sake. Later in life 'Women tend to manifest behaviours that can be described as socially sensitive, friendly, and concerned with others' welfare, whereas men . . . can be described as dominant, controlling and independent' (Eagly, 1995: 154). Women are found to suffer much more from anxiety and guilt feelings. They also take more responsibility for providing social support and maintaining relationships in the family and other social groups. Women are orientated to people where men are often more interested in things. Women often do caring and nurturant jobs, such as nursing, teaching and social work.

These characteristic female traits are more compatible with a religious outlook and life-style. Being caring and nurturant is what religion demands. Being aggressive and dominant is not. Guilt feelings often make people turn to religion.

These gender differences are partly due to differences in the way boys and girls are socialised. In nearly all cultures boys are trained to be self-reliant and independent, and in some cultures to be aggressive; girls are trained to be nurturant, obedient and responsible (Barry et al., 1957). Socialisation of girls in the past has often included expecting young women to help with the Sunday school, and to do other supportive and caring work in the congregation, under the direction of the vicar. There have been massive changes in the role of women in recent years – most have jobs, most do not want to be subordinated to males – so it is possible that these jobs in the church will be done with less enthusiasm in future.

Parental projection

The Freudian theory of religion is that God is a projected father image, replacing that of the real father. According to the oedipal theory girls should have a positive attachment to their fathers, while boys feel more ambivalent about them. We have seen that the images people hold of God are similar to their opposite-sex parents, and that women see God as more benevolent. So the Freudian theory gives a possible explanation of why women are more religious and why they have a different image of God. Rasmussen and Charman (1995) confirmed one interpretation of the Freudian theory that God is a projected super-ego. With 124 subjects they found that believers had stronger super-egos, on Cattell's scale, and an external locus of control.

Psychoanalytic theory also offers an explanation of Protestant–Catholic differences here. For Catholics the Virgin Mary and other saints are very prominent, and God is experienced more as a mother (Rees, 1967). For Protestants Jesus is an important figure, and this would appeal more to women. We have seen that the proportion of women is very high in radical Protestant sects. Jacobs (1987) in her study of those who had deconverted from sects found that these individuals were greatly devoted to God the father and to his representative the charismatic leader, for whom they had powerful feelings of love. There is a second psychoanalytic explanation of Catholic–Protestant differences in sex composition. Women have stronger guilt feelings, and Protestantism emphasises guilt and sin and the need to be saved more than Catholicism does (Argyle and Beit-Hallahmi, 1975).

The effect of employment

Women with jobs go to church less than those not working, as has been found in large-scale surveys in the USA, Canada and Australia (e.g. de Vaus, 1984). This could be because women who are not at work have more time, feel socially isolated or that they are not filling a valued social role, or have less conflict with worldly economic activities. Since there are more women not working than men, this could explain some of the gender difference in church attendance at least. However, precisely the opposite effect of work is found for men – those who are not at work go to church *less* than those who are. There would have to be a quite different explanation for this; it could be because out-of-work men are less educated and of lower social class – two groups who go to church less – or perhaps they are too demoralised to appear in church.

Conclusions

1 Religious activity and beliefs have little relationship to major personality variables like Extraversion or Neuroticism, but there is a negative relation with Psychoticism (tough-mindedness), and a positive relationship with Openness to Experience.

2 Church members are more authoritarian, but only fundamentalists as opposed to members of more liberal churches, and for Extrinsic, rather than Intrinsic, religiosity.

3 Some narrower traits relate to particular aspects of religious behaviour, or to members of particular groups, as with dogmatism (for members of strict churches), and suggestibility (for those who get converted or undergo religious healing), and cognitive factors like Purpose in Life. Some of these results are of general importance; for example, dogmatism seems to be a normal aspect of religious belief, and purpose in life is one of the benefits of religion.

4 Jung's personality types have been used to classify people for religious purposes such as advising on spiritual life.

5 Women are more active in nearly all aspects of religion. This is partly

due to personality differences between men and women innate or acquired, and partly to an interest in opposite-sex parents in a setting when God is seen as a father. The religious life and beliefs of men and women are different, and male and female clergy have different approaches to the job.

4

THE EXTENT AND VARIETIES OF RELIGIOUS EXPERIENCE

Introduction

Religious experience (RE) is one of the central facts of religion. Without it there would be no religions. It is one of the classic, and most convincing, arguments for the existence of God. Otto (1917) thought that the core of religion was the irrational emotional experience of the Holy. We shall see in Chapter 6 that religious beliefs may be attempts to put REs into words. Psychological research on this topic can add a great deal to our knowledge of these phenomena – what exactly they are like, who has them, what varieties they take, whether they have a common core. In the next chapter we shall look at the conditions that produce them and the effects that they have.

William James (1902) began research into these experiences by the analysis, from literary sources, of the experiences 'in their solitude' of individuals famous for their religious visions, such as Tolstoy and Walt Whitman. This was not a sample of the normal population.

Subsequent research has used larger and less exotic samples of subjects, and has not been confined to experiences in solitude. Much of the research on religious experience, from William James onwards, has used questions which elicited fairly intense and infrequent kinds of experience. The range of experiences that are collected by research depends on the exact question asked. Alister Hardy (1979) in 1969 advertised in British papers and magazines, inviting anyone to write to him who had 'been aware of or influenced by a presence or power, whether you call it God or not, which is different from your everyday self'. This has resulted in a collection of about 7,000 accounts; the first 3,000 were analysed by Hardy (1979) and the full collection is still being studied by the Alister Hardy Centre for Religious Experience at Oxford. This was not a sample survey, but Hay (1982), starting from the Alister Hardy question, found that while 31 per cent in Britain reported such experiences the majority had had them only once or twice (17 per cent) or 'several times' (9 per cent) (Table 4.5). These were mainly intense and infrequent experiences. The question also turned out to be a rather broad one; the result of leaving out religious terms was that psychic experiences were reported too.

Pratt (1924) first drew attention to the 'milder type' of religious experience – which many people might experience most Sundays, or more often, and these will be described later.

Elsewhere in this book we shall describe other kinds of RE. Conversion experiences, for example, are very common, and in evangelical and charismatic circles experiences of 'coming to know Jesus' or being 'born again' are normal.

The varieties of religious experience

The varieties probably have *something* in common that identifies them as religious experiences. This may be a common sense of awe or religious presence. However, there are quite a number of varieties. We have looked at the 'Alister Hardy question'. One result of using this question was that the answers included paranormal as well as strictly religious experiences. A proportion of those who reported these regarded them as religious, others did not. There were also experiences of evil, of angels, of visions of the Virgin Mary and many others. However, there is a lot of evidence of experience of a transcendent being, and most of the experiences were very positive.

An important distinction is often made between two kinds of RE: (1) experience of contact with a transcendent being or of the presence of a holy other, what Otto (1917) called a 'numinous' experience; (2) experience of the immanent unity of all things, sometimes called 'mystical' experience. We shall see that questionnaire measures of REs find that factors corresponding to these two kinds are somewhat independent.

Buddhism emphasises the second, mystical kind of experience. Zen monks are trained to empty the mind, to seek inner unity, and lose the distinction between self and others; there is no numinous, transcendent object. This tradition is found in Christianity too; for example, in *The Cloud of Unknowing*.

There may be more varieties than these two. Hay and Heald (1987), in an English survey, used the Alister Hardy question, and asked people if they had had experiences in some of his main categories. In answer, 48 per cent reported having had an experience of a presence or power, and those reporting each variety are shown in Table 4.1.

Out of this list, the first three kinds represent transcendent experiences, the last one, experiencing that all things are one, is the most clearly immanent, and the fourth category, awareness of a sacred presence in nature, could also be described in this way. However, synchronicity and contact with the dead are psychic experiences, and the experience of evil is another, quite separate kind.

The experience of evil was also reported by 4.5 per cent of Alister Hardy's original subjects, and 155 examples have recently been studied from the Alister Hardy Centre collection by Jakobsen (1999). The most common type was experienced when half waking, the so-called 'hypnopompic' state; others were due to hostile facial expressions or emotions; but there were no references here to antisocial individuals. Glock and Stark (1965) found that 32 per cent of their Protestant Church members thought they had been tempted by the Devil, and Poloma (1996) found that 55 per cent of a Toronto Blessing group thought they had been 'delivered from Satan's hold'.

The list in Table 4.1 did not include *aesthetic experiences*, and we shall see later that these can be very similar to religious ones. In particular, REs can be triggered by music or other aesthetic stimuli, and experiences in church and at concerts can be very similar.

Table 4.1 did, however, include *awareness of a sacred presence in nature*. Wuthnow (1978) surveyed 1,000 individuals in California; one of his questions was 'Have you experienced the beauty of nature in a deeply moving way?'; 49 per cent had and said that this had a lasting effect on their lives, and another 33 per cent had but without such lasting effects. All religions have sacred places, and places may become sacred because

TABLE 4.1 The varieties of religious experience in Britain

Type of experience	(1) % reporting this	(2) % interpreting religiously	% religious experience (1 × 2)
Awareness of the presence of God	27	80	21.6
Awareness of receiving help in answer to prayer	25	79	19.8
Awareness of a guiding presence not called God	22	58	12.8
Awareness of a sacred presence in nature	16	61	9.8
Awareness of patterning in synchronicity	29	32	9.3
Awareness of the presence of someone who has died	18	35	6.3
Awareness of an evil presence	12	38	4.6
Experiencing that all things are one	5	55	2.75

Source Hay and Heald, 1987

they have striking features; they may be believed to give access to transcendent reality. This is experienced in the course of everyday life (Bartkowski and Swearingen, 1997). Nelson (1997) studied two church communities for poor Blacks in Chicago. Their REs were in their ordinary lives, they saw the hand of God in providing food, jobs or apartments, seeing him as healer, provider and shepherd, and they saw the hand of Satan in drugs or other social evils. They were much influenced by religious language and metaphor, which was sustained by the church community, seeing themselves as children of God, but oppressed by spiritual forces.

There are some other varieties which are not found in the Hay and Heald survey, though they do occur in the Alister Hardy collection of reports. These reports contain many examples of experiences of *the presence of Jesus*, or *visions of the Virgin Mary*. I am grateful to Professor Laurie Brown and Mrs Polly Wheway for analysing the first 1,000 cases for me, since this kind of experience was not noted by Alister Hardy himself. Visions of the Virgin Mary have long been common in the Catholic Church in Europe. Individuals who are converted in charismatic or evangelical groups commonly refer to 'getting to know Jesus'.

There is another variety which this time may really be different in content, and that is the '*milder type*' of religious experience, first described by Pratt (1924). Such experiences are not those that occur only once or twice in a lifetime, but may happen every Sunday morning. We shall present data later to show that these are different from the intense kind of RE, and have a stronger social component. Probably most of these milder REs occur in church. In Chapter 9 we shall describe charismatic services, which are intensely social, and highly arousing – it is a misnomer to call them 'mild'. In several parts of the world charismatic behaviour such as speaking in tongues is very common. The experience of being 'born again' is described as particularly strong, and is often accompanied by being healed. Those involved feel that they have been reborn with a new kind of self, freed from sin, and feel great joy.

The majority of the REs studied by William James and later, on the other hand, have been in solitude, and often brought about by silence and meditation. In Hay's survey (1982) 61 per cent of the REs occurred when completely alone, another 9 per cent alone but in a public place, and only 7 per cent in a communal setting.

Paranormal or psychic phenomena cause us some problems, partly because they are more readily falsifiable than REs proper, and there is little evidence that they really occur. At least one, precognition, is generally believed to be logically impossible. However, many people report having experienced them, more altogether than report REs proper. Table 4.7 gives some examples of survey results. And many people believe in them – 46 per cent in foretelling the future, 62 per cent in ghosts and 31 per cent in exchanging messages with the dead (see p. 58).

There is some evidence that reports of these phenomena have been increasing, in the USA and also in China; for example, reported ESP went up from 58 per cent to 65 per cent between 1973 and 1988 (Levin, 1993). Sceptical psychologists put the whole lot down to inaccurate perceptions or mistakes about probability. What they may all have in common with REs proper is apparent evidence for a non-material world.

Psychic experiences are sometimes reported by the same individuals who report REs proper (Hood et al., 1996). However, Wuthnow (1978) found that psychic and religious experiences happened to rather different kinds of people. He found that *déjà vu*, ESP and clairvoyance happened to the young and Black among male subjects, and to people from unhappy homes with unhappy marriages. Religious experiences, on the other hand, happened to older, more educated, religious believers, from happy homes. Those who had been talking to the dead tended to be widowed, female and Black. He also found that while REs led to positive affect and life satisfaction, occult ones had no such effect. Greeley (1975) similarly found that while REs led to happiness, occult experiences had the opposite effect.

While these psychic experiences are of interest in themselves, and while some regard them as religious, there are grounds for considering that they are different from REs proper.

Near-death experiences (NDEs) may be rather different from the psychic experiences above – these are not so obviously in conflict with how we generally understand the material world, and they have clear positive effects. A lot of people say they have had one – 15 per cent of American adults, and 23 per cent of those who report REs (Gallup and Proctor, 1982). There is a lot of similarity in the NDEs that people report. Greyson (1990) analysed 183 cases and found that they reported:

- time stopped (74 per cent)
- incredible peace (74 per cent)

- a bright light of other-worldly origin (72 per cent)
- leaving the physical body (55 per cent)
- encountering an other-worldly being or voice (50 per cent)
- incredible joy (57 per cent)
- entering a mystical or unearthly realm (56 per cent).

Is there a core religious experience?

There must be some shared features for the term 'religious experience' to be applied to them at all. William James (1902) thought that there were four basic features of REs:

1 ineffability, i.e. they can't be expressed in words
2 Noetic quality, i.e. they are experienced as authoritative sources of knowledge
3 transiency, i.e. they last a short time but leave a lasting impression
4 passivity, i.e. there is a sense of being controlled by the Other.

Stace (1960) studied the features of REs in different religions, cultures and historical periods and produced his famous list of the core or universal features which they all shared, and these are given in Table 4.2.

We referred earlier to the distinction between transcendent and immanent experiences. Stace's list has more of the second kind, items 1 and 8 being the clearest examples, and fewer transcendent items, really only item 5. Hood (1975) used these categories to construct a 32-item scale of mystical experience. Factor analysis of this scale produced two factors, 'General Mysticism', which contained most of the items, and 'Religious Interpretation'. The first corresponds to immanence, the second to transcendence, but also positive affect. These scales were not independent, but

TABLE 4.2 Stace's list of core features of religious experience

---
1. Unifying vision, all things are one, part of a whole
2. Timeless and spaceless
3. Sense of reality, not subjective but a valid source of knowledge
4. Blessedness, joy, peace and happiness
5. Feeling of the holy, sacred, divine
6. Paradoxical, defies logic
7. Ineffable, can't be described in words
8. Loss of sense of self

Source Stace, 1960

correlated at .47, so that in a sense there is only one dimension here, not two. Some religions combine the two in their thinking, as in the Hindu Upanishads (Smart, 1964). Some experiences are hard to classify; Greeley (1975) cites this experience from F. C. Happold, an author of religious books:

> The room was filled by a Presence, which in a strange way was both about me and within me, like light or warmth. . . . I was overwhelmingly possessed by Someone who was not myself.
>
> (Greeley, 1975: 46)

Hood and colleagues (1993) have produced a longer version of the Mysticism scale, with thirty-two items, which produced three factors, which are an Immanent or Mysticism factor, a clearer Transcendent factor than before, and a Noetic, i.e. inexpressibility, factor.

It is good that transcendence has been given more importance than it received from Stace and in the previous Hood scale, since major religious writings often describe feelings of unity with God, fear, awe and transcendence, dependence, a journey inwards or upwards, love and marriage, and the goal of union with the divine (J. M. Smith and Ghose, 1989). Here is an example from one of Hay's subjects:

> At this time, if I'm lucky (during yoga), I seem to latch on to something akin to a pure emotional state, a sense of happiness. There is definitely some sort of power there which seems to greet me, to embrace.
>
> (Hay, 1982: 134)

There are other features which are not included in Stace's or Hood's lists. One is the social component of RE, a feeling of love, equality and union with others, as with Turner's 'communitas', experienced during religious rituals (see p. 127). For example:

> This sense of oneness is basic to what I understand of religions. . . . The effect of the Experience has been, I think, a permanent increase in my awareness that we are 'members of one another, a consequent greater openness towards all and a widening of my concern for others.
>
> (Hardy, 1979: 58)

The Stace list and the Hood scale do not mention imagery or visual aspects of REs. In the Alister Hardy collection 8.5 per cent mentioned light, 4.5 per cent being bathed in a glowing light, and 18.3 per cent visions; others mentioned music, voices or warmth. We have just seen an example of this from Greeley.

Greeley (1975) used an expanded version of these lists with a national US sample of 1,467 individuals. Of those who reported REs, 35 per cent of the total, the percentages who reported certain descriptors are given in Table 4.3.

This list includes some of the topics that we have discussed, such as sensory experiences, social aspects, and in addition some of the consequences of REs, such as joy and optimism. However, it is still weak on transcendent components, apart perhaps from 'The sense that my personality has been taken over by something much more powerful than I am'.

Argyle and Hills (in press) studied a group of 235 adults in Oxfordshire, many of them members of churches, to investigate the nature of milder and more intense REs. We used a set of twenty-five scales for religious affect, drawn from some of the sources which have been

TABLE 4.3 Greeley's descriptors of religious experience

Descriptor	%
A feeling of deep and profound peace	55
A certainty that all things would work out for the good	48
Sense of my own need to contribute to others	43
A conviction that love is the center of everything	43
Sense of joy and laughter	43
An experience of great emotional intensity	38
A great increase in my understanding and knowledge	32
A sense of the unity of everything and my own part in it	29
A sense of a new life and living in a new world	27
A confidence in my own personal survival	27
A feeling that I couldn't possibly describe what was happening to me	26
The sense that all the universe is alive	25
The sense that my personality has been taken over by something much more powerful than I am	24
A sense of tremendous personal expansion, either psychological or physical	22
A sensation of warmth or fire	22
A sense of being alone	19
A loss of concern about worldly problems	19
A sense that I am being bathed in light	14
A sense of desolation	8

Source Greeley, 1975

discussed, but adding more transcendental and social elements. Factor analysis of the twenty-five scales yielded three clear factors, as shown in Table 4.4.

It can be seen that the first factor contained the transcendent, relations with God, items, and also most of the positive affect ones. The second factor contains the social, feelings of unity with others, items, and the third the immanent, mystical ones. Church members reported stronger emotions on the first two factors, those who reported REs proper scored higher on the third factor only.

TABLE 4.4 Factor analysis of the religious affect scales

Item	Item label	$F_1{}^a$	F_2	F_3
G19	contact with God	.82		
G25	being at peace with God	.80		
G12	feeling supported and helped	.74		
G11	feeling uplifted	.72		
G13	feeling loved	.72	.46	
G14	feeling 'at home'	.72		
G03	refreshment	.68		
G07	obtaining guidance	.66		
G09	joy/elation	.65		
G05	positive feeling about life	.65		
G20	calmness	.62		.48
G16	excitement	.59		
G04	quieting of the mind	.57		.52
G18	enjoying company of others present		.81	
G22	being united with other people		.78	
G23	being part of a family		.75	
G06	opportunities to help others		.61	
G02	taking part in a shared performance		.61	
G17	enjoying familiar practices		.57	
G15	experiencing a unifying vision	.49	.49	
G01	timelessness			.78
G08	loss of sense of self			.66
G21	bodily well-being			.56
G24	being bathed in warmth and light		.49	.56
G15	glimpsing another world			.54
Cronbach's α		.95	.95	.79
Variance explained		49.6%	7.0%	6.1%

All factor loadings ≥.45 are shown.
^{a}Factor labels: F_1, immanent; F_2, social; F_3, transcendent.

Source Argyle and Hills, in press

We cannot say how far there is a core, universal kind of RE, but we have seen the elements of which most REs consist. These include both transcendent and immanent elements. We would like to add more social and transcendental elements to some earlier lists of essential components, and also sensory experiences such as 'being bathed in warmth and light'. Mild experiences may be different from the traditional REs in being more social, and charismatic REs are both social and associated with high arousal. However, some of the differences may really be in the triggering conditions or the socialisation involved rather than in the experiences themselves. In addition there are different traditions of religious practice and experience, including intensive training in different forms of meditation, which we shall describe in the next chapter.

Surveys of religious experience

Many surveys have now been carried out, with population samples, in Britain, the USA and Australia. The main finding has been replicated often – a large section of the population report having had an RE. Some investigators used the Greeley question ('Have you ever felt as though you were very close to a powerful spiritual force that seemed to lift you out of yourself?'). In the USA 35 per cent said 'yes', and in Britain 31 per cent (Table 4.5; Hay, 1982). More recent surveys by the American National Opinion Research Center between 1983 and 1989 with a total of 5,420 respondents found an average of 40 per cent (Yamane and Polzer, 1994). In a British Gallup Poll using the Alister Hardy question (see p. 47) Hay and Heald (1987) found 48 per cent of positive responses; in Australia it was 44 per cent. This question as we saw brings in a wider range of responses, including paranormal ones. Many people have been surprised by the large proportion of individuals who seem to have had REs. The reason that it is surprising may be that often people keep these experiences to themselves; Hay and Heald found that 44 per cent had never discussed their experience of a sacred presence in nature with anyone, and 38 per cent had not mentioned their awareness of the presence of God. The same thing has commonly been reported by members of the Alister Hardy Society, who say they have never spoken of their REs before.

These surveys have asked how often people had their REs and how long they lasted. The frequencies for the Greeley question are given in

TABLE 4.5 'Have you ever felt as though you were very close to a powerful spiritual force that seemed to lift you out of yourself?'

	Great Britain %	United States %
Once or twice	17	18
Several times	9	12
Often	5	5
Total	31	35

Source Hay, 1982

TABLE 4.6 'Approximately how long did the experience last?'

	%
A few seconds/Ten minutes	51
Up to a day	23
Up to a month	9
Up to a year or longer	6
Unclassifiable	10

Source Hay, 1982

Table 4.5. Over half of those who report them had the experience only 'once or twice', while 5 per cent had them 'often'.

The duration of the experiences is also interesting (Table 4.6). William James thought that they were all 'transient', and for 51 per cent of those who had them this was the case. A few seconds or minutes was the most common duration, though for 6 per cent the experience was said to have lasted a year or more.

We turn to the frequency of different kinds of RE. Looking back to Table 4.1, Hay and Heald found that the most common kind of RE in Britain was:

- 'awareness of the presence of God' (21.6 per cent)
- 'awareness of receiving help in answer to prayer' (19.8 per cent)
- 'awareness of a guiding presence not called God' (12.8 per cent).

These were the three items which we identified as Transcendent measures. There was only one Immanent or Mystical item in the study:

'experiencing that all things are one' (2.75 per cent)

The low rate of reporting mystical experiences is confirmed by Thomas and Cooper (1978), who used the Greeley question with an American sample but then asked them to classify open-ended descriptions of the experiences; only 2 per cent of respondents produced mystical experiences. However, 12 per cent reported milder 'traditional, church-related' experiences.

Several surveys have investigated the frequency of reports of psychic experiences (Table 4.7). ESP refers to experience of being in touch with someone at a distance, often with close friends or relatives who are ill or dying. Other psychic experiences commonly reported are precognition, clairvoyance (i.e. seeing things that happened at a distance), synchronicity, out-of-the-body experiences, and near-death experiences (Fox, 1992; Greeley, 1975; Wuthnow, 1978).

These surveys also provide evidence of the demographic distribution of REs. Here are the main findings, from the surveys by Greeley (1975), Hay (1982) and others:

- *Age*: we looked into religious age differences in more detail in Chapter 2. REs are reported by 6-year-olds, many of whom said that they sometimes felt God was near or was directing their lives (Tamminen, 1994). The percentages who report having had REs increase with age, perhaps because this is cumulative.
- *Gender*: most surveys found that women report more REs than men, 41 per cent v. 31 per cent for Hay (1982).

TABLE 4.7 Psychic experiences reported

	Never	Once or twice	Several times	Often
Déjà vu	38	29	24	6
ESP (thought you were in touch with someone when they were far away)	40	26	24	8
Clairvoyance (seen events that happened at a great distance as if they were happening [to you])	72	14	8	2
Have felt that you were really in touch with someone who had died	70	16	8	3

Source Greeley, 1975

- *Occupational class*: in Britain 47 per cent of those with upper-middle-class jobs and their families reported REs v .32 per cent of unskilled workers (Hay and Morisy, 1978).
- *Education*: in British and American studies many more college-educated individuals reported REs than those who left school at 15 or earlier, 56 per cent v. 33 per cent for Hay (1990).

Conclusions

1 About a third of the population, in Britain, the USA and Australia, report definite religious experiences, in most cases occurring rarely and for a short period of time.
2 There are a variety of REs, including transcendent, mystical, aesthetic, in nature, of evil, and 'presence'.
3 Milder REs are much more common, and unlike the experiences studied by William James many MEs take place as part of social events, i.e. in church.
4 Psychic and near-death experiences are also common but have quite different causes and effects.
5 Although REs vary, between different religious traditions, there appear to be a number of 'core' features of REs, transcendent and mystical components, and also sensory and social aspects. Milder experiences are similar except that the mystical part is weaker.

5

THE CAUSES AND EFFECTS OF RELIGIOUS EXPERIENCE

Introduction

We now turn to the conditions under which religious experiences take place, that is, the environmental settings in which they occur, such as prayer or drugs, and the kinds of people who have them and what is happening inside their brain. Next we consider what effects they have, whether they are good for us, and finally we look at possible psychological explanations for them, at any rate for when these doors of perception are opened, though we may not be able to explain what is seen. Then we shall consider what has been found out from a theological point of view.

Triggers for REs

Religious experiences can be aroused by a number of conditions. Greeley (1975) questioned a number of individuals and found that their experiences were produced by different triggers (Table 5.1). It can be seen that music is the most common trigger, followed by prayer, and there are some surprising ones like sex and having a baby. Although drugs scored 0 (in 1975) we shall report experiments in which drugs have been very effective in producing REs.

TABLE 5.1 Triggers of religious experience

Trigger	%
Listening to music	49
Prayer	48
Beauties of nature such as sunset	45
Moments of quiet reflection	42
Attending church services	41
Listening to sermon	40
Watching little children	34
Reading the Bible	31
Being alone in church	30
Reading a poem or novel	21
Childbirth	20
Sexual lovemaking	18
Your own creative work	17
Looking at a painting	15
Physical exercise	1
Drugs	0

Source Greeley, 1975

Music

Music came top of the Greeley list, and we shall describe in Chapter 8 the long history of music in connection with religious worship. In primitive shamanism trance states are produced by repetitive drumming, chanting and dancing, probably the earliest form of music, used here for religious purposes (West, 1987).

Hills and Argyle (1998) compared the affective states produced by music and church, for individuals who belonged both to churches and to choirs or other musical groups. We assumed that we were dealing with 'milder' REs here. We used a number of scales, including the Stace ones, and the differences are shown in Table 5.2. The surprising finding was that there were higher scores for music than for church on several of the scales, including scales intended to measure religious experience, such as loss of sense of self, and the only ones on which church scored higher were 'positive feelings about life' and 'taking part in a shared performance'. If all subjects were included, regardless of membership of religious or music-al groups, the differences in favour of music were greater on all scales apart from the one just mentioned, presumably because more people respond to music than to church. Factor analysis of the music scales found the factors shown in Table 5.3. Factor 2 contains the mystical scales, Factor 3 the

TABLE 5.2 Comparison of common items of the music and religious affect scales

Item	Music scale Mean	SD	Religious scale Mean	SD	r
Being bathed in warmth and light	2.70	1.43	2.32	1.49	.53***
Glimpsing another world	2.79	1.51	2.69	1.52	.52***
Loss of sense of self	2.65	1.48	2.34	1.41	.48***
Timelessness	2.73	1.52	2.60	1.50	.41***
Bodily well-being	2.75	1.43	2.45	1.36	.43***
Taking part in a shared performance	2.62	1.75	2.89	1.38	.27***
Enjoying company of others present	3.09	1.33	2.97	1.34	.24**
Joy/elation	3.61	1.07	2.93	1.40	.22**
Excitement	3.60	1.13	2.11	1.33	.21**
Positive feelings about life	3.53	1.14	3.62	1.19	.20**
Feeling uplifted	4.16	.89	3.41	1.35	.15*

Key * p < .05
     ** p < .01
     *** p < .001

Source Hills and Argyle, 1998

social ones (including shared performance), and Factor 5 is specifically about satisfaction from music.

Musical and religious experiences may have similar origins in the brain, in that both depend on right hemisphere activity, and depend heavily on non-verbal and non-rational processes. In addition music and church are both primarily social phenomena, carried out in a co-operative group, with shared experiences.

Prayer and meditation

Prayer and meditation were the second most common source of REs on Greeley's list of triggers. We shall see in Chapter 8 that many people pray every day, and that one kind of prayer, 'meditative prayer', is most likely to lead to REs, and produces the greatest benefits to the one praying. This is prayer where individuals spend time just feeling or being in the presence of God.

There are many kinds of meditation, some under the headings of Zen

TABLE 5.3 Factor components of the scale for musical experience

Factor (variance explained)	Item	Item label
Factor 1 (33.6%)	F03	being bathed in warmth and light
	F04	bodily well-being
	F09	feeling uplifted
	F08	excitement
	F16	mental well-being
	F01	achievement
	F13	joy/elation
Factor 2 (9.6%)	F24	timelessness
	F11	glimpsing another world
	F22	self-discipline
	F14	loss of sense of self
	F12	identification with performers
Factor 3 (8.0%)	F06	enjoying company of others present
	F10	getting the best out of one's self
	F05	challenge
	F23	taking part in a shared performance
	F18	positive feelings about life
Factor 4 (7.0%)	F21	reminders of happy occasions
	F07	entertainment
	F20	relaxation/calmness
	F19	recognising the familiar
Factor 5 (5.4%)	F02	appreciating a good performance
	F17	pleasure in musical structures
	F15	mental stimulation

Total variance explained = 63.5%

Source Hills and Argyle, 1998

or Yoga, using controlled breathing or deep relaxation. Transcendental meditation (TM) uses repetition and the focusing of attention on a mantra, and passive opening of the mind to thoughts which come and go. Others involve the repetition of religious words or prayers, or concentrating attention on a candle-flame or a crucifix. Some aim for detachment and emptiness, a Buddhist method. Many of them, such as the method used in transcendental meditation, are devoid of religious intentions or imagery (West, 1987).

There was an interesting experiment by Deikman (1963) where subjects were asked to concentrate their attention on a blue vase for a number of 15-minute sessions, with no religious instructions, in the Zen style.

These subjects all experienced more vivid perceptions of the vase, with increased colour saturation; some saw it as radiating or transfigured, or experienced a merging of self and vase. All felt the experience was pleasant and valuable. This has some similarities with core REs though, as with drug experiences, these were primarily visual. Van der Lans (1987) asked subjects to concentrate on their breathing for fourteen sessions, and in later sessions on any object; subjects identified as religious were asked to anticipate religious experiences. Half of the religious subjects reported having an RE, none of the others, but all felt more vital and energetic.

Drugs

There is a long history of the use of drugs for religious purposes. Mescaline is found in the cactus peyote, which was used by the Aztecs in 300 BC and is still used in the Native American Church. Marihuana is used in parts of India, and by Rastafarians; psilocybin was used for a long time in Siberia and is still used in Mexico – it is the famous 'Mexican mushroom'. These are all 'psychedelic' drugs; that is, they produce hallucinations. Alcohol is not one of these, but this too has sometimes been used; coffee is useless (Aaronson and Osmond, 1970).

Many studies have investigated the effects of these drugs. They produce striking visual sensations, of intense brightness or colour, eidetic images, objects come alive. The self may be dissolved, or there is union with the surrounding world, there may be visions of other-worldly reality. There can be experiences of death and rebirth, bliss, terror, love, forgiveness, sacrifice, and execution (Wulff, 1997).

For some who have taken these drugs the experience is described as religious, and the proportion who do so has varied from 5 per cent to 90 per cent in different studies, but typically is 35–50 per cent – we shall see shortly how this varies with the setting and the religiosity of the individual. But perhaps they are not quite the same as REs. Oxman et al. (1988) analysed the words used to describe drug-induced and mystical/ecstatic experiences. The drug experiences were described in terms of visual and auditory sense impressions, the mystical/ecstatic experiences as life-altering and religious encounters with God. REs sometimes include visual experiences, and more rarely auditory ones, but a non-sensual experience of 'presence' is more usual.

The best-known study of the effects of drugs on REs was the 'Marsh Chapel miracle' by Pahnke (1966). Twenty theological students were taking part in a 2½-hour Good Friday meditation in their chapel. Half were given a psilocybin pill, and the others a placebo. Immediately afterwards they all wrote an account of what they experienced, and within a week and then six months later they were all given a 147-item questionnaire, and they were also interviewed. The data were converted into scores on the Stace dimensions and some new ones, and the differences between the two groups are shown in Table 5.4. This has been described as the psychology of religion's most famous study. It can be seen that there were large differences between the two groups. Although the psilocybin group did not obtain maximum scores on the Stace dimensions, for eight out of ten of the drug subjects there were substantial effects six months later. This experiment can also be seen as a kind of validation of Stace's list.

Pahnke (1967) replicated this experiment with forty older professionals, not in a chapel, and the control group were given some psilocybin

TABLE 5.4   The effects of psilocybin on mystical experience

Category	Percentage of maximum possible score for 10 Ss		
	Experimental	Control	p*
1. Unity	62	7	.001
(a) internal	70	8	.001
(b) external	38	2	.008
2. Transcendence of time and space	84	6	.001
3. Deeply felt positive mood	57	23	.020
(a) joy, blessedness and peace	51	13	.020
(b) love	57	33	.055
4. Sacredness	53	28	.020
5. Objectivity and reality	63	18	.011
6. Paradoxicality	61	13	.001
7. Alleged ineffability	66	18	.001
8. Transiency	79	8	.001
9. Persisting positive changes in attitude and behaviour	51	8	.001
(a) towards self	57	3	.001
(b) towards others	40	20	.002
(c) towards life	54	6	.011
(d) towards the experience	57	31	.055

Key * Probability that the difference between experimental and control scores was due to chance.

Source Pahnke, 1966

but a much lower dose. This time seven out of twenty of the experimental group obtained a high score on the Stace dimensions, and one out of twenty of the control group. The high rate of RE in the first Pahnke study was probably because the conditions were exactly right – religious individuals in the chapel and on Good Friday. Masters and Houston (1966) also carried out a drugs study, using LSD, and with larger numbers of subjects. Out of the ninety-six who were given drugs in a religious setting 83 per cent reported having had a religious experience, compared with 32 per cent of the seventy-four in a non-religious setting.

Isolation and sensory deprivation

Isolation and sensory deprivation are not a common source of REs in the modern world, though they may have been for those early holy men and women who lived in the desert, up trees, on top of pillars or in small caves or cells. Hood (1995) used a sensory deprivation tank to experiment on the possible effects of sensory deprivation. The subjects floated in a 10-inch-deep solution at skin temperature, and there was no light or sound. In one experiment he asked subjects to attain 'as total silence as possible of heart and mind. Having attained it you will expose yourself to whatever religious revelation/insight it brings.' There were two alternative wordings here. The subjects were interviewed while in the tank, using Hood's Mysticism scale. Those high in Intrinsic religiosity had elevated scores with the religious instruction, but only on the Transcendent factor. In another experiment the Intrinsics were more able to form images of religious figures, situations and settings.

Distress

William James and others have thought that one of the main triggers for REs is distress. This did not appear in Greeley's list of triggers, given in Table 5.1, but there is other evidence. Hay (1982) found that 50 per cent had been 'distressed and ill at ease' and another 6 per cent 'confused' before their RE. Alister Hardy (1979) found that 18.4 per cent had been in a state of depression or despair, 8 per cent had been ill, 3.7 per cent had a crisis about personal relations and a few worried about death. We have seen that religious conversion often takes place when people are in a state of anxiety or conflict. The kinds of stress which produce REs are of a special kind: they are distress over death and loss, fear and dread, and crises of meaning (Spilka and McIntosh, 1995). However, there is no evidence that stress is a source of mild REs.

Personality factors

Only about one person in three reports having had an RE, so who are they? The main factor is that they have a stronger religious background; Hay and Heald (1987) found that 56 per cent of those who attended church sometimes reported REs compared with 26 per cent of those who never went. Experiments in which REs were aroused by drugs or sensory isolation produced more REs for theological students, or for those high in intrinsic religiosity. Hood et al. (1996) found that among those who pray or meditate regularly, the intrinsics had higher scores on the Hood mysticism scale. It is more surprising that so many of the non-religious individuals also report REs.

Do those who have REs differ in personality as well as in religious background? They do not differ much on familiar personality dimensions like extraversion or neuroticism, but differences have been found on more specialised aspects of personality. Several studies have found that they are higher in measures of 'cognitive openness', that is, are open to unusual, unconscious, or illogical aspects of experience. One of these measures is Claridge's 'schizotypy' (1997), a disposition to develop schizophrenia, but which at lower levels is associated with religious experiences and creativity. Two of the items which predicted REs best were 'Do things sometimes feel as if they were not true?' and 'Do you believe that dreams can come true?'. Jackson (1991) found that this scale correlated with a numinous scale and with the Hardy question. McCreery (1993) found that schizotypy also discriminated between those who reported having out-of-the-body experiences (OBEs) and others. These individuals were somewhat hypomanic, low in anxiety, and he called them 'happy schizophrenics'. McCreery was able to produce OBEs by the 'ganzfield' method, in which sensory deprivation is produced by asking subjects to wear goggles made from semi-ping-pong balls; they were asked to relax and imagine themselves out of their bodies. The OBE subjects had more such images and there was more EEG activity in their right hemispheres while this happened. It has sometimes been suggested that there is a connection between REs and schizophrenia. Jackson (1991) compared the REs of schizophrenics and a normal sample. The schizophrenics had higher RE scores, but these were more negative and higher on the mysticism factor; these people were also higher on schizotypy. Jackson suggested that an evolutionary basis for RE can be found here: schizotypy produces heightened creativity and hence the ability to deal with crises. Oxman et al. (1988) also found that schizophrenic experiences were different from REs in containing low self-evaluation and being less religious. In any case schizophrenia is far rarer than REs, so could not explain many cases.

It has also been suggested that there is a connection between having REs and epilepsy. Some epileptics who have fits have during their fits profound experiences which they may experience as religious. It has been suggested that some great religious figures in the past, like St Paul, and also shamans in primitive religions, suffered from epilepsy, though there is no good evidence for this. Thapa and Murphy (1985) compared the altered states of consciousness experienced by meditators, schizophrenics and epileptics. They were all somewhat different: the epileptics had hallucinations and perceptual illusions; the meditators had body-image changes, perceptual distortions, disturbed time sense, feelings of rejuvenation and alteration in thinking, loss of control, changes in meaning and significance; the schizophrenics also had changes in body-image and shared other parts of the meditative experience.

Persinger (1987) suggested that over the normal range of personalities some have more electrical activity in the temporal lobe; at the upper end of the scale they would be likely to have epileptic seizures, but lower down they could have religious and paranormal experiences. It would be expected from this theory that there would be a higher level of REs in epileptic patients, and some investigators have found this, but others have not.

There is better evidence that the right brain hemisphere is important in the production of REs. Fenwick (1987) concluded that meditation leads to increased right hemisphere activity, especially in the early stages of meditation. This connection was also found in McCreery's OBE research. The neurologist Penfield (1975) found that electrical stimulation of the right temporal lobe led to patients hearing distant voices. The thinking behind the sensory deprivation research was that the quieting of the verbal and rational left hemisphere would make the activity of the right more evident. However, it seems that in advanced meditation both hemispheres are either inhibited or automatised (Earle, 1981).

Jaynes (1976) produced another speculative theory: that before 1,000 BC minds were more divided and hallucinations from the right hemisphere were experienced by the left as the voices of the gods. These voices directed action in times of crisis. The directions from the 'gods' were interpreted and organised by hierarchies of priests. At about 1,000 BC the 'bicameral mind' broke down, as the result of increased trade and social contact producing conflicts between different priests and gods. We are now left with REs, glossolalia, hallucinations and other manifestations of the right hemisphere impinging on the left. This theory is consistent with the religious importance of the right hemisphere, and with the frequent occurrence of the voice of God in Old Testament times, but postulates a most unlikely piece of rapid evolution of the brain.

Research on meditation has found that there are definite physiological effects of Zen, Yoga and TM. A number of studies have shown that these forms of meditation produce reduced oxygen consumption, a lower heart rate, reduced blood pressure and a certain pattern of brain rhythms in the EEG – reduced alpha waves (8–12 cycles per second) and increased theta rhythms (4–7 cps). This corresponds to a deep form of relaxation or trance (e.g. Kasamatsu and Hirai, 1966). However, other forms of relaxation, or even resting, have much the same effect. And these are not the effects of religious experiences, but rather the effects of deep relaxation which may or may not produce such experiences. Deep relaxation will produce REs only in those who are religious.

Effects of tradition and socialisation

We shall see in the course of this book that different traditions each have their own form of RE. Examples are speaking with tongues, snake-handling, the Toronto Blessing, eating peyote, seeing visions of the Virgin, and Zen meditation. In some cases the origins of the tradition are known; for example, snake-handling in church and the Toronto Blessing were each started by one person, and others followed them.

In Chapter 2 we looked at the social learning of religious beliefs and attitudes in children, from their family and friends, and these social learning processes are familiar in psychology. Spilka, Ladd et al. (1996) compared the nature of REs on thirty-seven rating scales by those who had experienced them with what was expected. There was a high correspondence between the nature of the experiences and what was expected, and what was rated as desirable.

Sunden (1959) proposed a theory of religious social learning, that children learn Bible stories or other religious writings, and are able to take the role of the characters, and thus perceive their life in a religious way. He supposes that there is 'role-taking' which involves identifying with a character and also taking the roles of others in the story, including that of God. They can now see their ordinary life in a religious frame of reference. They may see themselves as prodigal sons, as prophets, as baptised in the spirit through speaking in tongues, or as Buddha by sitting in the lotus position (Wulff, 1997). The theory has been used by Sunden's Scandinavian followers mainly to interpret the religious development of famous historical figures like John Wesley. There has been no attempt so far to test the theory by using measures of role-taking ability. We cited earlier a study of the everyday religious experiences of poor Blacks in two Chicago churches; they too saw biblical themes being re-enacted in their lives (p. 50).

The world religions differ in the nature of the REs that they encourage. In all the main religions there is a tradition, or several traditions, of meditation, each with a set of aims or ideas which meditators will have in mind, and which are likely to affect the experience. In Hinduism there is a quest for transcendence and union with God through contemplation of God and spiritual disciplines like Yoga (Puhakka, 1995). In Buddhism on the other hand there is a mystical search for nirvana through loss of self and emptiness. For Jews the observation of complex rules and rituals is a source of REs, but there are also mystical traditions such as ascending the ladder through the heavens to the throne of glory. However, surveys of REs among Jewish Israelis in 1995–6 found that only 9 per cent reported REs, while Palestinian Muslims in Palestine reported 4 per cent (Beit-Hallahmi, 1996).

Sceptics would say that social learning can account for and explain away REs. However, it is notable that many REs occur to individuals who do not go to church – though they may have received some social learning from other sources. It is also interesting that new traditions of RE continue to be started, and we will discuss the growth of new movements in Chapter 15. Another way of looking at these social influences is to say that they are accumulated ways of interpreting the basic religious vision, the core experience.

The effects of religious experiences

In several of these studies there were both immediate effects and also longer-lasting ones, for six months or more. The usual design of these studies has been to compare the behaviour or attitudes of those who have had REs and those who have not, after the event. In the case of the experiments with drugs or sensory deprivation this is quite a strong design since the two groups of individuals were initially similar.

Positive mood, happiness

Positive moods and happiness have often been found to be produced by REs. Pahnke (Table 5.4) found that six months after the experiment the experimental, psilocybin group reported 'persistent and positive changes' in their attitudes to life. Hay (1982) found that 61 per cent of his Nottingham sample said they were 'at peace or restored, happy/elated, or uplifted/awestruck'. Greeley (1975) used statistical models of causal paths and found that positive affect was predicted by classic mystical experiences, e.g. 'being bathed in light', at .60. Regular REs correlated .39 and psychic experiences not at all. We shall report the effects of prayer experiences in Chapter 8; these too are very positive. Argyle and Hills (in press) found that the three main factors describing milder REs were each associated with well-being or positive mood items.

Altruistic attitudes

Pahnke found that his experimental group had another persistent and positive change six months later, of more positive attitudes to other people. Alister Hardy (1979) found that 18.4 per cent of his 3,000 cases reported an enhanced sense of purpose or meaning in life, and 7.7 per cent a more positive attitude to others. Wuthnow (1978) found that those with a number of peak experiences, religious or otherwise, were less likely to value having a highly paid job, job security or a beautiful house (11 per cent) than those who had not had such experiences (49 per cent). More of the peak experience group (79 per cent) valued working for social change, social problems or people in need, than the others (52 per cent). The peak experience group also claimed to be less concerned with social status, fame or having a lot of friends. Argyle and Hills (op. cit.) found that milder REs scored on a social factor which included feeling united with other people and wanting to help them.

Religious life

Another effect of REs is enhanced religious life. Hay (1982) found that 24 per cent said the experience had 'confirmed or intensified' their beliefs, Downing and Wygant (1964) found deepened commitment, Spilka, Brown et al. (1992) that REs led to a greater sense of feeling united with God. REs also lead to religious action; Poloma and Pendleton (1989) found in the Assemblies of God that REs were a strong predictor of evangelical activity. Near-death experiences have particularly strong effects – less fear of death, greater belief in the after-life, increased religious activity, a sense of mission (Wulff, 1997).

Attitudes to the self

Sometimes people are in a state of low self-esteem before having an RE. Pahnke found that 57 per cent of his experimental group, but none of the control group, had more positive attitudes towards themselves, Spilka, Brown et al. (1992) that they felt more at one with themselves.

General health

Supporters of TM in particular have made many claims for the benefits of this method, and consistently produced data to prove it. However, these supporters clearly lack objectivity, and the subjects would be familiar with what was to be proved, and have strong anticipation of what is supposed to happen (Wulff, 1997). In addition most of these studies were poorly controlled (Holmes, 1987). Some of these claims are unlikely, such as the abolition of crime when there are enough meditators, and claims to be able to 'fly'.

The explanation of religious experience

REs can be looked at as purely human psychological phenomena which may be capable of explanation by psychology. Or they can be looked at as real, in which case what psychologists are doing is examining the 'doors of perception'.

Some of the findings which we have looked at can be seen in the context of Schachter's two-factor theory of emotion (1964). He found that an emotional state is produced by the combination of a physiological condition, such as can be produced by drugs, and cognitions suggesting how this state should be interpreted. We have seen that certain drugs produce REs in some people, and that certain religious practices produce alpha rhythms and more of the slower theta waves. Perhaps the conditions of medieval monastic life, with fasting and flagellation, were also conducive to REs. Some of the other triggers of REs listed in Table 5.1 also involve altered physiological states, such as having a baby, but most of them do not. The most common trigger is music, and this directly produces emotions which can be given a religious interpretation. We have to extend Schachter's original theory, in two ways. REs are not produced by general physiological arousal, but by a special physiological state such as that produced by hallucinogenic drugs. And there is a third factor in addition to arousal and environmentally created cognition: the personality of the individual and his or her history of religious socialisation.

We have seen several ways in which having religious ideas makes REs more likely – they happen more to church members, in religious settings, and when people are encouraged to think about religious images. So in the Pahnke experiment there was a high rate of REs for theological students, in the chapel and on Good Friday.

William James thought that the main trigger for REs was some kind of stress or disharmony. We found that this was present in some of Hay's and some of Alister Hardy's informants. And as we have seen, many feel better afterwards, as if the RE had solved their problem. Another version of this approach is that of Hood (1995), who thinks that REs are produced when experiences go beyond normal limits, cannot be accepted or understood without a transcendent interpretation of them. Such strange experiences can be produced by nature, by sensory deprivation or by psychic experiences. This probably applies only to a subdivision of REs, and does not include milder ones, for example. Batson et al. (1993) have a view of religious conversion which is similar: that individuals in a state of distress undergo cognitive restructuring in which a religious solution to their problems is found (see p. 21). This fits the finding that individuals strong in 'schizotypy' are more likely to have REs, since creativity is part of this trait.

Milder REs can also be explained by means of the Schachter model. Those who have these experiences have been aroused primarily by music, which we saw was the most common trigger of REs, and church music is designed to create the right kind of emotion, or is strongly associated with it. And there is cognitive input from prayers and sermons, while hymns combine the two kinds of influence. And regular church-goers, who have these milder experiences, have been thoroughly socialised into religious ways of thinking. However, there is a third factor in milder religious experiences. They usually occur in church, so they are generated in part by the social event, shared worship in the company of others.

Conclusions and discussion

1 REs are aroused by certain triggers, especially music, prayer and meditation, hallucinogenic drugs, sensory deprivation and distress.
2 They are more likely to occur to certain kinds of person, those with 'cognitive openness'; the connection with epilepsy is doubtful, but REs do depend on activation of the right brain hemisphere.
3 Socialisation into religious traditions is important, and can produce special varieties of RE.
4 There are strong positive effects of REs, for happiness, altruistic attitudes, religious life, and self-esteem.
5 Some of the findings can be explained by an extension of Schachter's two-factor model of emotion, as a product of physiological arousal and cognition. Milder REs can be accounted for in the same way, but also depend on the presence of others.

REs convey to those who have had them a feeling of having been in contact with a powerful force, usually a feeling of unity in the whole of creation, and also of contact with a transcendent being. Those experiencing them have a sense of joy, feel more integrated, perhaps forgiven, have a sense of timelessness, and are convinced they have been in contact with something real; the experience carries its own validity for them. There are fruits of the spirit in that many who have REs want to lead a better life and do more for other people.

This does something to strengthen the 'argument from experience', regarded by some theologians as a foundation for theology. Even social scientists have to recognise that 'religious traditions cannot be adequately understood without the assumption that transcendent objects are believed to be real by those who experience them' (Hood, Spilka et al., 1996). And it is an empirical option that at least part of the sense of God may come from God (Bowker, 1973).

Transcendent experiences are very widespread and form the basis for belief in God; experience of timelessness and near-death experiences can be the basis for belief in eternity and the after-life. Perhaps there is a world beyond psychology, as there is in the case of mathematics.

6

RELIGIOUS BELIEFS

Introduction

Beliefs are often assumed to be the centre of an individual's religiosity, and define whether he or she is religious or not. Beliefs are what sixth-formers and undergraduates argue about, changing beliefs is the focus of evangelical activity, and holding 'unsound' beliefs is what gets bishops into trouble. Medieval philosophers produced arguments for the existence of God. It is beliefs that can be experienced as an obstacle to faith, an obstacle that has sometimes been countered by offering weaker, more abstract, or more symbolic interpretations of what beliefs mean. However, other aspects of religiosity are emphasised by different churches, which may require members to have certain experiences, or to perform certain rituals, or to display the correct degree of excitement during the services in the right way. An American national survey found that only 20 per cent thought that faith consisted of 'a set of beliefs', while 51 per cent said it was 'a relation with God' and 20 per cent the finding of 'meaning in life' (Gallup and Castelli, 1989). In some religious traditions belief plays a minor role or none at all. Bellah (1970) argues that religion does not consist of beliefs, except for intellectuals in the western world, and that beliefs play little role in Buddhism or other oriental religions. Zen is mostly about mediation, for example. He maintains that 'religion is transmitted more by narrative, image and enactment than through definitions and logical demonstration' (1970: 20).

We shall see that religious beliefs are quite unlike, for example, believing that there are tigers in China; they are about assent to verbal statements, but this is only the tip of the iceberg; underneath are powerful emotions, attachments and a commitment to action; and these are all supported by social bonds with a believing community. Nevertheless believers still entertain beliefs that take the form of verbal propositions, although these may be different from beliefs about tigers in India or the existence of Julius Caesar.

We shall start by looking at surveys of what people say they believe, and measures of orthodoxy of belief. Then we look at what is in people's minds, the images of which beliefs consist. It is found that while some think that beliefs are literally true, others do not, and that their beliefs are symbolic or in some other way not literal. The psychology of attitudes holds that attitudes have three parts – cognitions, emotions and behaviour. Whatever beliefs consist of they are not just the cognitive part, so we shall examine the emotional and behavioural components that go with them.

Surveys of beliefs

We will start by seeing what people say they believe – and there have been many surveys of this. Table 6.1 is an example of one of these surveys – the International Social Survey Programme for 1991, which included large national samples from Britain and the USA (Greeley, 1992).

It looks as if believing in God and in heaven are the two most widespread beliefs. There are considerable differences between the two countries – more Americans say they hold religious beliefs, especially 'fundamentalist' beliefs such as believing in hell and the literal truth of the Bible. It is notable that there is such a high level of reported beliefs; for example, 69 per cent in Britain believe in God, which is much more than the numbers who belong to or attend churches (see Chapter 14).

These surveys also reported differences between social groups, and found that women held religious beliefs more than men – in Britain 76 per cent of women and 60 per cent of men believed in God, and better-educated people believed less – 43 per cent of those who left education at 19 or later believed in God v. 75 per cent of those who left at 15 or before (Greeley, op.cit.). Older people also believed more. We examine

TABLE 6.1   Religious beliefs in Britain and the USA

	Britain %	USA %
Believe in God	69	94
God concerned personally *	37	77
**% believing in: **		
Life after death	55	78
Heaven	54	86
Religious miracles	45	73
Hell	28	71
the Devil	28	47
The Bible is the 'actual' or 'inspired word of God'	44	83

Key *The percentages combine 'strong agreement' with 'agreement' to the appropriate item.
    ** The percentages combine 'definitely' and 'probably' believing in each item.

Source Greeley, 1992

further the different nature of belief at different ages, for men and women and in different sections of society, in other chapters.

However, a problem with this kind of survey is that different people may understand the questions differently, in particular some may take them literally, others as symbolic or mythological. Two individuals may say that they believe in 'God', but may really have quite different beliefs. An example is what happens if respondents are offered alternatives; for example, a British Gallup Poll (1986) found that while 68 per cent said they believed in God, 31 per cent believed in a 'personal God' and 41 per cent believed that 'there is some kind of spirit/life force'.

The measurement of religious orthodoxy

Fullerton and Hunsberger (1982) produced a scale of central Christian beliefs, reduced to twenty-six items. Factor analysis produced a single, central factor, a consistent dimension of Christian orthodoxy. Here are some of the items:

1 God exists as Father, Son and Holy Spirit.
3 Jesus was the divine Son of God.
7 Jesus was born of a virgin.

Fullerton and Hunsberger also (1982) developed a Fundamentalism scale, with twenty items such as 'The basic cause of evil in this world is Satan, who is still constantly and ferociously fighting against God' and 'God will punish most severely those who abandon his true religion'. A dimension of fundamentalism has often appeared in American attitude research, usually at the opposite end of a dimension from humanitarianism. These studies have all been done in the USA, and British fundamentalism is different – less about the Devil and punishment, more about literal belief in the Bible, being saved, and knowing Jesus (these three items would be enough to define British fundamentalists). Evangelicals are also devoted to the truths of the Bible but are less committed to its literal truth; their main concern is with the conversion of others and holy living (H. A. Harris, 1998).

We shall deal with the relations between religion and prejudice later, but part of that story belongs here. Many studies have found that individuals who hold fundamentalist or orthodox beliefs are also more authoritarian, more dogmatic and more racially prejudiced. This is not true of other forms of religion, such as those with 'intrinsic' religiosity or 'liberals', who hold non-fundamentalist views (Beit-Hallahmi and Argyle, 1997). Particularly striking is the finding that those with fundamentalist and orthodox beliefs have 'closed' minds; they are not free to question their beliefs. Batson et al. (1993) developed a measure of 'cognitive bondage' with items such as 'I do not think that anything could make me change my present religious beliefs'.

However, it could be argued that irrational dogmatism is part of the essential nature of religious belief, and is to some extent present in all believers. We shall see that those who are converted make a 'leap of faith' on incomplete evidence, and try to make it work – rather like marriage. And as with marriage, religious beliefs are more than agreement to verbal propositions; they are deeply rooted emotional attitudes.

Thouless (1935) in a famous early study asked subjects how certain they were of the truth of various propositions. For factual propositions such as 'Tigers are found in parts of China' the distribution showed that most were uncertain, but for 'Jesus Christ was God the Son' there was a quite different distribution – the subjects were certain one way or the other (see Figure 6.1).

As Batson et al. (1993) argue, religion gives several kinds of freedom – from fear of death, from fear in life, from temptation, social conventions,

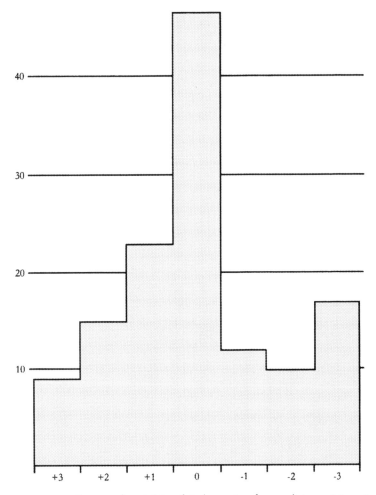

FIGURE 6.1a Degree of certainty of judgements of non-religious statements: 'Tigers are found in parts of China'
Source Thouless, 1935

and sexual desire; we shall see later in the book how true all this is. However, Batson and colleagues argue, religion also gives a loss of freedom – some churches do not allow drinking, smoking, or gambling, most do not allow promiscuity, some are against contraception, abortion,

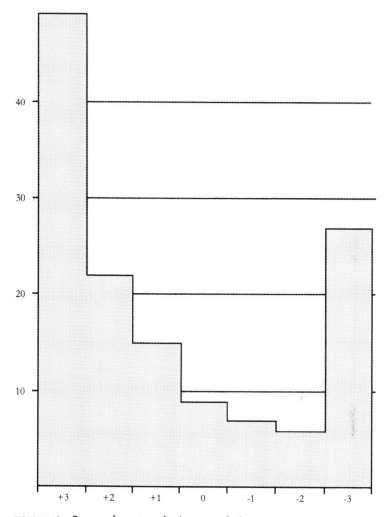

FIGURE 6.1b Degree of certainty of judgements of religious statements: 'Jesus Christ was God the Son'

Source Thouless, 1935

or divorce; but above all there is a loss of freedom to doubt basic religious beliefs. This is more true of some religious bodies than others, but it may be a universal feature of religion. Kelley (1972) ordered American churches along a dimension of strictness in enforcement of beliefs, and his order is given in Table 6.2. At the other end of the strictness dimension are churches that are very ecumenical. Part of Kelley's thesis is that it is the strictest churches that are growing fastest. We will look at the evidence for this in Chapter 14.

What is in the believer's mind?

Beliefs are formulated in words, but what do believers understand by these words? What do they think is meant by 'Son of God', 'Holy Spirit' and the rest? To be believers people have to learn this language. This happens in other spheres of life: if you want to be psychoanalysed you have to learn about the Ego, Super-ego and Id, if you want to be a

TABLE 6.2   Kelley's exclusive–ecumenical continuum

Jehovah's Witnesses	< Most exclusive
Evangelicals and Pentecostals	
Churches of Christ	
Latter-Day Saints (Mormons)	
Seventh-Day Adventists	
Church of God	
Church of Christ, Scientist	
Southern Baptist Convention	
Lutheran Church – Missouri Synod	
American Lutheran Church	
Roman Catholic Church	
Russian Orthodox	
Greek Orthodox	
Lutheran Church in America	
Southern Presbyterian Church	
Reformed Church in America	
Episcopal Church	
American Baptist Convention	
United Presbyterian Church	
United Methodist Church	
United Church of Christ	
Ethical Culture Society	
Most universal >	Unitarian–Universalists

Source Adapted from Kelley, 1972: 89. Copyright © 1972 by HarperCollins Publishers. Adapted by permission.

musician you have to learn about keys and harmony. After all, children learn new words at the rate of about seven a day. The learning may take the form of direct instruction, but it also occurs by hearing the language in use in the church community.

Several methods have been used by psychologists to study the meanings given to words. Part of the meaning of religious ideas takes the form of visual images. This is what religious art is all about – all those Virgins and Children, pictures of God as an old man with a beard, and crucifixion scenes, as well as elaborate portrayals of biblical scenes. These works of art show how artists and sculptors imagined those people and events; many churches have them, so many have been exposed to them, though more in Catholic churches.

It is possible to study images of God, for example, by asking people how much they think that God resembles various possible models. We saw in Chapter 2 that children commonly see God as similar to their father or their mother. They see God as a kind of person. C. W. Roof and J. L. Roof (1984) looked at the associations people made to the concept of 'God'. The percentages who said that they were 'extremely likely' to think of God in various ways were as shown in Table 6.3.

TABLE 6.3   Images of God

Image	%
Creator	87
Healer	76
Friend	68
Father	68
Redeemer	67
Master	64
Lover	60
King	58
Judge	52
Liberator	50

Source Roof and Roof, 1984

These were the percentages of the American Protestants studied; those for Catholics were a little lower.

This and other studies have found that God is widely seen as having human attributes, as being a kind of person. This is different from usual theological views of God as being quite other, and beyond human categories. Barrett and Keil (1996) found that which kind of image people reported depended on the experimental instructions; if indirect methods were used, such as recalling and understanding religious stories, more anthropomorphic images were obtained than by direct questions about the nature of God, which produced more abstract, impersonal images. They concluded that the subjects held both images, despite the contradictions between them.

Hutsebaut and Verhoeven (1995), in Belgium, asked 1,438 students at the Catholic University of Nijmegen an open-ended question: 'What is the meaning of God for you?' Some saw God as a person with whom one could have a relationship, others did not:

• 30 per cent described a relationship: God was a friend, father, someone who loves us, is near, forgives, etc.;
• 19.4 per cent gave transcendent descriptions: God is all-powerful, all-knowing, a mystery, cannot be represented;
• 14.8 per cent described an immanent God: present in everything, God is the power in me, is in justice and love, the deepest dimension of my life;
• 20.5 per cent gave vague answers: a feeling, an experience, everything we can't explain;
• 12.6 per cent were agnostics;
• 13.6 per cent denied Christian beliefs, despite being at a Catholic university.

This is consistent with the transcendent and immanent dimensions found in studies of religious experience. In our study of milder religious experience (Argyle and Hills, in press) we found a transcendent factor which also included relationship items as in the Hutsebaut and Verhoeven study.

Gustafsson (1972) used free associations to explore the meaning of 'the cemetery'. He found a rich set of meanings; for example, 61 per cent of non-believers used a cemetery for meditation, some of them found in it 'their own lack of hope and the bitterness of a finite existence', while some believers found 'the rediscovery of the order inherent in their faith and their very existence'. We do not know what the after-life may be like, but our images of it are in human terms, since we cannot imagine a life that is totally other. In Gorer's survey *Exploring English Character* (1955) he asked the 67 per cent who believed in an after-life what they thought it would be like. Their answers were far from symbolic, indeed, the next world was seen by most as very similar to this world. Examples were 'When I die all the jobs I have ever neglected I will have to sit and do everything twice over with burning fires around', and 'Similar to life here but no sex life'.

In large-scale studies it is possible to trace the causal relations between one belief and another. Ellison and Sherkat (1993) found that for American Protestants the holding of 'conservative Protestant' beliefs led to believing that human nature is evil and believing in the literal truth of the Bible; both of these views in turn led to believing that sinners should be punished and to support for corporal punishment. This causal sequence was not found for Catholics.

Beliefs can come into conflict with one another. Lenski (1963) found that 32 per cent of American Catholic graduates thought there was a serious conflict between science and religion, for example, over evolution; only 17 per cent of Protestant graduates thought this. In America at least there are very few successful Catholic scientists – they are more likely to be Jews, atheists or liberal Protestants. Lenski (1963) found that fewer than 1 per cent of scientists were Catholics, though 26 per cent of the American population were Catholics. The conflict between science and religion does not always result in those concerned abandoning religion, and some scientists have a great interest in religion. De Jong and Faulkner (1972) gave in-depth interviews to fifty-six American faculty members and found that many of the 71 per cent who were church members held a non-traditional, demythologised faith. These surveys have found that the least religious are psychologists and other social scientists, the most religious are physicists, while those pursuing education and economics are intermediate. This has been interpreted in terms of the different degrees of 'scholarly distance' between religion and these branches of knowledge (Lehman and Shriver, 1968), though it could also be due to the unconventional personalities of those who study the social sciences, or to the mysterious nature of modern physics, which now brings up fundamental, almost religious issues, about the beginning and end of time, the nature of consciousness, etc. Attempts to survey the beliefs of philosophers have famously failed – because they 'can't understand the questions'.

Conflicts between beliefs, even conflicts with empirical facts, often fail to worry theologians and other religious folk. Conflicts are described as 'paradoxes' and thought to be a good thing; in Zen Buddhism thinking about these is a form of meditation. Christianity has some paradoxes too, of which the 'problem of evil' is the most serious – how can God be wholly good and all-powerful and yet allow so much evil and suffering in the world? This suggests that religious beliefs do not follow the same logic that is applied to the scientific or the ordinary worlds. Failing to fit empirical facts is another problem for belief; for example, for those religious groups which predict the end of the world at a certain date and it doesn't happen. Two kinds of reaction have been common: revising the date; and reinterpreting the predicted event in a more abstract, less easily verifiable form. When the world failed to end in 1843 the Millerites in New England first revised the date by eleven years, and then at the later date revised what had happened to refer to events in heaven. This movement shortly developed into the Adventists and the Jehovah's Witnesses; clearly failure to fit the facts had little effect on the beliefs of members (Bainbridge, 1997). The best-known case this century was observed and described by Festinger et al. (1956).

In 1953 Mrs Keech received messages from 'Sananda' in outer space about the imminent destruction of the world with widespread floods and cataclysms. She and her followers gathered by an air force base in August to meet visitors from space. These failed to come, but after further messages some of the group gathered several times at her house between 17 and 24 December, expecting to be taken off by flying saucers. There were still believers after three failures but not after the fourth.

How are religious beliefs verified? Clearly not by the methods used by scientists, but people must have some way of deciding on them. One way seems to be via religious experience, reported by about 34 per cent of the population, and described in Chapter 4. This usually includes experience of contact with a powerful, holy and transcendent being. It also contains the experience of 'timelessness', i.e. eternity, and this is a route to belief in an after-life (Hood and Morris, 1983).

Are beliefs literal or metaphorical?

Many people do not hold their religious beliefs as if they were literally true. Strauss and Bultmann started the idea of 'demythologization' in which Christian beliefs are restated in less metaphysical terms. For example, the resurrection can be said to have happened in the minds of the disciples, and was described in the mythological language common at that time (McGrath, 1997).

Hunt (1972) devised a set of scales to measure (1) literal beliefs, (2) anti-literal beliefs, i.e. disbelief, and (3) mythological beliefs. There were twenty-four items to represent alternative versions of central Christian beliefs. Table 6.4 shows an example. Subjects are asked to choose one item, or to place them in order. A later version of this scale has recently been devised by van der Lans (1991) replacing the 'mythological' versions by 'metaphorical' ones; Table 6.5 shows one of the items. It was found that those individuals who opted for the metaphorical choices were more imaginative in their interpretations of religious photographs.

Another attempt to find a non-literal form of belief is Batson's Quest dimension (Batson et al., 1993). This is a measure of interest in religion but which emphasises complexity and doubt. Table 6.6 gives the complete list.

This scale has a small negative relation with measures of orthodox belief, and a stronger negative correlation with measures of cognitive

---

TABLE 6.4 An example from Hunt's scales measuring beliefs

Item 2. I believe in God the Father Almighty, maker of heaven and earth

> (*Literal belief*) Agree, since available evidence proves that God made everything.
> (*Anti-literal belief*) Disagree, since available evidence suggests some type of spontaneous creation for which it is unnecessary to assume a God to create.
> (*Mythological belief*) Agree, but only in the sense that this is an anthropomorphic way of talking about whatever Process, Being, or Ultimate Concern stands behind the creative process.

Source Hunt, 1972

TABLE 6.5 An example from the van der Lans scale

Restless is my heart until it will find rest in God.

> (*Metaphorical*) Agree. This is a manner of saying that finally we are longing for something greater that transcends human existence.

Source van der Lans, 1997

TABLE 6.6 The Quest scale

Item	Response
1.	As I grow and change, I expect my religion also to grow and change.
2.	I am constantly questioning my religious beliefs.
3.	It might be said that I value my religious doubts and uncertainties.
4.	I was not very interested in religion until I began to ask questions about the meaning and purpose of my life.
5.	For me, doubting is an important part of what it means to be religious.
6.	(−) I do not expect my religious convictions to change in the next few years.
7.	(−) I find religious doubts upsetting.
8.	I have been driven to ask religious questions out of a growing awareness of the tensions in my world and in my relation to my world.
9.	My life experiences have led me to rethink my religious convictions.
10.	There are many religious issues on which my views are still changing.
11.	God wasn't very important for me until I began to ask questions about the meaning of my own life.
12.	Questions are far more central to my religious experience than are answers.

Source Batson et al., 1993

bondage, which we described above. It has been objected that what Quest is really measuring is not belief at all but religious conflict. Perhaps it represents the sceptical and questioning views of students. Quest does not represent the view of committed members of any religious community. We argued earlier that commitment and some degree of dogmatism are central features of religion. On the other hand some religious individuals regard doubt as an important part of their faith; this is probably doubt combined with confidence that the problem will be solved. Hutsebaut (1996) produced a less sceptical Quest scale with items like 'In spite of the fact that in religious belief not everything is clear, I will follow the way of belief', and 'Through my belief in God, I can give a more profound sense to my life'.

Wulff (1997) suggested that beliefs can be classified along two dimensions: literal–symbolic, and transcendent–non-transcendent, as shown in Figure 6.2.

Beliefs may refer to entities in this world or in the other world, of transcendent religious beings. Non-transcendent theories say that religious beliefs are false, as with behaviourism (literal) and psychoanalysis (symbolic). Transcendent beliefs may be held as literally true (fundamentalism) or as symbolically true. A number of philosophers and theologians hold the last position, that religion expresses some transcendent truth, but in a symbolic or metaphorical way, a position sometimes called 'symbolic realism' (Bellah, 1970).

A number of attempts have been made to draft scales which assess symbolic realism. The van der Lans scale for mythological belief is one; an example is shown in Table 6.5. Hutsebaut (1996) gave a number of belief scales to 381 Catholic adults at Leuven, 45 per cent of them regular church attenders. He found a cluster of measures in the symbolic realism

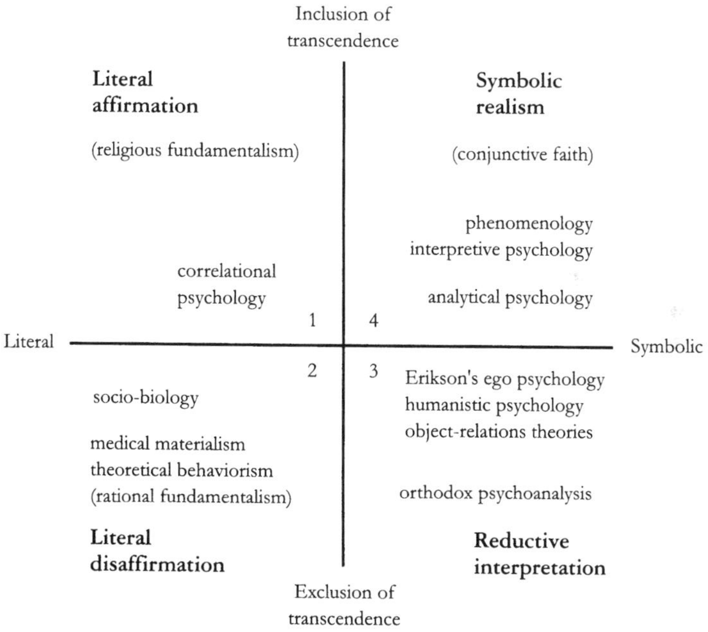

FIGURE 6.2 Wulff's schema of types of belief
Source Wulff, 1997: 635

domain, quadrant 4 – Hunt's Symbolism scale, his more positive form of the Quest scale, positive God images, and a symbolic interpretation of Bible stories. Individuals in quadrant 1, Orthodoxy/Fundamentalism, on the other hand, scored high on Literal thinking on the Hunt scale, religious certainty, positive God images, anxiety and guilt, and ethnocentrism.

Children are capable of symbolic forms of belief quite early in life as Goldman (1964) found (see p. 26).

Fowler (1981) interviewed 359 individuals aged from 4 to 84 to discover the nature of their faith, and claims to have found six stages. The earlier stages are literal; stage 3 is conforming to the religion of the community; in stage 4 there is questioning, awareness of other world-views, and some demythologising; stage 5 is a return to faith, but through accepting paradoxes and being moved by symbols and myths. On the other hand Barrett and Keil (1996) argue that people hold both anthropomorphic and abstract views of God; as they get older they learn to inhibit the simple anthropomorphic images.

Empiricist philosophers argue that propositions are meaningful only if they can be empirically verified, as most of those in science can be. And it has become widely recognised that religious statements of belief are different from those of science, though it has not been so clear what exactly they are or how they work. Susanne Langer (1942) in her influential book *Philosophy in a New Key* proposed there is a second kind of communication which she called 'non-discursive', which operates in fields like religion and music, and which has meaning in a quite differ-ent way. We have shown how belief for many people is symbolic. We will now look more closely into how such symbolism or metaphors work.

Some theologians think that the other-worldly, transcendent side of our experience is best expressed by metaphor, parable, poetry and story, and it is not superseded by abstract, conceptual language. This is 'the only legitimate way of speaking of the incursion of the divine into history' (McFague, 1975). A metaphor is when a more remote, abstract or obscure phenomenon is made more understandable by saying that it *is* some more familiar one. To say that God is a father is an example. In such cases there is some tension because of the obvious dissimilarity between the two entities, and these metaphors also have an emotional impact, which is lacking from the abstract version. Parables are a kind of extended metaphor. The story of the Prodigal Son has an emotional impact and implications for behaviour, and it also has a message about the love of God (McFague, 1975).

Religious ideas can be expressed by poetry, which is all metaphor, and by the other arts. The state of timeless eternity has been put into poetry in Eliot's *Four Quartets*. The passage to the next world is so described in the *Dream of Gerontius*. Poetry with its metaphors is one of the main forms of Langer's 'non-discursive' communication. Music can convey quite complex meanings. If people are asked to describe the message of a piece of music, they can often put this into words to some extent. Valentine (1962) did this; one person interpreted Beethoven's Pastoral Sonata as 'The joyful uplifting of the oppressed soul that feels itself released from the depths of anguish', and Hindemith's Piano Duet 'as if the composer is fighting against something, and . . . eventually there is triumph and peace of mind after great emotional disturbance'. As in the case of religion, these emotions also find expression in verbal terms, though this does not convey the full meaning.

Some religious ideas are more like myths, that is, they are not believed to be literally true but are believed to be true in some symbolic way and to express metaphorically some basic feelings and ideas about the world. Myths are a solution to life's mysteries, such as what is the origin of the universe, why are we here, what is the purpose of life, what is our destiny? There is no scientific answer to such questions, but people still ask them. The story of Adam and Eve is part of the Christian creation myth – and all religions have such creation stories, to give some account of how it all started (Hick, 1989). Myths refer to universal features of human life, so, for example, the 'fall' refers to our universal human failings. The best-known theory of myths is Jung's, and this is discussed in the next chapter.

But what is the referent of religious metaphor? What is it describing? It appears to be about the transcendental spiritual world, but there are other possibilities. (1) It could refer to underlying human emotions, of dependence, guilt, struggle, rebirth, etc. It could refer to parents, as Freud thought, or to society, as Durkheim thought. This is a quadrant 3 analysis. However, beliefs are more than emotions, they have a cognitive part too. To which theologians answer that parables and other religious metaphors are supposed to be about God, not mere human experiences (Soskice, 1985).

(2) The real meaning of beliefs, and the sphere to which they refer, may be religious experience. Although religious experiences are said to be 'ineffable', i.e. indescribable, they are often described in words. The most basic religious experience is perhaps of contact with the 'holy' or sacred, which may be the main evidence for many that there is a spiritual sphere in addition to the material world. The experience of contact with God may also be described in terms of human relationships, such as love and caring, which reflects the transcendent dimension of common religious experience which was described earlier in Chapter 4. Religious experiences for most of those who have them are of being confronted, of contact or encounter with a transcendent entity that has some of the properties of a person. Those who have such experiences are in no doubt of the reality of this entity; they are symbolic realists. These are not just individual experiences, since they are widespread in the religious community, which has its authorities and its traditions of interpretation. This is the quadrant 4 story.

Watts and Williams (1988) argue that this is the basic method of religious knowing, whereby religious experiences are rendered intelligible by the discovery of the right symbols, by individuals and by society. Symbols are not so much invented as discovered; something similar happens in psychotherapy when an individual gains emotional understanding of himself or herself. This involves effort and struggle and leads to a change of life. Such metaphorical understanding is a kind of inner vision, which is different from both faith and reason. This doctrine has not yet led to any empirical testing. One limitation is that it deals only with religious experience and not with ritual or any other aspects of religion.

It is possible that symbols can refer to both human and supernatural referents. The reason that parental images of God are so common may by because these are valued and emotive symbols, and the most immediately available for referring to God. Watts and Williams cite Jung's archetypes as an example of both referents being combined – except that, as we shall see, Jung did not himself believe in the supernatural part – he was not a symbolic realist.

Belief and emotion

Emotion is the second of the three components of attitudes which are commonly found by psychologists. For example, a racial attitude might consist of (1) positive feelings towards group X, (2) beliefs that members of this group are intelligent and virtuous, and (3) discriminating in their favour for jobs or other favours. Unfortunately most racial attitudes are more negative than this. It is assumed that the three parts are linked, but which causes which? When children develop these attitudes what comes first is basic liking or disliking, together with other emotions such as fear; beliefs about other groups come later. The same is true of political attitudes, which start as positive or negative feelings towards political parties or social groups and only later develop any ideological content. Attempts to change racial attitudes by purely educational, i.e. cognitive, methods may influence stereotypes but have little or no impact on the emotional side of prejudice.

A number of thinkers have argued that religion is primarily a set of emotions. Watts and Williams (1988) and Watts (1996) argue that emotions such as awe and reverence are central to religion, and that emotional responsiveness is a special way of knowing. It is argued that emotions are usually functional, rather than disruptive, and play a positive role in life. This kind of emotional response is found in aesthetic appreciation, in empathetic understanding of another person, and in coming to know oneself in psychotherapy.

We saw that beliefs are closely associated with patterns of emotion. Emotions may be communicated and aroused more strongly by communications other than verbal ones, i.e. by non-verbal communication. The study of this phenomenon in psychology has shown, for example, how facial expression and tones of voice express more clearly than words the emotional state an individual is in. They also show more clearly than words what one person's attitude is to another; for example, liking or disliking them (Argyle, 1988). A lot of use is made of non-verbal signals in religious rituals; for example, postures of bowing or prostration show reverence, the laying on of hands conveys healing or passing on of authority, putting on a new costume shows a new status, e.g. as a monk, or a ring indicates marriage (see Chapters 8 and 9).

Symbols for bodily healing are another example of non-verbal religious communication. Turner (1967) described a Zambian ritual for healing barrenness, which used red clay to symbolise menstrual blood, figurines for infants, and the death of a cock to stand for the end of being troubled by a spirit. Such symbols would arouse powerful emotions, and Turner thinks that there is evidence that this ritual worked.

The main factor found in the Hills and Argyle study of attenders at the Church of England (Table 4.4, p. 55) was of awe and reverence for a transcendent and loving God, together with well-being, the second of joy in shared religious activity, and the third a mysticism factor. These are different aspects of religious emotion, which individuals may experience in different degrees and combinations.

In other churches and other religions different emotions may be emphasised. In charismatic churches the dominant emotion seems to be joy combined with excitement. In monastic settings the main feeling seems to be of quietness, devotion and peace.

We saw earlier that the most common understanding of 'faith' in an American survey was that it is 'a relation with God', reported by 51 per cent, and this was also the most common image of God in a European study. We saw in Chapter 2 that the relation with God is experienced as similar to human relationships – for example, in providing social support – while 'religious coping' can consist in having conversations with God and taking joint decisions with him. In normal human relationships the emotional side is often strong and the cognitive side weak. Love usually involves a leap of faith with inadequate and often inaccurate information about the beloved (Argyle and Henderson, 1985). In the same way the relationship with God is not really a matter of beliefs. There may be beliefs – for example, that my children are good people or that Oxford University is a good university; the important part of such beliefs is my attachment to these objects.

The behavioural basis of beliefs

We said that attitudes are often thought of as having three components; we have now discussed the cognitive and the emotional parts, but what about the third, behaviour? In the case of racial attitudes this is the part that really matters – engaging in hostile or discriminatory behaviour. Sometimes people recognise this in the case of religion. Church attendance may be expected by members of a church, and those who do not attend are not regarded as proper believers. Good works may be seen in the same way. One of the reasons that people give for doing voluntary work is 'it is part of my religious belief' or words to that effect (p. 194). We have emphasised that religious beliefs are different from believing, for example, in Julius Caesar, in that religious beliefs are combined with emotions, personal attachments and commitment to action – indeed, commitment to a whole way of life. Perhaps the most important difference is in the commitment to action, the implications of religious beliefs for moral behaviour.

Beliefs, especially about the effects of possible behaviour, can certainly influence behaviour. In the field of health those who believe that some treatment will work are more likely to have it. This doesn't always work; for example, people may believe that cigarettes, drink or drugs are bad for them but the belief doesn't stop them smoking, drinking or taking drugs; they are addicted, the behaviour is outside conscious control. On the other hand behaviour can influence beliefs, rather than vice versa, as when public behaviour, for example under social influence, influences what people believe, via reduction of dissonance, the state of conflict produced by not acting in accordance with beliefs.

Followers of Wittgenstein have taken up the idea that there are a number of 'language games'; language may have various functions inside a community or interest group, and these may be different from the way language works in science. One of these games may be the religious language game. The philosopher Braithwaite offered a famous behaviourist definition of being religious – 'acting as if the beliefs are true' (1955). He proposed that religious statements are basically moral statements intended to influence behaviour, and these are backed by moral stories and parables which need not be true, or even believed. Don Cupitt, author of *Taking Leave of God* (1980), is an Anglican priest and theologian, famous for not holding beliefs, in a similar way to Braithwaite. However, this position does not do justice to the fact that believers do have certain beliefs in their minds; it does not describe what they are doing or thinking.

Sunden (1969) proposed that the study of Bible stories enabled people to apply them to their own life-situations by playing similar roles (see p. 70).

Prayer may also be interpreted in terms of its implications for the future behaviour of the person praying rather than any more spiritual impact on the object of prayers. Phillips (1966) argues that confession and intercession should be understood in terms of their effects on behaviour in this way, the immediate influence is on the believer's behaviour.

I have left to last what is in some ways the most important behavioural side of belief – its expression in ritual. Praying, praising, confession, sacrifice, expressing commitment, services of baptism, marriage and burial, are all forms of religious behaviour linked to beliefs. Some anthropologists have maintained that ritual is the primary form of religion. The words used in the course of the ritual have meaning as part of the ritual, not to express beliefs (Alston, 1967). Ritual is the topic of Chapters 8 and 9.

Conclusions

1 Perhaps the most important point to emerge from this chapter is that religious beliefs are quite different from other beliefs; they do not usually consist of assent to verbal propositions.
2 Beliefs consist in part of images, which act as metaphors, e.g. 'God is like . . .'.
3 Surveys find that many people hold basic religious beliefs, and that they have images of God, either as a kind of human with whom they have a relationship, or as a more abstract creator, or of both these images.
4 Beliefs express feelings and attitudes symbolically, and this can be done with music or poetry, and by religious ritual.
5 Beliefs are thought to refer to a transcendent reality, and may refer to experience of God and the relationship with God.
6 Beliefs are sometimes not logically consistent with each other or with worldly facts, and this is not felt to be a matter for concern.

7

FREUD'S AND JUNG'S ACCOUNTS OF RELIGIOUS BELIEF

Introduction

Freud and Jung produced elaborate psychological theories about religious beliefs and other aspects of religion. Furthermore they gave explanations of aspects of religion on which more orthodox kinds of psychology have had nothing to say, such as sacrifice, sacred meals, religious rituals and symbols. However, their theories are based more on the history of religion, anthropological studies of primitive religion and clinical case studies, rather than on the experimental and statistical data with which psychologists are familiar. Nevertheless a certain amount of solid empirical research has been done on some of the topics with which Freud and Jung were concerned, and we will see how far their theories have been confirmed.

Freud on religious symbolism

Freud's first contribution to the psychology of religion was his 1907 paper which said that religious rituals are a form of obsessional neurosis. Since this paper is about ritual and not about belief we will discuss it in the next chapter, where we deal with religious behaviour.

God as a projected father-figure

Freud's most influential theory about religion is that God is a projected father-figure, based on early experience of the real father, and who like him is needed as a source of protection, but who is also the source of fear and guilt (1910, and later papers). This theory is based on the theory of the Oedipus complex, according to which small boys between the ages of 4 and 6 or 7 have a kind of love affair with their mothers, including infant sexuality with genital stimulation, which is frustrated by the father, a feared rival, with a fear of possible castration. This is resolved by identifying with the father and internalising his image as the super-ego. Ambivalent attitudes to fathers develop during the long period in which children are dependent and need protection. The hostility to the father is repressed but guilt feelings remain. For girls there is said to be a similar sequence of events, but it is less traumatic and the super-ego less strong, less concerned with justice (see Wulff, 1997). There has been a lot of investigation of the Oedipus theory, using projective tests and other indirect methods, and the theory has been well supported (Kline, 1981). On the other hand, it has not been found to be universal; for example, it is not found in the Trobriand Islands, where fathers are neither disciplinarians of children nor sexual partners of mothers (Malinowski, 1927).

This theory explains why God is seen as a father, and why guilt feelings are associated with religion. This is essentially a quadrant 3 theory (see Figure 6.2), where the reference of the divine metaphors is to the actual father, and not to any transcendent being.

Freud's theories are famous for being very interesting, contrary to common sense, but also very hard to test scientifically. However, many attempts have been made to test this particular theory, and here are some of the main results.

1 In many religions there are father-figures; occasionally there are mother-figures.
2 Studies comparing perceptions of God and of parents find that God is seen as similar to both parents, but on the whole more similar to the father, though with a preference for the opposite-sex parent and for the preferred parent (Beit-Hallahmi and Argyle, 1997). This may not show a causal influence on perception of God; it could be because both are attitudes to a powerful, admired figure.
3 Hertel and Donahue (1995) studied 3,400 members of families and

found that God was seen as loving rather than as an authority, especially by girls; children's images of God were similar to those of their parents and to the style of child-rearing they reported, but again it is not clear which really causes which.

4 Cross-cultural studies also have found that where real parents are punitive then gods are also seen as punitive, and where real parents are kind so are the gods. Again the causal interpretation is not clear (Lambert et al., 1959).

5 Ullman (1982) found that absent fathers and poor relations with parents were more common among converts than among others, as the father-projection theory would expect.

There has been little investigation of the Oedipal part of the theory. However, it has been found that males rate God as more punitive, females as more benevolent (Larsen and Knapp, 1964), as predicted.

6 It has been suggested that belief in female gods is due to ineffective fathers; this was supported by Carroll (1983), who found that visions of the Virgin Mary are more common in cultural regions where fathers tend to be absent, and that these visions are far more common among the celibate or unmarried, who are assumed to be sexually frustrated.

7 The super-ego part of the theory has received some support. There is a strong correlation between super-ego strength and religiosity (Rasmussen and Charman, 1995).

8 The non-religious parts of the theory have also been tested. The Oedipus theory has been confirmed in cross-cultural studies; for example, Whiting et al. (1958) found that severe initiation ceremonies for young males occurred in those societies where mothers slept with babies and enforced a long period of sexual abstinence. There is also evidence that the super-ego is similar to the demands of the opposite-sex parent (Argyle, 1964).

Totem and Taboo

Freud's most remarkable book on religion was *Totem and Taboo* (1913). Here he uses a piece of speculative early history due to Darwin, that over many generations 'hordes' of primitive men had been dominated by single dominant males, who had appropriated all the women and driven off or killed the other males, including their sons. The brothers then co-operated to kill and eat the father, and seize the women. This led to great guilt feelings, and possible collapse of the social group; the result was a taboo on killing the totem animal, taken to symbolise the tribe, and now symbolising the father, and becoming the god, and a taboo on sex with female members of the in-group. Both the totem animal and the god symbolise the father.

The father, who was both loved and feared, is mourned, and as a result introjected as the super-ego. Eating and drinking together are symbols of fellowship and mutual obligation, and make those involved feel like kin, as blood brothers. They also feel they are kin with the sacrificed totem animal and with the god. The memory of these events was inherited by later generations, and was commemorated in the regular ritual killing and eating of the totem animal, a basic feature of primitive totemism. It lives on in later religions, in guilt and fear of god and avoidance of sex, in the Christian eucharist (eating of the god), and in atonement, leading to reconciliation with the father.

This theory has often been ridiculed; for example, as 'a wild gothic novel' (Eliade, 1987). However, a similar method of surveying primitive religion and ancient mythology was used by Girard (1972), who was very sympathetic to these ideas; his theory is discussed in the next chapter.

The theory was partly based on the work of the anthropologist Robertson Smith (1889) who thought that the totemic system involved an annual totem meal when the totem was eaten. However, this has not been found to be universal, nor is father murder reported. As we shall show in Chapter 9, Girard argued that the sacrificial victim was not the father but a scapegoat representing all. He also points out that Freud's explanation of the incest taboo is not convincing. In any case we would now explain it by the principles of socio-biology, through the undesirable genetic effects of in-breeding.

And totemism has not been found to be a universal stage in religious development. However, animal sacrifice is common in primitive religion, and sometimes there is a regular meal at which the totem is eaten. The Dinka sacrifice an ox and they eat the raw flesh, which is taboo. This is described as 'flesh of my father' and identified with God (Lienhardt, 1961).

Jolly (1970) showed that the gelada baboons have a social organisation like that of Freud's primitive horde: they have 'one-male breeding units' where the head male has exclusive sexual rights. This is enforced by the aggression of the main male, not by the incest taboo. In the next stage of evolution, primitive men did have an incest taboo and aggression to the father was suppressed. How did this happen? Badcock (1980) suggests that the shift to co-operative hunting groups, which would survive better than one-male groups, required a new origin of the super-ego since they could no longer depend on guilt over killing the father. It could be found in violent initiation rites, including circumcision or worse.

The Future of an Illusion

Freud's book with the title *The Future of an Illusion* (1927) develops his atheistic ideas. He restates the idea that religion has its origins in the infant's relations with its parents, and can be seen as some kind of neurosis. Projection is one of the Freudian defence mechanisms: when there is stress, internal parts of the person are projected and seen as external. The stress now is fear of death, natural disasters, and social problems. What are projected are parent-figures and the conscience. Religion helps us deal with suffering and powerlessness. A major part of civilisation and culture, it makes human life possible by social bonds, moral rules and the protection of the weak, restraining aggression by internalised moral rules. Freud was much concerned about the destruction of the First World War, and recognised the importance of controlling it. However, he believed in cultural evolution and thought that religion is an illusion which will disappear as we move into the rational age of science.

However, there seems little sign of religion fading away, and we shall show in Chapter 15 how it has been increasing in popularity in many parts of the world. In Chapter 11 we shall show that religion is associated more with mental health than with neurosis. In Chapter 12 we shall also show that religion has some power to control anti-social behaviour, though more by internal than by external restraints. The attempt to discredit religion by finding its childhood origins has been countered by the finding that atheists have often suffered early loss of parents or other traumata, so that a psychological explanation might be provided for them too (Wulff, 1997). As for the age of science, while it is true that technology has become increasingly important in the material culture, in the public mind science has become increasingly obscure and mysterious.

Sexual symbols in religion

A central part of Freud's general theory is about sexual symbolism. He thought that there is widespread interest in and attachment to physical objects of certain shapes, which resemble the penis, breasts, or other sexual organs, and to certain movements; for example, trains going into tunnels may represent intercourse. Religious practice is full of strange ritual objects and practices, and psychoanalysts believe that these are often sexual symbols.

The idea that objects act as sexual symbols has been confirmed in research into non-religious aspects of symbolism; pointed objects are recognised as male, rounded ones as female, males prefer the first, females the second, for example (Kline, 1981).

One of the clearest examples is the use of snakes in worship, still common in Tennessee and other parts of the USA (see p. 129).

Psychoanalytic theory has also been used in biblical exegesis, to interpret otherwise mysterious biblical events. Adam and Eve and the garden of Eden have often been commented on in this way. This extraordinary story is full of possible sexual symbols, but there is little agreement on what they all mean. It has been suggested that the snake represents sex, the apple is a breast, eating it is intercourse, the tree may be father, mother, or sexuality, Eden and the early paradise may represent the early blissful relation between mother and child (Wulff, 1997).

However, there is a variety of these interpretations, and there seems to be no way of deciding whether any of them are correct. Nevertheless, this and other religious stories are very difficult to interpret psychologically, and this is one possible way forward.

Sex does have some important links with religion, and it is certainly plausible that some religious symbolism refers to sex. It is familiar that the experiences reported by some of the classic Christian mystics were of a sexual nature – experienced by young women who were celibate. There has been great concern with chastity for the most religiously committed in several religions, and in sexual restraint for followers generally. We shall see in Chapter 12 that religious people in our own culture do have somewhat less sex, outside marriage at least.

Religion as a neurosis

A persistent theme of Freud's writings on religion is that it is a kind of neurosis, 'the universal neurosis of mankind'. It is neurotic because it is based on repression of early quasi-sexual desire for the mother and hostility to the father, and is associated with guilt and obsessional tendencies, keeping people immature. Freudian sympathisers see all kinds of neurotic tendency in religion, or worse. Badcock (1980) thinks that Christianity is ascetic and world-rejecting, making it psychotic, paranoid in rejecting other religions, sometimes megalomaniac.

We shall see in the next chapter that the theory that ritual is an obsessional neurosis has not been confirmed. And we shall see in Chapter 11 that there is a positive relation between religion and mental health, not the opposite as Freud's ideas would suggest. For those who are already religious it is a successful way of coping with stress, including fear of death. But does stress make people more religious? It can do, and we have seen in Chapter 2 that sudden religious conversions are more common in individuals who are in a state of distress; this includes those who join small sects and cults. However, the result of such conversions is usually positive; those involved are in much better form afterwards than they were before.

Conclusions on Freud and religion

1 The theory that gods are projected parent-figures has received quite a lot of empirical support – images of gods are similar to the way parents are seen, for example. Some corrections are needed to the original view: for example, mothers are as important as fathers in the origins of gods. We saw in Table 6.3 that God is seen in terms of a number of models, of which father is one – king, and some others (creator, healer) are more common. What Freud showed was that these models had an emotional force of their own; perhaps this is the sense in which they are true. Freud also believed that the god image was derived not only from childhood experience but also from 'inherited memory images of the primal father'. This comes very close to Jung's ideas (Watts and Williams, 1988).

2 Freud's most exotic theory, in *Totem and Taboo*, is consistent with some primate research and some anthropological findings, about tribes that kill and eat their totem animal, which symbolises God. This theory does give an interpretation of religious sacrifice.

3 His theory that religion will fade away has not come true, since religion is expanding in much of the world.

4 The idea that there are sexual symbols in religious practices has received

some support from snake worship, but is difficult to test, and the same applies to sexual interpretations of biblical stories.

5 There is no ground for thinking that religion can be regarded as a neurosis, or that ritual is an obsessional neurosis.

However, psychoanalytic ideas can be used in another way, to criticise those parts of religion that have negative results. Several psychoanalysts believed that psychoanalysis could lead people away from neurotic conditions to freedom and independence and that religions can do this too, but they can have too much emphasis on sin and guilt, too much attention to obsessional details of ritual, for example (Pfister, 1948; Fromm, 1950).

Jung and religious symbolism

At first Jung's ideas were similar to Freud's, and he saw religious ideas as projections of parental figures. This all changed with his 'discovery' of the collective unconscious. He did not think that religion was a neurosis, but saw it as needed for personality growth. He did not think it was based on sex because libido is much wider than that. And he did not think that images of God were based on an individual's father but rather on the universal father archetype. Unlike Freud, Jung was in favour of religion, thought that religious experiences were in some sense real, and held that religion was needed by society.

His main 'discovery' or new idea was that certain common themes could be seen in the dreams of his patients, in a number of world religions and myths, and in alchemy. Later he recognised that these themes also appeared in works of art (1968). Dreams often have numinous moments, he thought, a feeling of the holy. They are the route to the unconscious, and he thought that some of his patients had ideas and dreams that could not have come from their ordinary experience. His method was to study dreams, both of patients and from historical records, and to study religion and myth. Anyone who has had such a dream, has had any acquaintance with primitive religion, or has paid a visit to an art gallery will confirm that symbols like these are indeed common and some of them recur. However, Jung did not produce any criteria to decide which ones were universal archetypes, and his ideas have proved impossible to test by any familiar scientific procedures. On the other hand they have been of great interest to religious thinkers, have been used in devotional practice, and have been widely used in psychotherapy. Kirk (1970), from an examination of myths in the ancient world and in primitive society, concludes that these themes are in fact far from universal. And when they do occur they could be accounted for in other ways than by positing a collective unconscious. They could reflect common human experiences, of mothers and fathers, birth and death, etc. Or they could be due to cultural diffusion. The patients who reported dreams with these interesting contents were probably well-educated individuals who had read a lot. There is no systematic way of deciding which archetypes there are or what symbolises them. Are there not archetypes for lover/spouse, friends and group, home and family, work and achievement, for example, all central themes of human existence?

The personal unconscious, like Freud's, consists of lost and repressed memories, some of them taking the form of complexes, autonomous and broken-off parts of the personality, seen by Freud as the source of neurosis, but by Jung as the source of new growth, and accessed by him with his word association test (1918). Below the individual unconscious, Jung claimed, lies the collective unconscious. Materials from here are different from those produced by the individual; they may be more intelligent, carry a sacred authority, seem to come from outside the person, and possess emotional force. The collective unconscious consists of primordial images derived from the early prehistory of the race, rather like instincts. These *archetypes* are dispositions to experience and respond to the world in the ways those ancestors did (Palmer, 1997). They are something like Platonic ideas or Kant's a priori categories. They cannot be known directly but only via symbols, and these are derived from the culture and personal experience. They are abstract forms, which give a readiness to have certain universal mythical ideas, dreams, delusions, and religious beliefs, when shaped by individual and cultural influences. The Father is a symbol, not of the individual's father, but of a more generalised entity, a source of magical power, which can be symbolised in a number of ways.

The archetypes

The archetypes are the sphere of religion for Jung, and it is accessed by dreams.

The sun is symbolised by a lion, gold, and a king, and represents the power for life and health. It has been worshipped in some primitive religions, and we can see why this is an archetypal theme – the other-worldly power and energy, the daily and seasonal rise and fall, life and death, and the night journey into the psychic world.

Mother means the principle of maternal care and sympathy, fertility and rebirth, but also the underworld of the dead. Mother is symbolised in many ways, by goddesses, the Virgin, the sea, night or moon, and her evil side by deep water and the grave.

Father is similar, but there are other male archetypes such as the *Wise Old Man*. This stands for understanding, meaning and moral qualities, and is symbolised by a priest, professor, etc.

The child is about the origins of life, growth and self-realisation, and symbolises the hidden potential for marvellous growth. Symbols for the child include a monkey, a jewel or a golden ball.

The treasure is symbolised by a jewel or other valued object, sometimes protected by a serpent or a dragon, in a cave. However, it is really self-realisation or salvation, the discovery of the self.

The Self represents God, and is the archetype of wholeness, the integration and perfection of the personality, the result of *individuation*. It includes conscious and unconscious, and contains the balance between opposites in the personality. It can be expressed geometrically by the mandala, by kings and queens, by religious figures like gods and goddesses, Christ and Buddha, by animals like the dragon or lion, by the alchemists' philosopher's stone, which is able to transform gold, and by the Holy Grail. One of Jung's patients reported 400 dreams, of which 71 contained the four-sided mandala. These different symbols all stand for an archetype that is both God and at the same time the centre of the self. The self and God are closely related, the self being God within us, 'God, who is present everywhere, is most accessible to us within our own souls' (Bryant, 1983: 41).

The shadow is the suppressed, unconscious part of the personality, and is symbolised by the Devil, a snake or original sin. It is in contrast to the *persona*, the public self, which conforms to social expectations.

The anima is for males the female principle, part of the shadow derived first from the mother; good parts of it are symbolised by saints or fairies, bad versions by whores. For women the shadow contains the *animus*, the male principle, which can be symbolised by a variety of male types.

Jung and some Christian beliefs

Jung was very sympathetic to religion, and assumed that religious experiences could be accepted at face value. But he saw them all as symbols of his archetypes.

God is an archetype, an unknowable part of the collective unconscious, but experienced through symbols. These have taken a variety of forms in the history of religion, including Christ, Buddha, kings and queens, dragons and other animals, and God is known through numinous religious experiences.

The Trinity: Jung observed that similar groups of three gods appear in other religions, but he believed that a symmetrical four-sided pattern, the mandala, would make it more complete. The fourth side could be Satan, a shadow, making further growth possible in the self, or it could be feminine, and he approved the promotion of the Virgin Mary by the Catholic Church.

The eucharist: Jung recognised that this has been a very pervasive symbol, but of what? First he traces it back to early shamanism, with its mysteries and sacrifices, including sacrifices of gods in order to be reborn and fertilise the crops. The Christian eucharist recalls how God sent his own son, who is also himself, to be sacrificed; however, the son rises again, and so do participants in the eucharist, who sacrifice the selfish, broken-off part of the ego, and the self is transformed (1954).

Christ: for Jung the main archetype is the 'self', which also corresponds to God. Christ is one of the main symbols for the Self, though there are others, such as the philosopher's stone. He is seen as perfect, but incomplete, since he lacks a 'shadow'. The separation of Christ from God, at his birth, symbolises our human separation from our parents. Christ's death symbolises the necessary sacrifice of the ego in order to become more complete.

Religious dogmas arise from religious experiences, and together with rituals give protection against further disturbing religious experiences. Protestantism abandoned the Catholic dogmas and rituals and as a result modern man has been in a state of restlessness and fear ever since (1938).

The spiritual journey, 'individuation': the integration of the personality is self-realisation, the achievement of wholeness, which consists of the combination of opposites, of conscious and unconscious, accepting what has been repressed, finding the *self*. This is a particular task for the second half of life, and for psychotherapy. It is also a religious quest, since the self is a religious archetype represented by religious symbols. The worship of God gives liberation from human inadequacy; such transformation is found in initiation rites. Symbols of transcendence represent man's striving to attain the goal of self-realisation. There are many symbols which point to these archetypes, such as the bird (transcendence), the snake (healing), animal sacrifice (suppressing our animal nature), human sacrifice and rebirth, also the rising sun (growth by abandoning part of previous nature). Watts and Williams (1988) suggest that seeking knowledge of God is like trying to find the true self and then living it. Individuation is a kind of therapeutic and also a religious process. Is all this true? We don't know yet; there is no relevant research.

Other religious ideas include gnosticism. The gnostic set of beliefs saw the world as in a state of conflict between good and evil; for Jung this symbolised the inner conflicts in the personality, an example of opposites. Salvation could be obtained by mystical knowledge which could reconcile the two sides. *Alchemy* was about experiments to transform base metals into gold, which Jung saw as symbolising the transformation of the personality as it achieves integration. Jung interpreted the biblical story of *Job* as revealing that God himself has a dark side, a shadow, which is violent and unjust. Job comes to know this and God has to atone by the incarnation. This part of Jung's writings is not popular with theologians.

Jung's psychological types

Jung is famous for inventing or discovering the dimension of introversion–extraversion, though this was taken further by Eysenck and is now usually measured with the *Eysenck Psychological Questionnaire* (1976). However, as we saw in the previous chapter there is almost no relation between this dimension and religiosity.

Two other Jungian dimensions of personality are thinking v. feeling and intuiting v. sensing, and these have been incorporated in the 'Myers-Briggs Type Indicator' or MBTI (Myers and McCaulley, 1985) (see p. 39). The MBTI is widely used on weekend courses and retreats to advise people on how to conduct their spiritual lives. For example, intuitive type personalities might be advised to adopt a contemplative waiting on God, while feeling types are advised to express gratitude, penitence, trust or love in their prayers (Bryant, 1983).

This test is not used in mainstream personality research, and it has been suggested that its two main dimensions are probably very similar to two more familiar ones. McCrae and Costa (1989) think that intuiting is the same as 'Openness to Experience' and feeling much the same as 'Agreeableness', two of the dimensions of the 'big five'. We showed in Chapter 2 that both are related to having religious experiences. Jung may have been successful, at a much earlier date, in locating aspects of personality that have turned out to be important for religion.

However, there seems to be no relation at all between the existence of these dimensions and the theory of archetypes.

Evaluation of Jung's views on religion
(Conclusions on Freud's ideas were given earlier, p. 103.)

1 The central claim of Jung's psychology is that the archetypes occur universally in all cultures and historical periods. Similar themes, it is said, can be found in the myths and religions of remote cultures, and in the dreams of patients who could not know about them. So far no one has been able to devise methods of research which could test Jung's ideas, as they have with Freud's.
2 The archetypes provide a way of interpreting dreams, art and myth, and also Christian theological concepts like the eucharist, the Trinity, and the spiritual journey.
3 Jung's psychological types are used for spiritual guidance but not in mainstream psychological work, and have no connection with the archetype theory.
4 From the point of view of social psychology Jung gives a very solitary view of religion, of what individuals find in their own experience. There is no relationship with God either, merely visions of God's symbols.

Jung's work is not part of scientific psychology. However, it is to some extent supported by research into comparative religion by Eliade and his colleagues. In Eliade's great *Encyclopedia of Religion* (1987), which he edited and partly wrote, every religious theme is traced, not just from the New Testament to the Old Testament, but to earlier and more primitive and quite different faiths, where they can also be found. Eliade, like Jung, does not decide whether this is because there is a transcendent reality behind these phenomena. Nor does he provide any more human explanation of these common religious themes.

Jung was very interested in and well informed about religious themes, and constantly expressed himself as being in favour of religion, because it is good for mental health, and people need a meaning in life, a set of higher goals. They need to integrate the personality, and come closer to the Self, and this is a religious task. In his book *Modern Man in Search of a Soul* (1933) Jung is famous for saying that it is essential to find a religious meaning in life. In 1938 he did not believe that his religious symbols had any transcendental existence.

> It would be a regrettable mistake if anybody should understand my observations to be a kind of proof of the existence of God. They prove only the existence of an archetypal image of the deity, which to my mind is the most that we can assert psychologically about God. . . . Since the experience of it has the quality of numinosity to a high degree, it ranks among religious experiences.
>
> (1938: 73)

However, in 1959, twenty-one years later, in a TV interview on the BBC with John Freeman in the *Face to Face* series, when he was asked if he believed in God, Jung said, 'Difficult to answer. I know. I don't need to believe, I know.' Elsewhere he had said that 'Religious experience is absolute, it cannot be disputed' (1938). God existed for him as a 'psychic reality', and he thought that this is all we can know.

Where does this leave Jung's symbols? They are different from Freud's in that they do not refer to the individual's experiences (of parents, for example), for they refer to universal underlying features of human life. The archetypes are like instincts, the results of human evolution. They carry a sense of religious meaning, a sense of the holy, and are found in all world religions, and are in some sense true, yet Jung did not believe that they have any existence outside human life. As with Freud's symbols, a transcendent world can be understood only in terms of more familiar symbols, and it is likely that the most important symbols would be chosen to do this. They may refer both to supernatural and to experiential realities.

8

WORSHIP AND PRAYER

Introduction

In Chapters 8 and 9 we now turn to the central forms of religious behaviour. In this chapter we discuss the most familiar – worship, including music and sacrifice, and prayer. There has been a historical continuity in these forms of behaviour since the most primitive kinds of religion, though sacrifice and dancing have largely disappeared, music has been elaborated, and charismatic religion has produced new forms of behaviour, which we take up in the next chapter. In all varieties, however, we can find a priest leading a group of followers in worship and ritual, carrying out symbolic activities.

Worship

Services of worship play a central part in most religions. A group of members gather in a sacred place, under the direction of a priest, sing hymns, and sometimes dance. To this may be added some of the other aspects of religious behaviour to be considered later – healing, sacrifices, rites of passage and other rituals, and prayers. The intention is to influence the deity, but it also has the effect of putting the participants in an elevated mood, and enhancing group cohesion.

The most primitive form of worship may have been of light. A species of South African baboons has been observed to bark in ecstasy at the setting sun, and the setting sun has been seen to excite meercats and other species; simpler organisms orientate towards the sun (Malan, 1932). The early Egyptians worshipped a sun-God, Re – the creator and sustainer of life – and early Hindu scriptures described the sun as the God of Gods (Wulff, 1997). Today, happiness research has found that when the sun is shining people are in a better mood. We have seen that religious experiences are often described in terms of light – for example, people report 'being bathed in warmth and light' (p. 54) – and that light is a common metaphor for describing such experience. We shall see the importance of candles in setting up holy places next.

Another feature of religion found in the most primitive peoples is the response to the holy or sacred, which may be found in special places, people or objects. Marrett (1914) thought that this was the origin of primitive religion. Certain people, objects or places are declared 'taboo', and must be avoided. This marks the value attached to them by the society, the equivalent of being 'holy'. Otto (1917) thought that the response to the 'Holy' was central to all religion, a sense of 'unapproachable awfulness', majesty or 'overpoweringness', and of energy or force. The response to the holy is of fascination but also of dread, and the numinous object is seen as a route to special powers and to salvation. Powerful taboos surround holy places and objects and help to generate their emotional force. Religious services are carried out in special places, which are set up to create a numinous experience – darkness and silence, but also candles, making the altar separate and unapproachable, elaborate decorations, incense and music. These non-verbal symbols can have a powerful effect, some from the emotions they naturally produce as in the case of music, others from their learnt associations. The priest and his assistants may wear impressive robes. The Church of the Holy Sepulchre in Jerusalem, with its many lights and decorations, is a spectacular example; it is also in a symbolically important place, the supposed site of the burial of Christ.

Worship is performed by the use of symbolic acts and objects. A holy person, such as the founder of the religion, may be symbolised by icons, photographs, parts of their body, or blood, or their clothes. Members of cults often carry a photograph of their leader. Attitudes and emotions (for example, guilt or reverence) can be symbolised by bodily posture, dance or other forms of expression. The social status or role of priests and others is symbolised by their robes. Past events of importance to the faith can be re-enacted symbolically, as in the eucharist. Desires, as for rain or health, can also be expressed symbolically, as in the rituals used in rain-making or healing services. Rituals acquire their meanings in two main ways. Some are 'iconic'; that is they are similar to or part of the referent, as wine is to blood, water to purity. Others may have associations which have become established, as flags stand for national groups (Firth, 1973).

As well as singing and dancing, worshippers express their religious feelings and attitudes in other ways. There are special postures – kneeling, bowing head or body, sometimes prostrating on the floor. There are special gestures – hands together, one or two hands raised in the air, hands clasped, clapping, making the sign of the cross, and other ritual moves, especially on the part of the priest and his helpers. There are special ways of walking, quietly and humbly, and avoiding sacred areas, sometimes walking round and touching sacred objects. Singing has to be performed with the right volume and in the right tone. Hats or shoes may have to be removed or parts of the body covered. This is a pattern of non-verbal behaviour which clearly expresses awe and deference, but could also be seen as reaching up to or greeting (Heiler, 1932).

Music in worship

Religious meetings usually contain music, the two being closely connected. Music has been said to symbolise the other-worldly, and to express the 'otherness' of religion, to convey the experience of the numinous or magical. It is connected with dancing and 'Singing and dancing serve to draw groups together, direct the emotions of the people and prepare them for joint action' (E. O. Wilson, 1975: 564). For primitive peoples 'dancing is more important than sacrifice' (Heiler, 1961).

In shamanism and in voodoo there is frenetic drumming, used to work people into states of excitement and trance. Music has often been accompanied by dance in primitive religions – by shamans, the Greek followers of Dionysus, the Turkish whirling dervishes, and the nineteenth-century American Indian Ghost dancers, for example. In all these cases the dancing lasted for hours, producing states of ecstasy and exhaustion, in which participants could, for example, walk on burning coals. This state was induced not so much by the music as by its loudness and rhythm (Wulff, 1997). It was believed that the participants were gods, or were possessed, or were able to give protection against illness or volcanoes, or could win battles. In the modern world dancing is not usually linked to religion, except in some charismatic meetings, but secular dancing has been found to give rise to great joy and social cohesion (Argyle, 1996).

In ancient Greece music was used to create states of celestial harmony, and various musical styles were invented to do this. In early Christianity music was used to teach and to accompany ritual to express the faith. The combination of these two ideas led to early church music, e.g. Gregorian chant, sung by unaccompanied voices. The Renaissance produced the church music of Bach, Palestrina and others, who created the religious sound as we still know it in the West. They used organs and later musical instruments; Bach wrote and conducted cantatas at Leipzig; the author recently attended the church, associated with Luther, in the nearby town of Jena, and the service included a Bach cantata. Here, as elsewhere, religious words are set to music, which greatly enhances their meaning and emotional impact. The music for services carried the sequence of acts and emotions of the ritual, as in the Mass. Winchester Cathedral installed an organ in the tenth century, famous for its size and loudness. The Reformation produced hymns, on which Luther was particularly keen. Evangelical meetings today use moving hymns – a choir of 1,500 led the singing for Billy Graham. Hymns are found very enjoyable, and may put participants in a good mood and attract new members, as well as enhancing the cohesion of the group. Charismatic churches now use instruments rather than organs, partly because they often meet in buildings without organs, and because forming a music group can create more cohesion. At a previous period churches adopted organs partly to distance themselves from the secular music of the jongleurs. They may have discovered the power of deep and rhythmic organ notes to generate religious feelings.

Research on emotions has found that music is a very easy and powerful means of arousing them, and it has often been used in the lab for this purpose. We can make people happy, sad, etc., and this can be done by sounds which are like the corresponding tones of voice. A sad person speaks slowly, in a low and falling tone, with low volume, a happy person speaks faster, with higher and more varied pitch, gentle pitch-changes and purer tone (Scherer and Oshinsky, 1977). There is a recognisable 'religious' feeling which can be evoked by religious music. Goodwin Watson (1929) carried out an experiment with different kinds of service with adolescent boys, and found that the service with deeply moving music was rated the most worshipful.

However, music can do more than this. It can create different religious feelings, suitable for weddings or funerals, for Lent and for Easter, for example. It can create peaks of religious intensity in the Mass. Beethoven's last quartets seem to give glimpses of eternity. Elgar's *Dream of Gerontius* gives a vision of the passage to heaven.

We saw earlier that music is the most common 'trigger' for major religious experiences (p. 61), and that music itself, even outside church, can produce experiences very similar to religious ones, including timelessness, loss of sense of self and glimpsing another world (p. 62). There is indeed a very close connection between religion and music.

Worship in groups

Worship is conducted in groups, usually at the church, temple or other holy place, or in the home. Turner (1969), studying adolescent initiation rites in East Africa, found that candidates feel a deep sense of unity, of love, equality and harmony, and an absence of status divisions (see p. 128). Argyle and Hills (in press) found that part of the milder religious experiences obtained in church are feelings of unity and concern for the others, feeling part of a family. This kind of social cohesion is perhaps a central part of religious experience. We shall see in Chapter 10 that some of the benefits of religion for happiness and health are due to the very strong social support and social cohesion of church communities. The reason for this strong social cohesion is not known, but one possibility is that it may be due to shared participation in worship and ritual, with the shared experience of deep emotions (Spickard, 1991).

Whether or not non-verbal expression impresses the deity, it has another effect on the members of a group: it can affect the emotional state of the performers. Smiling makes you feel happy, clenching the fists makes you angry, through a phenomenon originally known as 'facial feed-back' (Argyle, 1988).

Priests and clergy

Worship is directed by the priest or other religious leader, who often dresses up in an impressive and symbolic costume, though less so for Nonconformist and evangelical bodies. There are also a number of helpers, to make the music, help at the altar, read from sacred books, and generally run the church or temple. For centuries priests in nearly all churches have been men, though Protestant churches are now increasingly run by female clergy, despite enormous initial resistance in some of them. In the most primitive religion, shamans were selected for their capacity to go into a trance, or for having odd bodily features. Candidates for the Catholic clergy are usually spotted when they are still at school by their priests (Fichter, 1961), but many Protestants feel themselves 'called', and some sects insist on this. Most clergy are now trained, though it was not always so, and may have to spend some years in a seminary. In addition to organising and leading the services, clergy are expected to preach, teach and look after their flock and the various groups attached to their church. Clergy are found to be deeply committed to their jobs, though they complain about overwork and having too little time for leisure.

In Chapter 15 we shall discuss another kind of clergy, the charismatic leaders or gurus of new religious movements. These individuals start their own churches, offering a new vision and set of beliefs and practices to their followers.

Sacrifice

Sacrifice plays a central part in all primitive religion, and is also found, usually in a symbolic form, in more developed ones. It is the offering to the deity of a gift, especially a living creature (*Oxford Dictionary of the Christian Church*, 1997). It is found in palaeolithic times, pre-literate societies, the religions of ancient Greece, India and Japan, as well as in Judaism and Christianity. Sacrifices are carried out by priests, or other qualified persons, after they have been ritually cleansed, at an altar, at regular times or special events such as rites of passage. Animals, sometimes humans as in ancient Mexico, sometimes vegetables, are sacrificed first by killing them, then burning them, sometimes eating them. The common element is offering living possessions to the gods (Henninger, 1987). Sacrifices are offered to the gods, to spirits, or to the departed, for various purposes. When there is propitiation of evil, this is represented by the animal and it is completely destroyed. When offerings are made to the gods of the underworld, blood is poured into the ground or streams. Anthropologists have found at least six kinds of sacrifice with different purposes:

1 gifts in the hope of favours being returned
2 propitiation, seeking forgiveness and avoidance of God's punishment
3 seeking a closer relation with God, by sharing a meal
4 killing the god, to prevent his becoming senile, so that he can maintain the fertility of the crops
5 eating the god to ingest his powers
6 funeral sacrifices to help the departed to the next world.

Some anthropologists have a longer list, with up to fourteen possible purposes of sacrifice. It looks as if there is no clear conscious purpose, rather that sacrifice is a fundamental form of religious behaviour which is not easily reducible to normal kinds of rational explanation.

However, there have been major historical changes in the use of sacrifice throughout the world. Literal sacrifice can now be found only in the most primitive societies; elsewhere it has become 'spiritualised', i.e. symbolic, and what is sacrificed is the self or part of it. Sacrifice of the gods, sometimes eating them, was common in agricultural communities, where the life, death and rebirth of crops were a central theme of life, and it was believed that it was the gods who fertilised the crops. Sacrifice was widely practised for centuries, and 'sacrifice as a religious act was part of the mental furniture of everyone in the ancient world, Jew, Christian and Pagan' (Hanson and Hanson, 1981: 107). However, sacrifice long ago ceased to be part of our mental furniture, probably by the end of the eleventh century (Hanson and Hanson, op. cit.).

Sacrifice was very important in early Judaism, and there were a number of different kinds of sacrifice. The best-known is that of the 'scapegoat' who was believed to 'carry all the sins of Israel with it'. In Christian theology the doctrine of the Atonement plays a central part, and in early Christianity this was seen as similar to animal sacrifice – Christ was the 'lamb of God', though it was recognised that repentance was needed as well. However, the sacrifice story is particularly found in St Paul's Letter to the Hebrews, and it has been suggested that sacrifice was emphasised in order to harmonise with the Jews. Later theologians have down-played sacrifice in favour of other models or images, such as the victory over Satan, legal and penal theories, or the demonstration of the love of God creating a right relation with him. As with theories of sacrifice, so there are a number of theories of atonement, including some of the same theories, such as avoidance of punishment and seeking a closer relation with God.

However, all agree that in some way the death of Christ had a momentous historical effect. And today the eucharist, which commemorates the death of Christ, plays a central part in Christian worship, and millions participate in it weekly. We have seen that very rewarding religious experiences are often obtained in church services, and we shall see that regular attenders at services gain great benefits for happiness and health from doing so. There is a further sacrifice in Christianity – not necessarily the giving up of all worldly goods or adopting a life of asceticism, but following definite restraints on sex and self-indulgence, and undertaking to do things for others.

The simple view of Christian doctrine is that 'Jesus died to save us from our sins', and we shall see in the next chapter that evangelical meetings and groups like the Toronto Blessing remind people of their sins and then make them feel better about them, their guilt feelings are removed in some way, they feel 'saved'. Hanson and Hanson (1981: 113) suggest that 'there is no reason why the doctrine of the Atonement should not be a therapeutic pattern of belief for modern man, and the cross a therapeutic symbol'. How does this therapeutic pattern of belief work? Freud thought, as we saw in Chapter 7, that the eucharist means eating the god, and that this derives from primitive totemism where there is ritual killing and eating of the totem animal, representing the god, to commemorate the earlier killing of the father of the primal horde (1913). This theory is consistent with several important facts about religion: the guilt and fear of the god, the incest taboo, as well as the regular killing and eating of sacrificed animals.

Girard (1972) proposed that sacrifice is central to religion, indeed is a cause of religious beliefs. He observed that there is a lot of violence in every society, which is repeated in endless 'mimetic' revenge, which can make society impossible. There is regular sacrifice of humans or animals, who are treated as scapegoats representing the violence of all, which ends the cycle of violence. There is collective violence in which the whole tribe takes part, this purges them of aggression and brings peace. The victim, who has been instrumental in this process, then becomes sacred, representing our evil nature transformed into good, thus preserving society. This theory is supported by reference to a number of anthropological field studies, for example by Lienhardt (1961) who studied the Dinka in West Africa, in which sacrifice of the totem animal is carried out by the whole tribe, and who then eat the victim. This is a modified version of Freud's

Totem and Taboo theory of the totem animal representing the murdered father. It does not, however, explain why the victim has to be eaten. It is also similar to Durkheim's theory that God is a representation of society. For Freud sacrifice is a shared meal, for Girard it is a re-direction of aggression; for neither is it a gift to the gods.

The change in attitude to sacrifice is reflected in the Protestant change after the Reformation from the stone altar, deriving from Old Testament sacrifice, to a table for a shared meal.

Jung, too, recognises that sacrifice and the eucharist are important in religion (p. 107). He relates the eucharist to shamanism and the death of gods to be reborn and fertilise the crops. God sent his son, who is part of himself, to be sacrificed and reborn. Those who take part in the eucharist or other sacrifices offer valuable gifts, which are part of the self; sacrifice is of the selfish ego for a higher purpose, to be reborn. The persistence of these rites shows that they 'rest on psychic conditions which are deeply rooted in the human soul' (Jung, 1954). Unfortunately, as with Freud's doctrine of sacrifice, there is no real evidence that it is correct, so we turn to more familiar psychological theories.

It is likely that more than one process is operating simultaneously. Evans-Pritchard (1956) in his famous study of the Nuer thought there were fourteen such processes taking place in their sacrifices at the same time. Social psychologists have studied relationships and the use of gifts in them. It is usually expected that gifts will be reciprocated (Furnham and Argyle, 1998), so this is one reason for giving valued objects to the gods. Animals were greatly valued, so this is the greatest 'gift' which can be given. Similarly it is usual to give thanks and gifts in appreciation of what has been received from another, so here is a second reason. If the other is feared, punishment may be averted by gifts; people throughout history seem to have felt guilt and feared punishment in this world or the next. Gifts can bring people together, with each other and with the gods, especially if they take the form of a shared feast, which is how communion is seen. Eating the god seems very strange, but it has been normal in some cultures to eat warriors or parts of them in the hope of ingesting their strength. What still seems strange is the emphasis on killing and blood – what would the gods do with dead or burnt animals? The answer may be that the sacrifice is symbolic, as Jung thought, that what is really given away is part of the self, the selfish part.

TABLE 8.1   Frequency of prayer in the USA

Frequency	%
Several times a day	17.7
Once a day	26.8
Several times a week	20.7
At least weekly	12.1
At least monthly	6.7
Less than monthly	8.0
Never	8.0

Source Poloma and Pendleton, 1991

TABLE 8.2   Types of prayer

Type
1. Meditative, e.g. 'How often do you spend time just feeling or being in the presence of God?'
2. Ritualistic. e.g. 'How often do you read from a book of prayers?'
3. Petitionary, e.g. 'How often do you ask God for material things you might need?' [another item asks about material things for others].
4. Colloquial, e.g. 'How often do you ask God to provide guidance in making decisions?'

Source Poloma and Pendleton, 1991

But if Girard (1972) is right sacrifice is not about giving God anything, but about discharging society's violence onto scapegoats.

Prayer

More people pray every day, or claim to, than go to church every week, about 40 per cent in Britain. In the USA over 60 per cent say they pray daily, and 76 per cent say that this is an important part of their daily life; some do it three times a day or more (Poloma and Gallup, 1991). Table 8.1 gives a more detailed breakdown.

We do not yet know how long these prayers last. We are thinking here primarily of private prayer, conducted in a room usually while alone, sitting or sometimes kneeling, except for some kinds of Eastern meditation, but making little use of the postures and gestures associated with worship.

TABLE 8.3 Frequency of engaging in four kinds of prayer 'often'

Kind of prayer	%
Colloquial	30.9
Meditative	4.6
Petitionary	5.3
Ritual	6.9

Source Poloma and Pendleton, 1991

However, we do know the main types of prayer that people use, as the result of two American studies. In the first, Poloma and Pendleton (1989) carried out a factor analysis of forms of prayer and found four clear factors, which are listed in Table 8.2. The same types of prayer were listed by Heiler, and have also been found in other studies.

The frequencies of people in Akron, Ohio, engaging in each kind of prayer are shown in Table 8.3.

Hood, Morris and Harvey (1993; cited in Hood et al., 1996) carried out a similar study and obtained four similar factors, the main difference being that the petitionary factor included asking for blessings for others and 'forgiveness for yourself'.

Social surveys show that women say they pray much more than men, indeed, this is the aspect of religiosity with the largest gender difference. Working-class people pray more, where middle-class individuals go to church more. Children pray from a very early age, if taught to do so. At 5 they may pray for new toys, and believe that prayer works. Young children think that God is present everywhere and can see everything. At 10–11 they have private conversations with God, and confide in him (Beit-Hallahmi and Argyle, 1997, and see our Chapter 2).

Petitionary prayer

This was regarded by Heiler (1932) as the prototype of all prayer. We have seen that it is typical of the first prayers by children. It is a spontaneous cry for help when self or family or friends are in serious need, when there is a threat to their well-being, when problems exceed our powers to deal with them. These may be material needs, illness, or other trouble. Prayer is resorted to when human agencies have failed, and is regarded as a means of coping with the situation. The prayer may become effective by directing or motivating the individual's own behaviour, such as visiting the sick.

When the problem has been solved and all is well there may be equally spontaneous prayers of thankfulness.

Meditative prayer

We saw in Chapter 5 that prayer is the second most common source of religious experiences (after music). The goal of meditation in most traditions is to be in the presence of God, to worship or experience a relationship with God, i.e. to obtain religious experiences, though as we saw different experiences are sought in different faiths. Secular meditation can also produce powerful experiences, as in Deikman's vase meditation experiment (p. 63). A number of meditational practices come under Zen, Yoga and transcendental meditation (TM). All are able to produce altered states of consciousness and deep states of relaxation. Probably most prayer, and especially individual prayer, involves some degree of contemplative effort, otherwise it will not be experienced as a religious activity. This is one of the less frequently used kinds of prayer, but as we shall see shortly it has the most powerful effect on the one praying.

Ritual prayer

Ritual prayers are usually spoken in public, read from a book or memorised, by the priest. What were once spontaneous expressions of need or devotion become hardened into standard ritual formulas, which may have to be intoned in a special way. Just saying them may be enough without any inner sympathy with the contents (Wulff, 1997). But what they have lost in spontaneity is compensated for by the emotional power of familiar and sacred phrases.

Colloquial prayer

Poloma and Pendleton found a factor of prayers where people talk to God in their own words, or ask for guidance in making decisions. This is much the same as what will be referred to as 'religious coping' later, which may involve taking God as a partner in making decisions, and being confident that he will help deal with the problem. The other prayer factor for Hood et al. is a little different, and is about seeking blessings for others and forgiveness for oneself. The common element to all these is talking to God as to another person in ordinary language, treating him as a very wise and helpful friend. This is the most common kind of prayer; 30.9 per cent of Poloma and Pendleton's subjects (1991) said they did it daily and another 21.6 per cent 'quite often'.

Does prayer work?

We have seen that prayer is very widely used; it is particularly likely to be used by those who are very ill or in danger or despair. Poloma and Pendleton (1991), with a sample of 560 adults in Ohio, found that meditative prayer was the main predictor of 'prayer experience', a variable consisting of feeling inspired to do something, obtaining deeper insight into religious truth, receiving an answer to prayer, feeling the presence of God, and a deep sense of peace and well-being. This in turn was a good predictor of existential well-being, i.e. having a sense of meaning and purpose, as well as happiness, life-satisfaction and religious satisfaction. Frequency of prayer did not predict these as well as the prayer experience variable, or the use of meditative prayer. These investigators found that prayer experience predicted existential well-being best for conservative Protestants, while for mainstream Protestants church attendance was a stronger predictor.

In another American survey 82 per cent said that they believed in the healing power of personal prayer, and 73 per cent believed that praying for someone else could help cure their illness (Poloma and Gallup, 1991). With a smaller sample Poloma and Pendleton (1991) found that 72 per cent believed in the power of prayer for healing and 34 per cent claimed that they had experienced this. Those who said they had experienced healing had higher scores on 'prayer experience', they felt closer to God, and they engaged in meditative prayer. They were also less educated, older and poorer. Furthermore they were in worse health, perhaps because only the sick needed such prayer. Nevertheless those who felt close to God had greater 'health satisfaction'.

Ellison and Taylor (1996) with a sample of 1,344 African Americans found that many turned to prayer, five times as many for bereavement or illness of self or family as for other problems, women three times as much as men, 3 per cent more for each year of life, more for those who prayed already, and more for those who felt a loss of mastery of the situation. During the Second World War American soldiers who were most frightened in battle said they were helped by prayer (72 per cent), more than those who were least frightened (42 per cent). Mattlin et al. (1990) found that religion helped people deal with loss of a loved one. Ellison (1995) found that religious variables helped whites avoid depression when under stress, but there was no effect for African Americans, indeed, prayer was associated with more depression; this could be because distress caused them to turn more to religion.

But does prayer work in the sense of influencing events directly, apart from the activities of the one praying? This is a real empirical question, and there have been occasional attempts to test it. One of the better ones was by Byrd (1988). In this study 393 coronary patients were divided randomly into two groups, of which one was prayed for by born-again Christians outside the hospital. The allocation to the two groups was kept secret from the patients and hospital staff, but those in the prayed-for group were in a slightly but significantly better medical state at the end of the study. However, there is not yet a substantial body of replicated results in this area.

The nature of prayer

Psychologists sometimes include prayer with other kinds of 'active cognitive coping', that is, seeking helpful ways of looking at things more positively. It is a cry for help when human resources have failed. For a religious person this includes seeking guidance, and the strength to do what ought to be done. The main effect of prayer, e.g. for others, may be on the behaviour of the person praying, a point recognised by some theologians (Phillips, 1966). The religious person may pray in order to have a conversation with God, to strengthen and enjoy this relationship, to give spontaneous thanks, and have some degree of joyful religious experience. We have seen that prayer is most helpful for bereavement, perhaps this relationship can compensate in some way for such loss.

Conclusions

1 Worship is the central theme of religious activity, and is accompanied by music and ritual. The study of non-verbal communication shows how beliefs can be expressed in bodily actions; taboos and awe for the sacred can be expressed by the reverence shown for the altar or other sacramental objects.
2 Music is widely used, to express the other-worldly, and to produce high levels of arousal.
3 Sacrifice is a common form of ritual, about which there are numerous

accounts of what is going on, and the same applies to the Christian doctrine of the Atonement; it seems that there is a deep human need for sacrifice, without a clear understanding of why. It may be intended to produce propitiation, or take the form of a shared meal, and may have the function of neutralising aggression in society.

4 Prayer can be looked at as a coping device, turned to when other methods have failed. Meditative prayer leads to experience of contact with God; other kinds of prayer are successful in producing healing in the form of improved subjective health.

9

RITUAL AND CHARISMA

Introduction

Ritual is a central feature of religion, charisma marks the holy, the religious sphere. We saw in Chapter 6 that beliefs are often expressed through ritual, symbolic behaviour like sacrifice and worship. Ritual and symbol are ways of expressing the inexpressible, the 'key to the unknown', the 'gesture language of theology' (Firth, 1973). There has been historical continuity back to the most primitive religion. More recently has occurred the emergence of various kinds of 'charismatic' religion, such as Pentecostalism, in many parts of the world, using glossolalia and religious healing, often involving high degrees of emotional arousal.

Rites of passage and other rituals

Rituals are repeated and formal patterns of social behaviour, which have no instrumental use, but which are expressive and symbolic. An example is shaking hands, which marks the beginning and end of an encounter, and may also indicate a positive attitude towards the other person. This is not a religious ritual, though it could have been if it had been the custom for a priest to officiate over and bless greetings. We are concerned here with religious rituals, which consist of 'a stereotyped sequence of activities involving gestures, words and objects, performed in a sequestered place, and designed to influence preternatural entities or forces on behalf of the actors' goals and interests' (Turner, 1977: 2). Rituals express transcendent religious ideas and feelings, and they do it by symbolic bodily acts (Zuesse, 1987).

Two main kinds of ritual have been distinguished: (1) confirmatory rituals, such as taboos and ceremonies that confirm the social order, and (2) transforming rituals, rites of passage that alter the state of individuals, such as marriages, funerals, and adolescent initiation rites. It is by rituals such as these that the stages of life are marked out; becoming an adult, for example, is a matter of society's definition of adults and children, and it is society that signals when the change takes place.

It was suggested by Bellah (1964) that rituals have gone through several historical stages. (1) *Primitive*, re-enacting earlier, mythical events: in early agricultural communities there was celebration of the birth and death of gods, and their role in regenerating the crops. (2) *Archaic*: in primitive religion the emphasis was on worship and sacrifice. (3) *Historical*: these emphasise the gap between sacred and profane, concern with salvation. (4) *Early modern*: ritual has now spread to secular activities as well as religious.

Rituals use non-verbal signals, some examples of which are given in Table 9.1. Research on non-verbal communication has shown how bodily signals are used to show emotions and attitudes to others. They are used because they have much more impact on others than putting the same message into words. We have seen that non-verbal signals seem to put others immediately into a state of emotional preparedness, and also affect the emotional state of the person sending them. Religious rituals also use bodily parts, such as blood, which has emotive significance as standing for life, and also such 'natural' symbols as water, fire and light, which are closely linked to central activities of life.

Rites of passage are the rituals used when individuals are passing from one state or status to another. Van Gennep (1908) observed that these rituals often had three stages. In the first the candidates (for marriage, graduation, etc.) appear with their friends and supporters and wearing their usual costume. In the second, or 'liminal', stage they remove some of this costume and leave their friends behind for the central part of the ritual. In the third stage they appear in the new costume which shows their new status, and in new company.

In primitive societies there are initiation rituals for boys (and some-times for girls), so that they can be separated from the world of women

TABLE 9.1 Non-verbal symbols used in rites of passage

Ceremony	Bodily contact	Symbolic meaning
Graduation Confirmation Ordination	Places hands on initiate's head	Passes on continuous chain of authority
Healing ceremonies	Anoints with oil or other substance	Application of medicine
Wedding	Places ring on bride's finger	Ring stands for marriage bonds
Monk taking vows	Puts his new clothes on him	Clothes represent his new status
Prize-giving	Presents cup or other prize, shakes hands	Prize is mark of group's recognition for success
Adolescent initiation	Inflicts physical damage	Test of manhood

Source Argyle, 1988

and children and initiated into the world of men. In the second, liminal stage they are taken outside the boundaries of the tribe and stripped of their clothes. They may be disguised, put on masks, wear clothes of the other sex, or have strange hair arrangements. A priest or senior male figure officiates and initiates them into adult life, telling them about sex, religion, and the secrets of the tribe, submitting them to painful ordeals and mutilations, such as circumcision. We described in Chapter 7 the neo-Freudian theory that this has the effect of internalising the super-ego (p. 98). These boys may be expected to go into trances or have religious experiences. They are 'born again' into the adult world.

Turner (1969) observed that in the liminal stage there is also play, joking and status inversion, in which future leaders are humbled. There is the ritual creation of an ideal state of society, where there is love, equality and harmony, and where there is no property and no status divisions. He called this state 'communitas', a religious and ecstatic condition in which people are freed from the sins of selfish and hierarchical society. It is the experience of the world of the spirit, but it consists of a certain set of social relationships. This state is able to purify candidates for transformation. Without this basic human bond 'there could be *no* human society'. The liminal phase is outside ordinary life, there may be reversals of status, dressing in special clothes, and revelry. Religion keeps communitas alive, especially at religious services. I will return to Turner's analysis of the symbols used in these rituals later. Meanwhile the three-stage theory has been generally accepted. The idea that religious rituals produce a state of communitas has been confirmed by research such as our own on the nature of religious experiences, particularly the mild ones commonly experienced in church, which are found to have a strong pro-social element, a feeling of fusion with others (p. 55).

Graduation ceremonies give a good example of the three-stage process and the wearing of different costumes. Candidates first appear at Oxford in their undergraduate gowns, which they later discard after they have had a ritual exchange with the Vice-Chancellor, who plays the role of 'priest' here. They then put on their graduate gowns. At Oxford there is a point in the liminal phase where candidates leave the Sheldonian Theatre, though there is no passing on of secrets, no mutilation, and the revelry comes afterwards. Indeed, revelry seems to be an important further stage of many rituals, graduations, weddings, even funerals.

Anthropologists like Geertz (1966) think that ritual celebrates the sacred, that it endows concepts with emotive force and thus unifies people into a community. Turner (1977) thought that the power of ritual was due to its double symbolism: first to bodily parts and acts – for example, red wine for blood, washing with water for purification of guilt – and secondly to social groups, as with taboo totem animals in some primitive societies. Some of this symbolism is totally unconscious and related to infantile experience or earlier. In this way ritual links group values to the body and thus charges them with emotion, and emotions are ennobled by being linked to group values. Zuesse (1987) suggests that ritual may have several more levels of symbolism, including the ideology or beliefs for which they stand; the cross is such a symbol. We saw in the last chapter that one particular kind of ritual, sacrifice, does indeed have a number of levels of meaning.

Snake-handling in Tennessee and other parts of the American rural south-east is an interesting case. Rattlesnakes are brought to church in boxes, passed round and handled. Sometimes they bite, and sometimes with fatal consequences. This was started by George Hensley in Holiness sects in 1910 and the tradition has been passed on; new members copy what the experienced handlers do and are trained. Hensley was often

FIGURE 9.1   Snake-handling in Tennessee
Source Sargant, 1957

bitten and eventually killed. There is some biblical basis for handling, treading on or not being bitten by serpents. La Barre (1962) studied these groups and found evidence that the snakes were believed to have phallic properties and were regarded as gods. Snakes are very symbolic, especially of the penis – snake dances are sometimes used to try to make it rain, and for death and rebirth; like other symbols the symbol is based on part of the body (Hood and Kimbrough, 1995). The intense arousal produced by snake-handling may be interpreted as a religious experience, and success would lead to enhanced self-esteem. This is an interesting example of sexual symbols being used in religion, giving some confirmation of Freudian ideas (p. 102). But another part of the story here is that those who engage in snake-handling come from the poorest and most deprived sections of the community; this activity gives them social status and identity.

But do these rituals 'work'? If they are intended to help in the trans-formation of individuals from one state to the next, do they do so? For example, does the wedding ceremony bind couples together more than if they only cohabit? The evidence is that formal marriage does lead to a longer period together, and that married couples are on average happier than those cohabiting (Inglehart, 1990). However, we do not know whether a religious wedding ceremony has more effect than a non-religious one.

Adolescent rites also may be effective. They are used more for boys in tribes where boys must be prepared for war or hunting, and in societies where boys sleep with their mothers during the first year of life, and it may be felt necessary to make more effort to make them into men, or it may be due to Oedipal jealousy and sexual frustration on the part of fathers (Whiting et al., 1958). Funerals are used in all cultures, ostensibly to help the deceased on their journey to the next world, but more to help those left behind to deal with their loss.

Bonta (1997) has argued that co-operation in co-operative societies is sustained by rituals. These may be religious, as in the daily worship of the Hutterites; in some primitive religions there are the trance-healing cere-monies of the !Kung and the pig sacrifices of the Buid, who also symbolise their co-operation by facing the same way, both for work and conversa-tion. The !Kung have frequent all-night dancing for the whole com-munity, which is also found in the Miri in the Sudan (Baumann, 1987).

These are contrasted with the 'rituals' of competitive sport in individualist societies.

Church services involve ritual, not rites of passage now, but rituals symbolising basic beliefs, re-enacting past events, recalling ancient myths, and as part of sacrifice and petition. We shall see in Chapter 10 that church services are successful in human terms in that those who attend them are happier and in better mental and physical health. The main reason is that church communities are very close and supportive. This may be due to their shared beliefs, or taking part in shared ritual may be the key to it; the participants will experience a sequence of shared emotions and actions which symbolise their beliefs and religious outlook, and this may create a special bond (Spickard, 1991).

Freud's theory of religious ritual (1907) is that it is a kind of obsessional neurosis, with similar compulsions to carry out certain acts, guilt if this is not done, and that the rituals are distorted symbolic versions of repressed instinctive desires. The main basis of this theory is the observation that religious rituals often do have a compulsive character, to carry out ritual acts with great precision. This is particularly marked in Jewish, Roman Catholic and Greek Orthodox rituals. On the other hand religious rituals are group rather than individual affairs, and there is no obvious sexual symbolism, as Freudian theory would predict. There is no endless repetition of the same act, like hand-washing, but rather the satisfactory completion of a ritual.

Dulaney and Fiske (1994) studied twenty-five symptoms of obsessive–compulsive disorder in twenty cultures. A number of these symptoms were more common for cultural rituals than for work – such as fear that something terrible will happen, and the carrying-out of repetitive actions. However, these authors did not see their results as supporting Freud's view, but as suggesting that there is a universal capacity for ritual, which is used to mark transitions and help with relationships. Pfister (1948) produced historical evidence which showed that the Jewish–Christian community has become more ritualistic in times of stress. And although religious rituals do not appear to express sex, we have noted already that the age of conversion has often been at the onset of puberty, when defence against sexual desires might be needed. Freud also related ritual to the memories of earlier generations about killing the father, with consequent taboo for totem animals representing the father (1913). Spiro (1966) developed this theme, and proposed that children learn that they can influence their powerful parents by carrying out whatever meaningless acts are required. We discussed Freud's theories of religion further in Chapter 7.

Jung's interpretation of ritual is in terms of the symbolic acts and objects which he sees as related to the archetypes. So the Christian eucharist is primarily a symbolic sacrifice, including sacrifice of the ego, while the bread and the wine have other symbolic meanings; we considered sacrifice in the last chapter. In his autobiography (1962) he describes how disappointed he was at the age of 14 to take his first communion, full of expectation of the mysteries to be seen, when nothing happened at all. Pratt (1950) could explain this: he thought that for religion to work it is necessary to be immersed during childhood in the worship of the church so that the symbols can acquire their emotional force. This does not seem to have happened with Jung, despite his being brought up in the vicarage.

Charismatic religion

Charismatic religion includes Pentecostalist Churches, defined by their emphasis on 'being baptised in the Holy Spirit', of which the main sign is speaking with tongues. There are also sections of mainline churches, Protestant and Catholic, which have incorporated charismatic elements into their services. In addition to glossolalia, which will be discussed later, several other 'gifts' are recognised, such as healing miracles (also dealt with later), and prophesying. The services are marked by a higher degree of emotional excitement than those of other churches, in some cases with uncontrolled singing and frenzied dancing, speaking with tongues, wailing, 'holy jerking', uncoordinated praying aloud, barking like dogs, or collapsing on the floor ('being slain in the spirit').

Such religious excitement is common in primitive religion, where these states are produced in several ways, including very loud drumming or other music, handling snakes, and periods of fasting and sleep deprivation. Hayden (1987) found in a cross-cultural study that they are more common in societies where men do dangerous hunting and fishing, and it is important to build up group cohesion. He said: 'Masked monsters or spirits, flames and darkness, bullroarers, drumming, and the whole panoply of sensory effects ensured total involvement and the forging of some of the strongest emotional bonds the human race has known' (1987: 86).

McClenon (1997) proposed that shamanism is the origin of religion.

For 30,000 years there have been these ecstatic group meetings with repetitive chanting, singing, dancing and drumming; those most susceptible go into a state of relaxation and eventually trance, lowering their heart rate and blood pressure, which benefits health and fertility, and they have religious experiences. Being easily hypnotised becomes selected in evolution since it gives these biological benefits. The event itself is immediately rewarding and hence endures.

The shamans, who conduct these meetings, are individuals who can go into a trance voluntarily; this is usually interpreted as spirit possession, and they dress appropriately; sometimes there is a spiritual marriage between the shaman and his spirit. Shamans have experienced 'chaos' in the form of dreams, visions and mental disorder, but they have overcome it and become 'masters of chaos'. They may have been oppressed in the past, but have found an aggressive and self-assertive solution and become primitive psychiatrists who can help others (I. M. Lewis, 1989).

Such religious excitement has been common in the modern world too, and we have seen that hell-fire preaching was important in early Methodism. Modern Pentecostalism started in the USA in 1901, and grew out of Holiness movements in the Midwest. 'At nearly every meeting there was speaking with tongues, prophesying, healings, exorcism, hand-clapping, uncoordinated praying aloud, running, jumping, falling, "dancing in the spirit", crying and shouting with great exuberance' (Anderson, 1987: 230). From 1960 there was a charismatic revival which led to its becoming more restrained and spreading to the majority American churches. It concentrated on speaking in tongues, which is seen as the main sign of baptism in the spirit. It has also become a world-wide movement, particularly strong in Australia, for example, but also in South America, Africa and Asia, sometimes in churches that would be regarded as heretical. The churches in Korea and Brazil are described later in Chapter 15. The world-wide membership in 1982 was estimated to be 100 million. In the USA a number of TV evangelists proclaim the charismatic message, and display dramatic cases of religious healing. This is discussed further in Chapter 15.

The regular services are now well organised with the usual liturgy, and are carefully staged with charismatic elements added, such as healing or speaking with tongues. There are also services in houses, and emphasis on the idea of 'intentional communities', that is on the love and commitment of members to each other.

Originally most members of charismatic churches, in America and elsewhere, were poor, Black or immigrants. During the period 1890–1915 there was great economic depression in America, mass immigration and a huge move of population to the cities. These very poor people were living under economic stress and in social chaos, in communities riddled with drugs, drink and crime. They had little education and poor verbal skills. What the Holiness churches offered was the promise of the early coming of the Kingdom, ecstasy, social acceptance and self-confidence. Speaking with tongues was chosen as the sign of baptism in the spirit, and gave self-esteem to those who did it. This was a non-verbal kind of religion, of expressive behaviour rather than theology.

However, the hard work and discipline which these churches encouraged led to a lot of social mobility and so there are now many middle-class members. Originally these churches were very strict and ascetic, they did not allow dancing, music or even coffee, for example, but this can now be found only in the Black charismatic churches (Anderson, 1979; Poloma, 1982).

The latest development in Pentecostal and charismatic Churches has been an emphasis on healing, by the casting out of evil spirits (Cox, 1996).

The Toronto Blessing

A recent manifestation of charismatic religion has been the 'Toronto Blessing', which began in what was then the Airport branch of the Vineyard Church, which met in a large airport hangar. It is noted for a particular pattern of ecstatic behaviour:

1 bodily weakness, falling to the ground, sometimes unconscious
2 shaking, trembling, convulsive body movements
3 uncontrollable laughing or weeping
4 apparent drunkenness ('drunkenness in the spirit')
5 barking, roaring or other animal noises.

At the same time those involved have an intense experience of 'the awesome presence of God, and human sinfulness'. Some of this behaviour has a good biblical precedent, in the behaviour on the original day of Pentecost, but animal noises do not, and this led to the Airport Church's being expelled from the Vineyard fellowship.

For those at the early meetings this pattern of behaviour was largely spontaneous, though with some historical antecedents. Many of the later followers have been instructed in what to do, some by hearing the testimonies of those who have done it, some by hearing them at the time, with microphones given to those who have already collapsed on to the carpet (Richter, 1995). Services are conducted by a Master of Ceremonies, who may interview individuals to elicit testimonies, there is a praying team who pray for those in need of it, and a music group who provide a sequence of emotive music. Sermons focus on God's mercy and love and preparation for the 'end-time' (Poloma, 1997). There is carefully staged healing or speaking in tongues.

Many have attended the Airport Church, it is estimated 235,000 over the first twenty-three months, most of them going several times, typically four times, and a total of 7,000 first-time converts (Poloma, 1996). The movement has spread abroad rapidly, the main centre in Britain being Holy Trinity, Brompton, where 2,000 were going to services for a time. Other churches are said to have 'invested' in the cost of sending members to Toronto, in order to 're-kindle the fire', that is, keep up the level of charismatic enthusiasm and attract new members.

Poloma (1996) surveyed 850 of the many thousands who attended over a two-year period. She found that out of her 850, 91 per cent said they had come to know Jesus, 50 per cent had been experiencing spiritual dryness or discouragement, 78 per cent reported inner or emotional healing, 21 per cent physical healing, 55 per cent had been delivered from Satan's hold, 34 per cent did more good works, and 88 per cent had greater married love. The large percentages reporting previous distress and later healing is interesting. However, 850 is a small and self-selected minority of those who chose to complete the questionnaires, which had been sent to all, and may not be representative of those who went to these services. Of the Poloma sample 18 per cent were clergy, 30 per cent church leaders, the average age was 45 and they had fifteen years of education.

Poloma and Hoelter (1998) studied various forms of healing in 918 who had been to the Toronto Church. 'Spiritual healing' (e.g. 'I received a fresh sense of God's goodness') was predicted from experiencing positive emotion, being prayed for at the service, and experience of manifestations. 'Inner healing' (e.g. 'I experienced an inner or spiritual healing') was predicted by spiritual healing, manifestations and positive emotions. Mental and physical healing was rare and could not be predicted well by these variables.

What is the explanation of these phenomena? At the sociological level part of the story is that this kind of collective excitement generates social cohesion, which we saw was useful for groups of men about to undertake dangerous hunting or fishing, where co-operation is important. At the psychological level several have pointed to the extreme arousal produced by very loud music, especially rhythmic drumming. Sargant (1957) suggested that this produced a state of over-arousal, like that found in animals when stresses exceed their capacity to respond, and that this produces a high level of suggestibility. The result is that uninhibited behaviour takes place and may be imitated. Those involved may experience it as religious experience, and regard their behaviour as an expression of their religious fervour. Religious conversion in such churches may be a result of the heightened suggestibility. Like other charismatic behaviour this is an expressive, uninhibited and non-verbal form of religion.

Shortly after the publication of Sargant's book, the present author was visiting Ghana, in West Africa, and took the opportunity to visit services of various African churches. All were very noisy. In one of them, 'The Lord is There', the service, which was in a large tin shed, lasted for twelve hours, the whole of Saturday night, during which there was continuous preaching or singing, the volume greatly amplified, and there was nowhere to sit down. On Sunday morning about 80 of about 1,500 present were said to have been converted, had their devils cast out and were baptised in the Atlantic surf under the palm trees at dawn. In addition to the continuous noise, it looked as if sheer exhaustion may have been a factor.

Another theory is that endorphins are released and produce states of euphoria and eventually trance. Endorphins can be activated by exercise, but also by sleep deprivation, fasting, and other stresses. Like other morphemes, endorphins are a drug which reduces pain, produces euphoria and is addictive. At discos today there is a lot of vigorous exercise, and music which is rhythmic and extremely loud; observation of those doing it suggests that a high level of euphoria is produced. However, there is no evidence of uncontrolled behaviour such as collapsing on the floor or barking like dogs, or of religious behaviour.

Glossolalia

Glossolalia, or speaking in tongues, was first reported on the original day of Pentecost. Then, and on later occasions, individuals in a group were found speaking in what were thought to be foreign languages which they had not learnt. The pentecostal revival started in the USA in 1901, and speaking in tongues was a central feature of it. The practice has spread to other churches and other countries. A recent Australian survey of all church attenders found that 14 per cent did it (55 per cent of Pentecostalists), and another 23 per cent approved of it (Kaldor, 1994).

Linguistic analysis has found that there is no real language here, since there is no vocabulary or grammar, but a string of words like 'alleluia' plus some biblical names. However, the utterances do have a pattern of pauses, stresses and changing intonation (Samarin, 1972). One theory is that it is learned, and that there is social pressure from the group to do it. Another view is that it is a kind of automatic speech produced by extreme emotion and near-trance, as found by Goodman (1972) in an ecstatic Mexican church. Stanley et al. (1978) analysed 120 letters describing these experiences, and found evidence for both kinds; for some it was the result of a crisis. It was once believed that glossolalia was a manifestation of mental disturbance, but a number of studies have found no difference between tongue speakers and others in this respect, though as we have seen some report themselves to have been undergoing a crisis. The only personality difference reported so far is that tongue speakers are more extraverted (L. B. Brown, 1987).

Glossolalia occurs in members of pentecostal churches, but also in Baptist and some other mainline churches, and is further predicted by devotional activity, desire for a deeper spiritual life, disillusion with existing traditions, a life crisis and the encouragement of friends (Malony and Lovekin, 1985). The conditions for a member to speak for the first time are an emotional meeting, prayers, laying on of hands, and an expectation that it would happen (Holm, 1991). The main effect is a feeling of joy and euphoria at having had the sacred experience.

Speaking in tongues in pentecostal circles is a way of showing that one has been 'baptised in the spirit'. It is a form of religious behaviour, more non-verbal than verbal, expressing worship and religious devotion.

Religious healing

We saw in Chapter 8 that people often turn to prayer when they or those close to them are ill, and that furthermore they believe that such prayer works, and they report that they feel better as a result, especially after meditative prayer, where people feel close to God. Healing is an important activity in charismatic churches, and this is how it is done: some diagnosis is made of the client's symptoms and it is said that they are due to the presence of a number of evil sprits. One or more elders of the church press their hands on the client's head and shout at the evil spirits. When he gives a sign such as by twitching, this is described as an evil spirit leaving him. But how far is health affected by such prayer or healing services? There have been several careful studies of the effects of healing services. Glik (1986) interviewed 176 individuals who had attended charismatic and other healing groups, and compared them with 137 who had received regular primary care. Those who had been to the healing groups reported better subjective health and well-being, though their actual physical state was unchanged. Pattison et al. (1973) studied 71 cases of individuals who had been 'healed' at these services, 62 of them during the service, half of them suddenly, and 50 of them suffering from serious conditions. Again they felt much better, and attributed this to the casting out of sin, but there was no actual change in their medical condition. In both studies there was extensive evidence for the improvement of subjective health but not of objective health. So were they healed or not?

Idler (1995) studied 286 people, many of them with disabilities. She found that when they became ill most of them sought help from religion, and most of them found it. Some found a new purpose in life as a result of the illness and recovery from it. For many religion led them to focus on an inner spiritual self, to which the body is irrelevant, which included emotional well-being, social relations, even the health of others, a non-physical sense of self which was felt to be well even if their bodies were not. This is what an improvement of subjective health is like. Furthermore several studies have found that subjective health can predict reduced mortality, with bodily health held constant (Idler and Benyamini, 1997).

We shall see later that religion can affect physical health, through the insistence on better health behaviour in some churches, through social support, and the emotional effects of shared rituals. Religion and religious healing have an effect on subjective health, but this in turn can lead to improvement in physical health.

Conclusions and implications

1 Many religious rituals take the form of rites of passage, to bring about changes of individuals or relationships; they achieve this by non-verbal communication, making symbolic use of bodily parts or acts.

2 Other rituals are used to express religious feelings and ideas, as in worship and sacrifice, making reference to religious beings or experiences, and have emotional force in the same way.

3 Rituals are group activities, which gives them social force, and relate people to groups and their values. The second or liminal stage of rituals has an emotive power and generates feelings of unity and altruism, and also has religious quality: the state of 'communitas'.

4 Religious excitement was common in primitive religion and is now found in charismatic worship, is produced by music and the verbal message, rather than by drumming, dancing or snake-handling, and is manifested in glossolalia and forms of religious enthusiasm.

5 Religious healing is part of charismatic worship, is found to be successful in terms of improved subjective health, but is less successful for objective health.

Ritual is a basic form of religious activity, it emphasises the bodily, emotional and non-rational side of religion, as distinct from beliefs, theology and doctrine. It is this behavioural side of religion which has now become dominant in much of the world. This is an important part of religion as a social phenomenon.

10

HAPPINESS AND THE OTHER BENEFITS AND COSTS OF RELIGION

Introduction

Pragmatist philosophers said that the proof of religion is whether it 'works'. Part of such working is whether religion makes people any happier, whether their marriages or jobs are more successful. From a religious point of view it would be very puzzling if religion conveyed punishments rather than rewards – unless these are to be received only in the next life. And if religion is an other-worldly affair, does it follow that the religious will be less successful in matters of this world? These are empirical questions and a great deal of research has been done on each of them. If it is found, for example, that religion makes people happier, we can ask why it does, in human terms at least. We can ask whether this is a special kind of happiness. We can also ask whether there are 'costs' of religion (traditional theology says that there are) and whether there are 'fruits of the spirit', in terms of kindness and altruism; this will be discussed in Chapter 13.

Happiness

Happiness is usually measured by asking people if they are happy. In the work by myself and colleagues we have used a 29-item scale, the 'Oxford Happiness Inventory' (Argyle et al., 1995), but in the big international surveys they can afford to ask only one or two questions. For example, Inglehart (1990) used data from the Eurobarometer surveys of fourteen European countries, with 163,000 respondents in all, and found that 85 per cent of those who went to church once a week or more said that they were 'very satisfied' with life, compared with 77 per cent of those who never went. Sometimes the relation is stronger than this, and with such big surveys it has been possible to hold constant such variables as age, sex and social class, so that the results are not due, for example, to women being both happier and going to church more. There is still the possibility that the direction of causation is the other way round, i.e. that happier people go to church more, and we do not have much experimental evidence yet to rule this out. The studies we reported in Chapter 5 on religious experience showed, however, that intense religious experiences did produce increased happiness, for a time at least. But in this chapter we shall be dealing with more common forms of religious experience and behaviour.

The Inglehart survey found a positive, but modest, effect of church on happiness. There have been many other surveys, of students or population samples. They have usually found a positive relation between, for example, frequency of church attendance, or orthodox beliefs and happiness, of about 0.15, but more than this with older samples (Veenhoven, 1994). Witter et al. (1985) carried out a meta-analysis of fifty-six, mainly American, studies and found a similar effect, actually 0.19 of a standard deviation in happiness between church members and others, but a much larger difference for old people, and greater for religious activity rather than other measures of religiosity. A survey of 1,343 people of 65 and over in Minnesota by Moberg and Taves (1965) found a strong effect of church involvement on happiness for old people (Table 10.1).

It can be seen that the benefits of church were greater for those who were single, very old, fully retired, or in poor health. This suggests that it may be the social support of the church community which is benefiting them. We show later that church communities are major sources of social support, especially for old people.

TABLE 10.1 Church membership and scores on an index of adjustment

	Church leaders	Other church members	Non-church members
Married	15	15	12
Widowed	15	11	7
Single	12	8	5
65–70	18	14	10
71–79	15	12	7
80+	13	8	6
Fully employed	18	18	17
Partly employed	16	16	13
Fully retired	15	12	7
Health (self-rated)			
Excellent	17	14	13
Good	15	14	11
Fair	17	6	8
More active in religious organisations than in fifties	16	13	9
Less active	14	11	7

Source Moberg and Taves, 1965

However, social support is not the only reason that religion makes people happy. It is found that reported 'closeness to God' correlates with happiness, independently of church attendance (Pollner, 1989). We have seen that both religious experience and prayer are found to enhance happiness, and it has been suggested that they give the experience of a social relationship with God which is in some ways similar to human relationships (Kirkpatrick, 1992). There is the old joke that if you talk to God this is prayer, but if he talks back it is schizophrenia; nevertheless those who have these conversations are happier than those who do not. We shall describe later some forms these conversations may take under 'religious coping'.

There is a third way in which religion may enhance happiness. Ellison (1991) found that having firm beliefs, 'existential certainty', correlated with life-satisfaction, independently of both church attendance and private devotions, especially for older and less educated individuals; we show in the next chapter that fundamentalists are more optimistic, and later that this certainty of belief may have been part of the reason for the rise of 'strict' churches (p. 210). There is some evidence that in the USA members of Baptist churches, who are mostly fundamentalists, are happier on average than members of more liberal churches (Ellison, Gay et al., 1989). The contents of beliefs matter too. Belief in the after-life is a strong predictor of happiness for the elderly (Steinitz, 1980) as is belief in a supportive, caring God; this all leads to a greater sense of optimism and control.

Research on happiness finds that it is related to, perhaps caused by, the frequency of positive emotional experiences. Argyle and Hills (in press) investigated the possible effects of such experiences in church. We found that happiness had a positive, though modest, correlation with two factors of religious emotion: (1) the Transcendental factor, with scales like 'Being at peace with God', and 'Contact with God'; and (2) the Social factor, with scales like 'Being part of a family' and 'Being united with other people'. This confirms what was said above about the benefits of church as a social community, and enjoying a relationship with God, and that the latter can be obtained in the course of church services. However, one of our factors of religious emotion was a 'Mystical' factor, with scales like 'Loss of sense of self' and 'Timelessness' (see Table 4.4); this had a small negative correlation with our measure of happiness.

We can also ask which aspects of happiness are most affected by religion. Some have found that having a sense of meaning and purpose is most strongly affected (Chamberlain and Zika, 1988). We described the effect on optimism and control above. We have seen in Chapter 8 that prayer particularly affects 'existential well-being', another name for purpose in life.

These studies show that belonging to churches has a weak positive effect on happiness, but a stronger one for old people, and that this is partly due to the social support of the church community, to the relation experienced with God, and the certainty of beliefs. However, it must be admitted that the relationship with happiness is weak for most of the population; we found that although going to church caused great joy, belonging to a church had less effect on happiness than belonging to a sports club (Argyle and Hills, in press). The reason could be that for most church members their joyful experience happens only once a week, and this is not often enough – happiness depends on the frequency of positive events. Those who play sports or exercise often do so every day.

We have seen other examples of the effect of religion on happiness, in the effects of religious experience (p. 71), of conversion (p. 24), and the effects of prayer (p. 122). The results in all these cases are positive, and they all show a clear before-and-after causal effect.

Fear of death

Death is a universal feature of the human condition, and one which some find very worrying. There may be anxiety about dying itself, or the loss of the good things of this life, or the sheer uncertainty about what is going to happen next. This is an area where religion does provide some kind of account, and an optimistic one, although it is very vague. Most religions provide such an account and this has often been regarded as one of the main roots of religion. It is assumed that there are two steps here, first fear of death (FOD) leads to acceptance of religious beliefs about the after-life and hence about religion in general, and second this in turn leads to reduced anxiety about death. We shall consider the evidence that all this happens.

We reported a recent survey earlier (p. 78) which found that in Britain 55 per cent believe in an after-life, and in the USA 78 per cent do. The great majority, 93 per cent, of those who believe in it, think that it will be happy, peaceful, etc. But 28 per cent in Britain and as many as 71 per cent in the USA believe in hell – perhaps the greatest difference in religiosity between these two countries. Jews hold these beliefs less; in the USA 30 per cent believe in heaven and 10 per cent in hell (Hood et al., 1996).

A number of methods have been used to measure FOD, including direct questions, and 'unconscious' measures such as physiological reactions to death words. From a number of American studies it seems that there is little conscious FOD for most people, but there is more at an unconscious level, shown, for example, by delayed verbal associations with death words compared with other words (Feifel, 1974). It has been found that the 'cemetery' is a very emotional word, and can inspire fear and sadness (Gustafsson, 1972).

Is FOD less for religious individuals? A meta-analysis of thirty-six studies found such a relationship in twenty-four of them (Spilka, Hood et al., 1985). If we look at different kinds of religiosity, FOD is less for those high in Intrinsic religiosity, with correlations of .4 to .5, but for those high on Extrinsic and Quest FOD is greater (Wulff, 1997).

Experiments are rare in the psychology of religion but they have been done on the effects of FOD on religious beliefs. Osarchuk and Tate (1973) produced strong FOD arousal by showing subjects forty-two slides of corpses and other death-related scenes, playing dirge-like music, and telling them about the dangers of dying from accidents or diseases. For those subjects who were already believers this experience produced lower FOD and increased belief in the after-life, but for those who initially had weak beliefs in the after-life there was no change. In the eighteenth century and later, revivalists tried to convert people by giving them frightening images of hell, and it seems likely that this was successful, for some of their listeners at least.

A recent development has been through the concept of 'terror management' (Greenberg et al., 1997). Terror Management Theory (TMT) proposes that human beings have a deep-seated fear of death and feel very vulnerable, because we are programmed for self-preservation but are also self-conscious, making us aware of our inevitable end. We control this anxiety by the creation of cultural world-views which enable us to transcend the natural world and elevate us to a higher plane of existence where we can transcend death. We need self-esteem, a cultural construction which enables us to see ourselves as valuable members of a meaningful universe.

A long series of experiments has been carried out, using fairly mild arousal of death anxiety. These have found that such mortality threats (1) increase prejudice and hostility to those with different world-views, including other ethnic groups, and 'moral transgressors' like prostitutes, (2) increase pro-social behaviour to those who uphold our world-views, (3) increase the desire for and perception of consensus, and (4) produce more conformity to cultural values. These effects are greater for authoritarians and for depressed individuals, and do not take place at all for those with high self-esteem. Although religious beliefs are implied in these 'world-views' there is no specific reference to religion, although it is clearly the main source of death transcendence.

We can look at some real-life situations where people face death. Several studies have compared the terminally ill with matched healthy individuals. Feifel (1974) found that the religious terminally ill were somewhat more likely to be unafraid, 81 per cent v. 70 per cent, but there was no difference between the ill and the healthy. However, in another study it was found that the terminally ill engaged in more avoidance and denial of this topic, and were less able to think about death.

Being in battle is another life-threatening situation. As mentioned above, in the US army in the Second World War 72 per cent of those who had been most frightened said that they had been helped by prayer, compared with 42 per cent of the least frightened. In a more recent war Florian and Mikulincer (1993) found that religious Israeli soldiers had lower levels of FOD even after battle experience.

Old age is another likely source of FOD. We have seen that older people believe in the after-life more than young ones, 100 per cent of those over 90 in one study (p. 28). And we have seen that this belief is a strong predictor of happiness for the elderly. Swenson (1961) studied 210 individuals over the age of 60 and found that both church attendance and fundamentalist beliefs correlated with looking forward positively to death, saying, for example, 'It will be wonderful'. Those in poor health looked forward to it more.

How people achieve this belief in the after-life and reduce their FOD we discussed in Chapter 4 – a combination of religious teaching and religious experience, including near-death experiences. And as we have seen, religious beliefs are successful in reducing the fear of death, particularly for those high in intrinsic religiosity and for fundamentalists. Even these, however, do not know what it will be like; all they know is that it will be wonderful.

Marriage

We shall see in Chapter 12 that most religions are strongly in favour of family values and keeping marriages intact, and are against divorce and extra-marital sex. Does religion have any effect on the success and happiness of marriage? The divorce rate is definitely higher for those who say they have no religion, 45 per cent in the USA, compared with lower rates for Catholics (27 per cent) and liberal Protestants (31 per cent), for example, though no lower for Jews (47 per cent; Davis and Smith, 1994). The lowest divorce rates are reported by Mormons, Mennonites and Hutterites.

Church attendance is also related to divorce rates. Heaton and Goodman (1985) combined several American surveys and corrected them for demographic differences, with the results shown in Table 10.2. This table

TABLE 10.2 Divorce rates by church and attendance

	Catholic		Liberal Protestant		Conservative Protestant		Mormons	
	Attendance rate							
	High	Low	High	Low	High	Low	High	Low
Percentage divorced	13.3	30.4	24.0	32.3	20.3	37.4	12.7	23.9

Source Heaton and Goodman, 1985

shows both the effect of denomination and the effect of church attendance. In a later, large-scale American study, Heaton and Call (1997) studied the break-up rate for 4,587 couples over a 5-year period. The best religious predictor of marital stability was regular and joint church attendance. Some of the apparent effect of attendance may be due to the divorced going to church less, but other studies have found that intrinsic religiosity is also correlated with a higher level of marital commitment, and there is no reason to expect a reverse order of causation here. The way that religion affects marriage may be that the religious have greater commitment, regard marriages as for life, engage in less extra-marital sex, and disagree less because of their beliefs (Hood et al. 1996); if couples go to the same church they are part of the same supportive network as well. The main reason, however, may be sharing religious beliefs and rituals; we have seen in this chapter and will see again in Chapter 13 how sharing beliefs and practices is a major source of cohesion in church groups, and the same may apply within marriage.

However, if partners have different faiths, the divorce rate is much higher. Lehrer and Chiswick (1993) studied American mixed marriages, and found that Protestant–Catholic couples were about twice as likely to divorce as pairs of Protestants or pairs of Catholics. The Catholic–Mormon combination was the worst, and any mixed marriages with Mormons or Jews all had high rates of divorce. The probability of divorce is less if one partner converts to the faith of the other, as often happens. The problems created by such mixed marriages are not confined to religious beliefs and practice: there are likely to be different ideas about marriage, child-rearing, money, work and other issues.

Marital happiness is also affected by religion as was found by Witter et al. (1985) in their meta-analysis of fifty-six studies of religion and happiness, especially for older couples. More surprisingly perhaps, religious couples report more sexual satisfaction in marriage, and we discuss later the view that religion and sex are related to each other, may even substitute for each other (p. 190). There are surprisingly high levels of contraception, abortions and oral sex in religious marriages (p. 188), though a little less than for the non-religious. Religion does not seem to impair the sex life of married couples; they have a little less sex but they enjoy it more (Hood et al., 1996).

The interest of churches in family values has often included wanting members to have a lot of children. Catholics, Muslims and Mormons used to have many children, and Mormons still do. The author knows a Mormon couple with forty-four grandchildren. Overall there is some relation between church attendance or membership and having children. In Canada women who belong to churches have 2.66 children v. 1.84 for those who do not (Heaton and Cornwall, 1989), and there is a correlation of 0.57 between family size and church attendance for Catholics, but not for Protestants (Sander, 1992). This may be partly because Catholics who limit their families may feel reluctant to go to church.

For many years Catholics had more children than Protestants, but this difference is now zero or very small. In Europe women in the Catholic countries of Spain and Italy have small numbers of children, 1.2 and 1.3, while in Britain and Denmark women have 1.8. In North America the most fertile groups are the Hutterites (5.28), Mennonites (3.31), Mormons (3.04), the Salvation Army (2.80), Catholics and Pentecostalists (both 2.80). So religion still makes a difference to fertility, but really only affects these small Protestant sect-like groups.

Work and achievement

Religions often say that material success and other worldly goals are unimportant. They may proclaim a special interest in the poor, the humble and the meek, or suggest that the rich may have difficulty in going to heaven. However, the Protestant reformers had other ideas and said that we would be judged on our life's work; but money should not be spent on oneself or on luxury but put back into the business. The lives of early capitalists often followed this model. Max Weber (1904–5) in particular noticed that there seemed to be a connection between Protestantism and economic success, though he thought that the ascetic accumulation of wealth applied only to first-generation capitalists.

Measures of the Protestant work ethic (PWE) have been developed, with items like 'Hard work is fulfilling in itself', and it is clear that there really is such a work ethic factor and some people still have it (Furnham, 1990). It is found to have a small positive correlation with measures of religiosity in general, regardless of denomination. For example, Furnham found a correlation of .29 with a 'religious and moral beliefs' factor. However, there has been more research interest in denominational differences. In Europe those in the Protestant countries like Britain and Denmark have higher average PWE scores than people in the Catholic countries (Giorgi and Marsh, 1990). Surveys in the USA find the same, but Jews score even higher than Protestants.

The results for actual achievement are similar. Homola et al. (1987) analysed the results of several American surveys with a total of 12,120 subjects, and some of the results are shown in Table 10.3.

Average job status is highest for Jews, closely followed by Episcopalians, then Catholics, and Baptists well below them, so there is no clear Protestant–Catholic difference here. These authors found that the differences were partly due to variations in years of education, shown in the first column, and to the education of fathers. Others have found more social mobility for Protestants. Earlier American studies had found larger Protestant–Catholic differences, but these have narrowed since 1930 (Argyle and Beit-Hallahmi, 1975).

The denominational differences in incomes shown in Table 10.3 are similar to those for occupational status, except that Jews are well ahead here. Homola and colleagues found that the income differences were partly due to education, but also to family size and, in the case of Jews, to living in New York. If national average incomes are compared there are striking differences between countries classified by the dominant religion; see Table 10.4.

Some of these differences can be explained as being due to different length of education, which in turn is due to differences in amount of parental education. But how does religion affect education? McClelland (1961) thought and found some evidence that Protestantism encourages self-reliance, and the early training of children to be independent, leading to higher achievement motivation. Achievement motivation, the desire to succeed, has a lot in common with the PWE. Those who have it would

TABLE 10.3 Denomination and achievement in the USA

	Education (years)	Job status (av. scores)	Income ($)
Episcopalians	14.6	49.9	19,250
Jews	15.8	50.7	24,765
Baptists	11.9	40.2	13,424
Italian RC	12.9	43.2	14,779
Irish RC	13.8	45.8	16,217
Methodists	13.2	45.2	16,901

Source Homola et al., 1987

TABLE 10.4 Median per capita income for groups of nations classified by dominant religious tradition, 1957

Type of nation (i.e. dominant religious tradition)	Median income ($)	No. of nations
Protestants	1,130	11
Mixed Protestant–Catholic	881	6
Eastern Orthodox	365	5
Roman Catholic	329	33
Muslim	137	20
Primitive religions	88	15
Eastern religions (Hinduism, Buddhism, etc.)	75	16
Others (including mixed types)	362	7
All nations	224	113

Source Compiled from data presented in Bruce Russett et al., *World Handbook of Political and Social Indicators* (New Haven, Conn.: Yale University Press, 1964), Tables 44 and 73–5. Nations with Communist governments are classified on the basis of their traditionally dominant faith.

engage in more educational efforts. However, high PWE scores have also been found in Japan, India and parts of Africa, which are presumably nothing to do with Protestantism, though they may reflect other religions (Furnham, 1990).

Religion can affect behaviour at work in other ways. Wuthnow (1994) carried out many interviews with Americans, and found that for 22 per cent religion affected their choice of job, favouring social or moral values rather than money. He also found that those who went to church placed more emphasis on fairness and honesty, and on humanitarian and altruistic considerations.

Benefits and costs to society

In Chapter 13, which is on the effect of religion on moral behaviour, we shall describe two major benefits of religions for society, the lower level of crime and the higher level of altruistic behaviour on the part of religious individuals – such as donations to charity and engaging in voluntary work. Churches and religious individuals played a major part in social welfare before the state took it over. There is a further benefit to society, which does not fall into the sphere of individual morality or altruism: that is, the benefits for social integration. We saw earlier that one of the main ways in which religion influences happiness and mental and physical health is through the high degree of social cohesion and social support found in church communities.

Compared with other comparable groups, such as leisure groups and political groups, church groups are very cohesive. Kaldor (1994) carried out a survey of the 310,000 who went to church in Australia on two Sundays; 24 per cent said that their closest friends belonged to their church and another 46 per cent had some close friends in it. For Pentecostalists 33 per cent said their closest friends belonged to their church, and for Seventh Day Adventists 38 per cent. We obtained similar results in the Oxford area. Belonging to the same church leads to social support, choice of friends and marital partners, and also to material help, such as food, clothing, advice or help when ill. The reason for this high level of cohesion is not clear; the study by Idler (1987) suggested that shared participation in religious rituals was the key variable that affected health. Rokeach et al. (1960) found that shared beliefs were more important than shared race in friendship choice.

Churches can also help in the social integration of those who feel they have been rejected by the wider society. Individuals who belong to minority groups, or who are just lower class, have been accepted and resocialised in disciplined ways of life, to become regular and prosperous members of society (D. R. Brown and Gary, 1991).

However, the opposite side of all this in-group positive feeling is a negative attitude often found towards out-groups, in the form of a higher level of prejudice towards ethnic minority groups, and to those who belong to other churches or to none. We saw from the work of Rokeach (1960) that prejudice is greater the greater the difference in beliefs, and that fundamentalist churches are the most likely to reject members of other faiths. Historically there have been serious Protestant–Catholic conflicts, though these have greatly diminished over the last three hundred years. The Jews have always kept themselves separate, and their rituals and food laws continue to keep religious Jews at least apart from others, and the same is true of some other groups.

Religion has been a factor in most wars, not as the cause, but as part of the social identities of the warring groups (Vrcan, 1994). And it must be admitted that religion has made such conflicts worse rather than better, for example, in Northern Ireland and Israel. It is ironic that each of the religions or churches that has become involved in such conflicts tells its members to love their neighbours and forgive their enemies, apparently without effect.

The costs of religion to the individual

Batson et al. (1993) conclude that religion gives several kinds of freedom – from fear of death, fear in life, temptation, concern over possessions, social conventions, sexual desire and existential concerns – but there is loss of freedom to think freely and to doubt the belief system itself. We discussed their scale for 'cognitive bondage' and reported that it is higher for those high in intrinsic religiosity, orthodoxy and other measures of religiosity. We have seen that religious individuals also score high on measures of dogmatism, and tend to have 'closed minds'. This is truer of fundamentalists than of members of liberal churches. On the other hand there is an irrational leap of faith for members of many faiths, who make a decision in the absence of complete evidence. The only people who keep their freedom to doubt are those scoring on the Quest dimension, but we have expressed doubts over whether they are really committed believers or are more in a state of conflict and indecision. Religious people are found to have more purpose in life, and worry less about death. Perhaps the loss of freedom to think about these things is really a gain rather than a loss; dogmatism means certainty, and we shall see that this may be one of the attractions of 'strict' churches.

If you are a Mormon, you are no longer free to drink alcohol, smoke, drink tea or coffee or various other things, and the same is true to a lesser degree of members of other churches. You will no longer be free to engage in sexual promiscuity in any church. Are these losses or gains? If you are a committed believer there is no longer any desire or 'temptation' to do these things, so there may be no sense of subjective deprivation. All moral and other rules have been developed because it was believed that they would be advantageous to individuals or the community, and we shall see that Mormons live longer as a result of their health behaviour rules.

There can also be costs to individuals who join some rare and extreme sects. They may be subjected to tyrannical discipline, have to leave their family, accept an arranged marriage, give up their career for menial work, or in some cases have to commit suicide (p. 226).

Conclusions

1 Church members are somewhat happier on average than others, espe-cially for the old. This is mainly due to church social support, but also the relation with God and the effects of beliefs on optimism. Church groups are more cohesive and give more social support than any other comparable groups, perhaps because their shared beliefs and shared rituals create a special closeness, seen in companionship, tangible help and emotional support. Religious beliefs, such as in the after-life, and that God is looking after us, lead to a sense of purpose in life, remove fear of death, and are a source of happiness. This process is strongest for fundamentalists and other dogmatic groups.
2 Fear of death is much less for the religious.
3 Marriages are happier and more likely to last for church members, but worse if they belong to different churches.
4 Achievement and worldly success are a little greater for the religious, and for Jews and members of some Protestant Churches. This may be due to the Protestant work ethic, which makes people work harder, get educated and lead a more disciplined life. This has led to economic success and social mobility on the part of sect members.
5 Religion gives benefits to society. In addition to lower crime and greater altruism, there is increased cohesion among church members and con-cern for outcasts. However, there are also costs to society in the conflict between different religious bodies, and religion is an extra source of conflict in most wars.
6 There are also costs to individuals, loss of freedom to think, and religious prohibitions, though these may not be experienced as costs.

11

PHYSICAL AND MENTAL HEALTH

Introduction

We have seen that religion does make people somewhat happier; does it also give them better physical or mental health, allow them to live longer? If religion has any survival value, there should be some positive effects here. There are historical links between religion and health. In earlier times and in primitive societies there were no doctors, but there were many healers, most of them using religious methods, including sacrifices, trances and other rituals. In Third World countries today there are thousands of such healers, and they can deal with problems arising from local interpersonal conflicts, which they will know all about. In Brazil and Korea the Pentecostal Churches place emphasis on healing, which is the main attraction of religion for many. In modern society, too, there are many for whom medicine has failed to work, and who seek alternative, often religious, forms of healing. We have seen that such healing is successful in increasing subjective health, which includes a positive attitude to life. Meanwhile some churches are opposed to medicine, and forbid their members to see doctors, as with Christian Scientists, or to receive blood, as with Jehovah's Witnesses. Mental health is another matter, and any subjective benefits produced by religion might be expected to enhance mental health.

Health

If religion was shown to lead to better physical health, this would be more impressive evidence for its real benefits than the effects on happiness. Religious individuals might say they are happy because they think they ought to be, but physical health is more objective. We have seen the difference between subjective and objective health; the two may be quite out of step, for example, neurotic individuals think they are in worse health, for the same symptoms. And some serious health indicators like blood pressure produce no subjective sensations. Health psychologists generally ignore subjective health, but we shall see that this may be a mistake.

Early studies showed positive correlations between church attendance or membership and how well people thought they were. However, we will look first at the effects of religion on objective health. A classic study of the relation between health and church is that by Comstock and Partridge (1972) using death rates for large samples (Table 11.1). There is nothing subjective about death.

It can be seen that the death rates for several major diseases were much lower for church attenders. This study can be criticised on the grounds that only those who were well enough could get to church, and this might indeed apply to a few elderly individuals. However, other studies have found the same effect, using rates of church membership in different counties and death rates from different diseases. Idler and Kasl (1992) studied 2,812 elderly individuals and found that church attendance was correlated with health in terms of reported functional ability (i.e. what they were able to do), and that this held up after chronic disability had been allowed for. The health of the church-goers also improved more over

TABLE 11.1 Mortality rates of regular church-goers and others (per 1,000)

	Once a week or more	Less than once a week
Heart disease (5 years)	38	89
Emphysema (3 years)	18	52
Cirrhosis (3 years)	5	25
Cancer of the rectum (5 years)	13	17
Suicide (6 years)	11	29

Source Comstock and Partridge, 1972

the next three years. Church particularly affects death from respiratory and digestive illnesses, but also several kinds of cancer, and indeed all the major diseases (Levin, 1994).

Hummer et al. (1999) studied 21,000 from the American National Health Interview Survey and concluded that, on average, church-goers had seven years' longer life-expectancy at age 20.

The most likely explanation of the effect of religion on health is in terms of better 'health behaviour'. Look at the diseases listed in Table 11.1: the church goers had lower rates of death from cirrhosis of the liver (due to alcohol), emphysema (due to smoking), cancer of the cervix (partly due to promiscuous sex), and heart disease (partly due to smoking and diet). Many religious groups prohibit some of these kinds of behaviour. And the strictest groups, which have very strong demands about drinking, smoking, diet, even exercise, have the lowest death rates, both overall and from heart disease and cancer. In the USA the greater longevity of church members is particularly marked for Mormons, Seventh Day Adventists, Orthodox Jews and the Amish (Jarvis and Northcott, 1987; Levin, 1994).

However, this is not the whole explanation of the effects of religion on health; it will not explain the effects of religion for mainstream churches, which make very few demands for health behaviour. We saw in the last chapter how the social support of churches affects happiness. It has often been shown how social support benefits health, and we have seen that churches are very supportive. Drevenstadt (1998) carried out a study of 11,000 Americans and found that church attendance correlated with subjective health for all groups studied. However, for middle-aged whites this was mainly due to social support, while for the young of all racial groups attendance only affected subjective health if there was also religious commitment. Social support may take the form of actual help, people looking after each other. In addition inside families, and perhaps inside churches too, social support activates the immune system.

There is an effect of religion after health behaviour and social support have been controlled for, as Idler and Kasl (op. cit.) found; they suggested that church attendance and participation in religious rituals work through the 'experience of sufficiently intensive collective religious life'. They found that there was a lower death rate for Christians for 30 days before Easter and for male Jews for the same period before the major Jewish feasts, and think that this is because of the increased participation in shared rituals. These authors did not find an effect of private devotions, though others have done so (Frankel and Hewitt, 1994). If the social relationship with God can function in a similar way to relationships with family and close friends, this would be expected. In each case the positive emotions and relaxation generated would have a biochemical effect. In one experiment watching a film about Mother Teresa was enough to bring about a substantial increase in salivary immunoglobulin – watching a film about Hitler did not (McClelland, 1987).

Religious practices are not always good for health. In 1831 half of the pilgrims to Mecca were killed by a cholera epidemic, many Hindus have perished from cholera in the Ganges, the plague was partly spread by gatherings of penitents, the Zen macrobiotic diet can lead to malnutrition, as can the 110–150 days fasting a year in the Ethiopian Orthodox Church, the water at Lourdes is infected by bacteria though so far they have not infected the visitors. Communion vessels can spread common diseases, though there is less infection if the vessel is wiped (Reynolds and Turner, 1995).

Health of the clergy

If church-going is good for health, the clergy should benefit even more. Clergy, monks and nuns have a lower death rate, i.e. live longer than others on average. They are less likely to die from heart attacks, most cancers, suicide and accidents. Protestant clergy do better than Catholic priests. The longevity of the clergy was particularly clear in the nineteenth century, but the difference is now less and clergy live to about the same age as university and school teachers. The benefits are mainly due to better health behaviour, such as smoking less (Jarvis and Northcott, 1987; Reynolds and Turner, 1995).

Religious healing

We saw in Chapter 9 that religious healing is very successful in improving subjective health – including subjective well-being. This effect is at least partly due to thinking of 'health' in a broader way, as more than the state of the body, and encompassing a happier view of life. There is little or no immediate effect on objective health, though this is likely to improve in the longer term.

Mental health

Are religious people in better or worse mental health than others? Some have said that being religious is itself a sign of mental disturbance, while others might say the opposite. We will look at studies which have used standard measures of mental health and disorder.

Intrinsic religiosity

Batson et al. (1993) analysed the findings of 115 such studies, all carried out in the USA, using various self-report measures of mental health, and three dimensions of religiosity: Intrinsic, Extrinsic and Quest. Most of these studies found that intrinsic religiosity correlated positively with mental health, extrinsic negatively. This was also found in a later study by Genia (1996), who found that intrinsic religiosity correlated with depression (negatively), and with measures of spiritual and existential well-being and self-esteem. Extrinsic predicted distress, Quest and Fundamentalism had no effect when intrinsic had been taken into account. Those who never go to church or have no religion are more likely to be mentally disturbed (Stark, 1971).

So intrinsic religiosity is related to good mental health; it also goes with high self-esteem and a positive image of God. However, intrinsics also feel guilty and worry about sin. How does this fit in? Watson, Morris et al. (1987) found that they believed in a loving and forgiving God as well as a punishing one; they felt that they were saved and in receipt of grace, felt worthy in the sight of God. We shall see shortly that fundamentalists also feel guilty, probably guiltier, but that it doesn't upset them.

It has been found that intrinsic religiosity buffers (that is, it removes the effects of) stress due to uncontrollable life-events, such as death and serious illness, which otherwise produce anxiety and depression. McIntosh et al. (1993) studied 124 individuals who had experienced the sudden death of a child. Regular church attenders reported more social support and finding meaning in their loss. Those who said religion was important to them also found meaning and engaged in ways of working through their loss by thinking and talking about it. Both aspects of religiosity predicted reduced distress 18 months later.

Religious coping

Pargament and his colleagues have found the positive effects of various kinds of 'religious coping'. By coping is meant a way of behaving or thinking which helps people avoid or reduce the effects of stress, and the negative emotions which it causes. Religious coping is when religious behaviour or thoughts are used in this way. Pargament (1997) has reviewed a considerable number of studies of this process, and showed that religious coping is used most by those who are religious, female, old, poor, uneducated, Black, or widowed, probably because these individuals have fewer alternative resources. And people use religious coping for certain kinds of situation – problems, like bereavement and serious illness.

There are many studies of the effectiveness of religious coping on mental health, with rather mixed results; 34 per cent out of 130 studies (not individuals) found significant positive effects on depression, anxiety, etc., 4 per cent showed negative effects and the rest no significant effect (Pargament, op. cit.).

However, some kinds of religious coping are more successful than others. Perception of guidance and help by God, 'collaborative coping' in which God is a partner in decisions, 'benevolent reframing' in which negative events are seen in a positive way as due to the will of God, and seeking support from congregation or clergy, are found to be the most successful. Other kinds of religious coping are not successful – anger or feeling abandoned by God, and thinking that negative events are due to God's punishment. Some religious moves have mixed effects; we shall see that conversion can have positive effects for some but negative effects for others.

While this coping research has produced an impressive body of data, it is open to the criticism that it is all correlational, and does not demonstrate that there is a causal effect of religious coping. So to take one of the unsuccessful methods, it is quite possible that being depressed makes some people feel more angry with God rather than that being angry with God makes them depressed.

Religion of psychiatric patients

The studies we have mentioned so far are of people in the community, or of students; we look now at more seriously disturbed individuals, many of them in mental hospitals. Surveys of mental hospital inmates find that a proportion of them have a definite religious content to their disorders. Rokeach (1981) studied the 'Three Christs of Ypsilanti', by putting them on the same hospital ward. Each denounced the others as imposters. More Messiahs can be found in the Jerusalem hospital ward kept for those who find the religious atmosphere in that city too strong for them. It is generally believed that in most cases these individuals were insane already and have simply chosen to express their troubles in a religious way, using ideas from their religions, just as other patients may use the latest technology to believe that they are being controlled by laser beams or TV. Religious delusions are most common in working-class individuals and members of fundamentalist churches.

There is a particular problem with religious leaders. As William James (1902) and others have pointed out most of the famous religious figures of the past, saints, mystics and religious leaders, have shown clear symptoms of mental disorder, from St Paul to Luther and John Wesley. Nevertheless they were clearly very different from the three Christs of Ypsilanti, in that they were not generally regarded as insane and they were able to organise not only themselves, but many followers. We discuss later the personalities of cult leaders or 'gurus'; they often go through a period of what looks like temporary insanity before revealing their new vision (p. 224). The ideas which these leaders introduced did more than solve their own problems: they had a very wide appeal, and met the needs or solved the problems of many others (Argyle and Beit-Hallahmi, 1975).

Fundamentalists

It has often been claimed that members of fundamentalist churches are mentally disturbed. Starbuck (1899) found long ago that two thirds of adolescent conversions were due to guilt feelings, probably over sex. The arousal of guilt, and its later reduction by being saved, plays a central part in fundamentalist life. Strozier (1994) interviewed a sample of fundamentalists and found that they had experienced early traumas, had strong guilt feelings, and obtained relief by being born again and using the rhetoric of the struggle against evil and other literal Christian ideas. Children are more likely to have experienced severe punishment and sexual abuse. Other investigators have also reported strong guilt feelings, as well as rigidity and authoritarianism, but these do not equate to mental disturbance. Furthermore there is a definite positive side to being a fundamentalist. Sethi and Seligman (1993) studied the cognitive style of 623 individuals from nine major religious groups. On their measure of optimism the fundamentalists (Calvinists, Orthodox Jews and Muslims) scored higher than members of 'moderate' churches like Methodists and Lutherans, who in turn scored higher than those from 'liberal' churches such as Unitarians and Reformed Jews.

Revivalism and charismatic services can also disturb people. During the Millerite Adventist revival in New England in 1842–3 nearly a quarter of local mental hospital admissions were said to be due to 'religious excitement'. Over half of these were diagnosed as manic, a few as depressive (Stone, 1934). The author has known psychiatrists and also some patients who have reported similar effects from attendances at Billy Graham meetings or regular charismatic services. The same has been reported in connection with evangelical preachers in Papua New Guinea, where 'revival hysteria' has taken the form of very violent and psychotic behaviour.

However, as we showed in Chapter 2, most individuals who are converted, including those converted 'suddenly', some of them at revival meetings, are in a better mental state after than before, with greater self-esteem and purpose in life. This is partly because they were at a low ebb to begin with, partly because the new beliefs, group membership and way of life are good for them.

Sect members

It has been widely believed that members of the Moonies and other sects are mentally deranged. Research has found that those who join these sects have often experienced recent crises or personal problems, and that many had already sought psychological help. Galanter (1982) studied members of the Divine Light Mission and the Unification Church; 30–40 per cent had sought such help before joining, and 6–9 per cent had been in hospital. Very similar rates have been found for members of Hare Krishna and other groups. Yet joining these groups, however strange they may seem, often has beneficial effects, partly because they provide a 'spiritual haven'. Laurie Brown said:

> Religious communities can also provide a haven for those who are disturbed or do not cope well with the world, and they can have a

therapeutic value because of that . . . participation is itself linked to psychological well-being and social integration, simply because it offers social involvement rather than isolation.

(1988: 57)

The social support, strict moral code and freedom from temptation and stress enable new members to get off drugs, gambling, sexual promiscuity or whatever their problem is. Many studies have documented these positive effects (Richardson, 1985). The concept of a haven can also be applied to nuns who enter closed orders, some of them silent. They are found to have a high rate of schizophrenia, probably because they had these tendencies before they joined (Kelley, 1958).

There are, however, some negative aspects to sects. In several recent cases the leader has decided that the members should commit suicide. At the People's Temple in Jonesville, Guyana, the Reverend Jim Jones ordered his followers to drink a mixture of cyanide and strawberry juice, with the result that 912 died, many of them children or elderly. Members of several other sects, such as the Solar Temple and the Branch Davidians, have had a similar fate. Other sect leaders have made less extreme but also unreasonable demands, including making members hand over all their money, prohibiting sex, deciding whom they shall marry, making them engage in embarrassing fund-raising, making it difficult for members to leave, or imposing punitive forms of discipline, none of which can be good for their mental health.

The clergy

Studies of American theological students have found that they often suffer from depression or other problems, probably because such individuals are drawn to the clerical role. Many of them leave, however, and research on clergy does not find the same pattern. Clergy do report being under a lot of stress, particularly from work overload and not having enough time to themselves, as well as low incomes and, for the unmarried, loneliness. However, personality measures show that clergy are above the normal population in mental health (Fletcher, 1990), especially in the case of female clergy (Francis, 1991). They have high job satisfaction, and are happier and more fulfilled than average; Anglican clergy 'would not think of doing anything else' (Fletcher, 1990). However, many Catholic priests do leave; over recent years 37 per cent of

American priests left in the first twenty-five years of their ministry (Schoenherr and Young, 1990), mainly young ones and because they wanted to get married.

Sex is a real problem for many clergy. About 50 per cent of American Catholic priests admit to breaking their vows of celibacy; 30–40 per cent are homosexual, as are many high Anglican clergy, which causes them a lot of stress, through fear of being 'outed' (Fletcher, 1990). The reason for this high level of homosexuality may simply be that the Church is a socially acceptable career for an unmarried man. About 25 per cent of American clergy admit to having been sexually involved with parishioners, and 10–15 per cent have had intercourse with them (Hood et al. 1996). Loftus and Camargo (1993) report a study of 1,322 male clergy sex offenders in Canada; of these 10 per cent had engaged in abuse of children, but were not otherwise abnormal.

The reason for all this sexual misbehaviour is probably the sexual deprivation, especially of unmarried clergy, and the exposure to temptation with parishioners and choirboys.

Suicide

Sociologists have been mainly interested in the differences in suicide rates between Catholics and Protestants, but we will start with the effects of religion in general. We showed earlier Comstock and Partridge's finding that the suicide rate for those going to church once a week or more was 11 per 1,000, but 29 for those going less than once a week over 6 years (Table 11.1). Others have found the same, using different methods; for example, Bainbridge (1997) compared the suicide rates for 75 American cities and found that they correlated −.40 with church membership. He and others have found that suicide rates also correlate with divorce rates, and the effect of church can be partly explained by the lower divorce rates of church members.

Durkheim (1897) is famous for his theory that suicide is partly due to 'anomie', or normlessness and lack of integration into social groups, which he thought has been increased by industrialisation and rapid social change. He predicted that Roman Catholics would commit suicide less because they are more strongly integrated into the Church by shared beliefs and rituals, compared with Protestants who are more free to make individual interpretations of religion. Early European research found that

Protestants had two or three times the suicide rate of Catholics, though some of this may be due to reluctance to give a verdict of suicide in Catholic communities. This difference has all but disappeared during the twentieth century.

In a careful American study Pescosolido and Georgianna (1989) compared suicide rates in fifty-two denominations. Suicide was lowest for Catholics, Evangelical Baptists and Nazarenes; it was *higher* than average for mainline Protestants like Presbyterians and Lutherans. When churches had divided it was the Evangelical branches which had the lower rates, and these were lower for weekly attenders and when spouses shared the same religion, and many had close friends in the church. These authors propose a revised version of Durkheim's theory, that suicide is prevented by social network support, which is high for Catholic churches and for some fundamentalist Protestant ones. Stack and Wasserman (1992) in a big survey also found that suicide rates were lower for churches with a policy of promoting social networks, and churches in conflict with society, which they argue would increase network support.

Jews also have low suicide rates, and so do Muslims. In an international study of seventy-one countries it was found that Christianity had no overall effect on suicide rates, but Islam did, with a correlation of −.55 (Simpson and Conklin, 1989).

Conclusions and discussion

1 Religion was traditionally linked with healing, which is very important in Third World churches. Religious individuals in modern society today are also in somewhat better health than others. This is primarily due to better health behaviour, but also to the social support of the church community and participation in shared rituals.

2 Mental health is associated with intrinsic religiosity, but not with extrinsic. Religion buffers stress, especially for life-and-death issues, and some forms of religious coping are used and with success by those with few other resources.

3 Some psychiatric patients are religious, their illness has taken a religious form. Successful religious leaders and gurus have often had a period of near-insanity. How can this paradox be resolved? The same is found with creative individuals in other fields, perhaps because they too are

high in schizotypy (p. 225). And when they solve their problems with a new vision, it is one with a wide appeal.

4 Fundamentalists tend to be optimistic and benefit from the certainty of their beliefs, but are also dogmatic, are prejudiced, have strong guilt feelings and may be encouraged to ill-treat their children. Their revivalist services can be emotionally disturbing. Sect members have often been disturbed before they joined, seeking a safe haven, but for most there are positive effects.

5 Some sects have made their members commit suicide; otherwise the suicide rate of church members is lower than for others, and for Protestants as well as Catholics.

12

RELIGIOUS AND OTHER ORIGINS OF MORALS

Introduction

There are close links between morality and religion. Indeed for most of human history the two were not really separated. Religion was thought to provide the authority for moral rules, which were backed by the possibility of divine punishment, in this world or the next. The experience of moral commands was one of the arguments for the existence of God. Religious leaders were the main source of moral laws, such as the Ten Commandments; religious and moral leaders were the same people.

Religion and morality now appear to be distinct spheres: religion is about our relations with God, and carrying out religious rituals and observing taboos; morality is about relations with other people and with society. However, religion is also about our relationships with each other, and these are usually central parts of religious obligations.

What is meant by morality is valuing and seeking certain goals rather than others, obeying certain rules, being able to resist temptations, and being able to make moral judgements. There are usually guilt feelings when people fail to resist temptations; they feel inside themselves that they have fallen short.

The historical development of morals and religion

How far, in the course of human history, has religion been the basis of moral rules and moral behaviour? Sociologists observe that moral rules are needed in all human societies, that they all have them, and pass them on to later generations. How far are they the same rules? Are they universal or arbitrary?

Pre-literate societies

All pre-literate, 'primitive' societies had moral rules, usually the same ones. There were rules about killing, stealing, adultery, deceiving, keeping promises, justice and caring for kin, much the same field covered by Moses. There were also variations in the details of these rules, especially about killing, which has often been allowed under certain circumstances, such as war and punishment, and occasionally for sacrifice. However, a serious weakness in these moral systems was that sometimes concern for others did not extend to those outside the tribe. There were also religious rules, about keeping taboos, and making sacrifices. Failure in either sphere was likely to lead to guilt feelings and to the prospects of human or divine punishment. Divine punishment could be avoided by appropriate rituals, conducted by shamans, including sacrifices, and confession (Bianchi, 1987). Moral rules in primitive society were obeyed partly because of fear of social sanctions, but also fear of religious ones. Although anthropologists like Malinowski (1936) thought that these moral rules had religious origins, Nowell-Smith (1967) suggested that moral rules may have other origins, as they are often similar in different tribes while the religious beliefs are not.

Greeks and Romans

For the Greeks, morality was not primarily based on religion but on rational self-interest. The right behaviour could be discovered by reason and was a matter of natural law. Virtue was good for the individual and for society, and virtuous behaviour led to happiness. Religion was separate; it produced festivals but not moral rules, and the gods did not act as moral agents and were not very moral themselves. However, religion did provide some supernatural support for morals, since bad behaviour was punished in this world or the next, though the Greeks were fairly indifferent to the next life. To prevent such punishment the Greeks used ritual, prayer, sacrifices, and also gifts – the rich could hope to influence the gods more by larger gifts (Parker, 1986).

In the early centuries of the Roman Empire, acts were valued by how much they contributed to the success of the race. In later centuries the influence of Greek and Middle Eastern religions produced an intense moral atmosphere. However, the Romans were notable for not valuing all human life, as shown by their killing of victims in their circuses for entertainment, and their treatment of slaves, both of these being morally offensive to us today.

The Jews

From the seventh century BC, religion took on a moral quality, as shown in the Old Testament. The Prophets were much concerned with moral behaviour, especially justice, mercy and love, and also behaviour to God. Scripture became the authority for morals. This took the form of many detailed rules of behaviour – there were a lot more than ten commandments. There was concern for the needs of the poor, the sick and the widowed, and people were supposed to give away 10 or 20 per cent of their income. However, the Jews still recognised the principle of an eye for an eye, and they did not think it necessary to treat outsiders as they treated other members of their own society. Forgiveness of others was a minor Old Testament theme, and it did not extend to treatment of Gentiles. They believed in supernatural sanctions, and attached importance to repentance and sacrifices.

Islam

For Muslims, religion has strong implications for morals. They believe in compassion and forgiveness, and have a special concern for the poor, the weak and the sick. They believe that moral principles are knowable by reason, and believe in reward and punishment after the last judgement. Mohammed himself was a moral reformer, he stopped infanticide and was in favour of moderation, but he allowed slavery and polygamy, and weakened the family by placing respect for parents below loyalty to the group, resulting in tribal wars. Muslims are ambivalent on religious tolerance; while they accept Jews and Christians as 'people of the book', social contact with them is not encouraged and marriage certainly is not. Part of the reason for Muslim intolerance is that this religion emphasises its concern with the whole of secular life, which should be conducted in a certain way, turning from 'human self-centredness to an individual and communal life in obedience to God's commands' (Hick, 1989). There are still 'fatwahs', in which individuals thought to have been disrespectful to Islam are condemned to death.

Other world religions

Not all world religions have provided the authority for morals. In Egypt and Babylon it was believed that the 'heart' was in contact with God and was the source of moral rules. Unlike the Greeks or Romans, the Egyptians had an intense interest and belief in the after-life. There was much concern with justice and care of the poor and the ill.

Hinduism provided religious support for morality, and proclaimed that ethical behaviour is the way to spiritual perfection. Believing in the oneness of God and of all humanity leads to the ethical requirements of giving, compassion, humility, etc., and the belief that those who benefit others will go to heaven (Hick, 1989).

In Buddhism morality is based on the ideas of co-operation and brotherhood, which would lead to Nirvana, so there is a spiritual reward. Egoism can be suppressed by spiritual exercises such as meditation. In Confucianism morals are based on reciprocity, not on religion, and the reward is peaceful inner life. Although all the world religions have had similar moral ideals of love, compassion and forgiveness, the detailed application of these ideals in society has varied greatly with the circumstances of life at different times and places, and this applies to Christianity too (Hick, 1989).

Christianity

Early Christianity broke away from the Jewish rules, in favour of the spirit of moral rules rather than the letter of the law, and an emphasis on love of God and man. It replaced the eye-for-an-eye principle by valuing forgiveness (which is also stressed in Islam). Forgiving others leads to being forgiven by God, or possibly vice versa (Cobb, 1913). It broke away from the Romans' ideas by valuing every human soul, opposing the Roman treatment of slaves and prisoners, and valuing humility rather than worldly success. Christianity extended the Jewish concern with outcasts and the underprivileged and recognised the need to love outsiders as well as members of the in-group. It was believed that God would forgive sins, after repentance, conversion and baptism. At first it was believed that the end of the world was imminent, and that rewards or punishments would follow, so at this period moral imperatives recommended giving away all possessions.

Later Christian thinkers developed the religious basis of morals in several ways. Augustine said that grace was needed to live a Christian life, Aquinas adopted Greek ideas of morals being based on natural law, reason and human nature, but William of Ockham thought that the only basis of morals was God's will, a view adopted by Luther and the early Protestants. The medieval Catholic Church allowed the sale of indulgences, as a way of evading later punishments, a practice condemned by the Protestants.

Later, Protestantism emphasised the Bible as the source of moral rules, and it was believed that salvation was by faith rather than by ritual or works. Early Methodists and others stressed punishments in hell. Sin, guilt and the need for atonement have been emphasised at several periods: by the Protestant reformers, later by Roman Catholics, and today by fundamentalists, especially in the USA, as we see later in this chapter. In the early nineteenth century Protestants developed the 'social gospel', with wider concerns for the underprivileged, with an awareness of the possibility of heaven on earth, as well as later, and hence for the reform of society.

Catholicism placed more emphasis on the role of priests and the church as the source of moral teaching, and on confession as the means of restoring relations with God. In the Orthodox Church the emphasis was on spirituality and the religious life as the source of moral behaviour (Singer, 1987).

Biological origins of morals

Morals can develop without religion: we have seen that there are a number of moral rules which are found in all human societies. It is possible that these are partly innate, as we shall see shortly: very young children are upset by the distress of another, and by age 3–4 seem to realise that hurting others is wrong. Alternatively all societies may discover that certain rules are needed for society to exist – against murder and violence, against stealing, and about telling the truth, for example.

Biological explanations have been offered for limited aspects of moral behaviour. W. D. Hamilton (1964) discovered the principle of 'inclusive fitness', popularised by Dawkins (1967) as the 'selfish gene'. The idea is that there is a basic biological urge for animals to promote the survival of their genes, and hence to look after their children and other close kin. This has been strongly confirmed for birds and bees; for example, birds help their sisters at the nest by feeding them, at cost to their own breeding, but thus produce more birds in the next generation. It is not known how far there is any innate basis to human concern for others. It would explain the lifelong attachment to close kin, and willingness to provide serious help when they are in trouble (Argyle and Henderson, 1985). However, this concern for close kin could also be explained in terms of early attachment, based on conditioning or some similar process, or could be due to socialisation into accepting obligations for kin. There is very little evidence in support of the biological theory of human pro-social behaviour, apart from the finding that such behaviour is partly inherited. There is also the question of how it is mediated; one solution is that inherited capacity for empathy is involved; we will return to this shortly.

However, the selfish gene cannot provide a basis for morals, since its demands extend only to members of the family. All systems of morals go much further than this, and every religion exhorts people to care for all members of the community, and some religions exhort their members to care for members of other communities too.

Campbell (1975), in a classic paper, argued that biological evolution can produce very little self-sacrificing altruism, that society needs such restraints on biological urges, and that these are provided by moral and religious systems which have emerged in the course of history by social evolution; many generations have found that they work, in making urban society possible and enabling people to meet their needs. Moral systems need to keep a balance between looking after the satisfaction of individual needs and restraint in the interest of society; moral leaders correct the balance by being on the side of unselfishness and restraint. Unrestrained biological urges can be equated with sin, possibly original sin, in theological language.

There is a lot of evidence that empathy is a major factor in human help and mutual concern; empathy here means concern for others and their feelings, which is the motivation for helping them; it is not the same as feeling distress. Batson (1991) has shown in many experiments that, for example, subjects will be willing to stand in for 'Elaine', who is about to receive some electric shocks, if they have been told that she comes from the same town, etc., as themselves – an empathy-inducing procedure. Other studies have found that individuals who feel more empathy, or can take the role of the other, will help more. The way this works may be that empathy enables a person to share the other's joy, and so one is rewarded oneself. Experiments have found that while empathy induces more helping it does so only if the actor will receive feedback on the other's outcomes – the helper needs to be able to share the joy (Batson, 1995).

A number of psychologists believe that the capacity for empathy is innate, and there is some evidence for this from twin studies. This could be the innate component of morality. Even new-born infants will cry in response to another baby's distress, and at 14–15 months infants will recognise the distress of another and in some cases help. At the age of 3–4 children recognise that it is 'very bad' to hit or otherwise cause distress to another child (Smetana, 1981); by this age they distinguish between behaviour which hurts others and behaviour which merely breaks social conventions (Mussen et al., 1990). However, this is not all due to adult instruction, but is at least partly based on the distress reactions of the victims (P. L. Harris, 1989). By the age of 6–8 children can to some extent see the point of view of others. Hoffman (1991) believes that these are the early manifestations of empathy. It develops into 'empathic distress' which is distress at another's distress and altruistic concern for the other, leading to a desire to help him or her. A number of experiments have found that subjects will help where they could more easily reduce their own distress in some other way, such as by leaving the situation (Batson, 1995). However, empathy is also affected by socialisation, such as training children to take the perspective of the other and to perceive their needs.

Social learning – the effect of parents

Biological factors may or may not be important in the development of moral behaviour, but there is no doubt of the importance of social learning. And the most important source of social learning here is from parents, or other care-givers. Parents control the behaviour of their children from an early age, first by rewards and punishments; moral and other rules are obeyed for these external reasons. After a time children begin to control themselves and obey the rules when the parents are not there; some will speak to themselves in a parental voice saying 'Don't touch', for example. At age 6 children may feel guilty as the result of a negative outcome, even though this was beyond their control, but by 9 only if they could have done otherwise.

A second form of social learning is by modelling, and the parents are the first important models. Bandura and Walters (1963) found that other children will be imitated if they are seen to be rewarded for what they do. And the other's behaviour has more effect than what they prescribe, if the two are in conflict.

Another kind of social learning is by verbal explanation of why some kinds of behaviour are good or bad. Hoffman and Salzstein (1967) found that there was most development of the consciences of 11-year-olds when their parents used 'induction', that is, appealing to empathy, and explaining the consequences for others, rather than use of power or love withdrawal. This has more effects on pro-social behaviour than rewards and punishment, since it induces empathy (Mussen et al., 1990). Certain styles of child-rearing are more effective – when there is warmth and consistent discipline, and when reasoning and explanation are used. At age 5 children feel pride, shame or guilt, depending on the presence and reactions of an audience, but by age 8 they may feel these emotions without an audience. They can learn to reward themselves by feeling good when they have behaved well, and punish themselves by feeling guilty when they have not (Bandura, 1977).

Some kinds of childhood experience have been found to enhance the development of morality. Being made responsible for others at an early age, such as for younger siblings, is one of these. Being at a school run on very democratic lines is another (Kohlberg and Higgins, 1987).

In a cross-cultural study Whiting and Child (1953) found that there is more guilt in cultures where there are nuclear rather than extended families. There are considerable class differences in the development of inner controls and restraints, due to different styles of child-rearing, and resulting in more middle-class restraint in sexual behaviour, less delinquency, and more acceptance of long-term goals (Argyle, 1994).

Freud maintained that the super-ego, or conscience, is the 'heir to the Oedipus complex', as we explained in Chapter 7. There is no question that a very strong relation is formed with parents, and that they influence morals, but the details of Freud's theory have not been strongly confirmed. Cattell and Pawlik (1964) managed to find three factors in the personality, one of them being the super-ego. It is certainly possible to locate an 'ought self', as Higgins (1989) called it, which has definite causes and effects. The main effect is guilt feelings and anxiety. This all gives some confirmation to the Freudian idea that the parent is 'introjected', a special form of social influence. And the super-ego, or conscience, is experienced as somewhat in conflict with the rest of the personality; when this is so there are guilt feelings (Kline, 1981). Guilt feelings can be interpreted as the inward direction of anger, 'intropunitiveness', and correlates with projection test measures of aggression.

A number of scales have been devised to measure guilt and conscience formation. Mosher (1968) produced three scales:

1 Sex-guilt: e.g. If in the future I committed adultery (a) I hope I would be punished very deeply, *or* (b) I hope I enjoy it.
2 Hostility-guilt: e.g. After a childhood fight I felt (a) like I was a hero, *or* (b) as if I had done wrong.
3 Morality-conscience: e.g. A guilty conscience . . . (a) does not bother me too much, *or* (b) is worse than a sickness to me.

Scores on all these scales correlated with moral judgements, guilt over transgressions, and production of sexual and aggressive materials in word associations and the Thematic Apperception Test (TAT) – a projection test in which subjects make up stories for vague pictures.

The effect of the peer group

Where do the contents of what is taught to children come from? Mainly from the social rules of society, which can be regarded as social norms of the peer group.

All human groups have rules of behaviour, and moral rules are social norms which are learned and enforced; those who break them will be disapproved of or punished. Some of these moral rules had religious origins, and this can explain some of the variations in moral rules. Piaget (1932) thought that it was in the course of playing games like marbles that children first came to follow rules. Before 2 they can't play marbles, but between 6 and 10 they try to follow the rules, and after 10–12 they realise these could be changed. Many other rules are developed when needed to solve a social problem. The rule of the road is a simple example.

Groups of children all find out that fairness and co-operation are necessary to make their social exchanges workable and satisfactory, and they evolve early moral rules of fairness, co-operation and justice. This is a kind of joint social construction, arising out of conflicts and negative reactions to their behaviour when at primary school level (Darley and Shultz, 1990). This has some similarity with the 'rational' ethics favoured by the Greeks. It happens in middle childhood, between 6 and 12, later than the influences of parents just described, and works in a quite different way (Youniss, 1980).

Individuals conform to the rules of social groups partly to avoid disapproval and rejection, and partly because they think the group may know best. Identification with the group, feeling oneself to be a member, leads to internalisation, that is, members believe that the rules are correct and enforce them on other members (Hogg and Vaughan, 1998).

School is another source of moral learning. Teachers may provide models of altruism and honesty, and may encourage moral behaviour by role-playing exercises or other kinds of moral education; for example, enabling children to understand what it is like to be handicapped or to be a member of a minority group. Some schools are run on highly co-operative principles. In America there is a clear 'college effect' on scores on the Defining Issues Test (see below). This is mainly due to general intellectual stimulation, causing students to think more about moral judgements. Moral Education courses have additional effects on such tests (Rest and Narvaez, 1991).

A central feature of social groups is the tendency of members to approve of and like one another, but at the expense of the out-group. Social identity theory has shown how self-esteem is enhanced by holding biased views in favour of members of the in-group, and hence of oneself. This leaves much to be desired in the morality that naturally flows from belonging to groups – they favour discrimination against other groups, especially when these are in some kind of competition. We saw earlier how this was a normal feature of Muslim and Roman Empire thinking, for example – they believed that behaviour is good which helps the in-group. However, recent research has found that this in-group bias is far from universal (R. Brown, 1995), and in my own work I have found that it does not happen in most kinds of leisure group, including churches (Argyle, 1996).

How religion can affect morals

We have seen that religion has had a powerful historical role in all cultures – religious leaders discovered or invented moral principles, and early societies and later on churches enforced or promoted them. We shall see in the next chapter that religion has an effect on behaviour today, in that church members do more good works, give away more money, are less likely to use drink or drugs, are more restrained in sexual behaviour and have lower divorce rates, and are less racially prejudiced, for the most religious at least. Their main failure is that many church members, especially of fundamentalist churches, are prejudiced to other ethnic and religious groups and other minorities.

One way in which religion may affect moral behaviour is that religious people may feel that 'God is watching us . . . at a distance', as a recent pop song put it. Tamminen (1994) surveyed over 2,500 Finnish Lutheran children, and found that 57 per cent of the 9–10-year-olds often felt close to God, when alone or in trouble but also for moral difficulties. The conscience is often experienced as the voice of God, and in 'religious coping' people talk to God about what they should do (p. 160). Church members and religious individuals have been found to do somewhat better on moral dilemmas tests than non-members and non-religious people (Hood et al., 1996).

It has been found in a number of studies that Protestants have stronger guilt feelings than Catholics, particularly in the case of fundamentalists (see p. 160). Protestants also score higher on projective test measures of intropunitiveness, self-directed aggression and blame (Beit-Hallahmi and Argyle, 1997). In a study of 700 schoolchildren Argyle and Delin (1965) found that guilt feelings correlated with church attendance at .30, but for Protestant females only. For a long time there was a higher suicide rate for Protestants (see p. 164), which can be regarded as aggression towards the self. Protestant, and especially fundamentalist, churches place more emphasis on sin and the need for salvation, and the fear of hell has often been used as a way of getting people to behave better, and as a means of conversion.

The belief in hell has occurred in many religions, but in the Christian Church it was at its height in the Middle Ages. It was used by John Wesley in Britain as a means of evangelism, sometimes at death-beds or to those on their way to their execution. He said:

I preach hell because it arouses their fears, arrests their consciences. . . . It is filling up every day. Where is it? About
eighteen miles from here. Which way is it? Straight down – not
over eighteen miles, down in the bowels of the earth.

(J. B. Pratt, 1924: 178)

Hell was widely preached in the Protestant churches in New England.
However, the hell theme gradually disappeared from sermons in America
and had gone by 1850 (Armstrong, 1977, cited by Wulff, 1997), though
it has had some revival in Southern Baptist churches, and now 71 per cent
of Americans say they believe in hell, compared with only 10 per cent of
Jews, and 28 per cent overall in Britain. The belief is much more common
for uneducated and working-class Americans (Hood et al., 1996). However, observers of the American scene think that this belief has been
'radically attenuated' and may be thought of more as alienation from God
(Wulff, 1997).

Frightening people about hell was used as a means of converting them.
We showed in Chapter 2 how converts, especially those experiencing 'sudden' conversions, were often in a state of guilt or other distress beforehand.

The moral impact of religion may come about through the search for
meaning and purpose in life. Frankl (1975) proposed that we have a need
for meaning in this way, and that without it life will seem empty and
pointless; this 'existential vacuum', he suggested, is the cause of depression
and other distress. A central part of this search is the conscience, which
conveys religious guidance on what we should do. This idea has led to the
development of 'Purpose of Life' scales, such as the PIL (Crumbaugh and
Maholick, 1964), which have been found to have strong correlations with
happiness. We shall see in Chapter 15 that in recent years 'strict' churches
have been prospering, and that the probable reason for this is that they
give clear guidance on how to behave.

The moral impact of religion may come about in several ways. Sarbin
(1997) described the myth of the American hero, the frontiersman who
stands up against the forces of evil, and uses violence to protect the
community. This story has been repeated in countless Westerns and similar American stories and offers a moral model – the need for violence to
protect American society. Religion offers a different model of good behaviour, which is also repeated many times and may influence behaviour in
a similar way.

Religious education and instruction

Does religious education influence morals? Research on the effects of Sunday school on religious attitudes and morals has found that the effect is quite weak, especially when the influence of parents has been taken into account. However, going to a Catholic school does have an effect on religious attitudes and later church attendance, and similar effects have been found in the USA for attending fundamentalist or Jewish schools. In Britain going to a Church of England school has no such effect (Francis, 1984). Hoge and Thompson (1982) found that American religious educators and parents who belonged to mainstream Protestant or Catholic Churches made moral maturity their main goal, but for Southern Baptists and other fundamentalists the main goal was conversion and personal religious life. In a similar study Philbert and O'Connor (1982) found that most religious educators were aiming at Fowler's fourth level of faith development, his 'individual reflective faith' level (see p. 28). However, Episcopalians were the group most interested in stage five, 'commitment to ecumenism and social justice', while Southern Baptists aimed only at stage three, 'conventional faith'. We shall see that there is some relation between the Fowler stages of faith and the Kohlberg stages of moral maturity (p. 197). So there is evidence, for some churches, that religious educators aim at developing moral maturity, but less evidence that they are successful.

Studies of conversion, especially sudden conversion, have found that there are immediate benefits for those concerned; they feel that they have more purpose in life, feel better about themselves, and are generally in better mental health. Does their moral behaviour also improve? Converts sometimes say that they look back on their former self with disgust and loathing. Conversion to new religious movements in particular has been found to alleviate problems with drugs, alcohol, gambling, or sex (Beit-Hallahmi and Argyle, 1997).

Having profound religious experiences also has positive effects on moral behaviour. In Chapter 5 we reported the results of studies which showed clearly that having religious experiences led to more pro-social attitudes. Wuthnow (1978), for example, found that those who had them were more likely than others to value working for people in need, and placed less value on having a beautiful house or a large salary.

Religious counselling

Religious counselling is not primarily directed at improving moral behaviour, but it has much stronger moral implications than ordinary counselling or psychotherapy. Moral failures are often seen as part of the problem, sometimes the main part. There are several kinds of religious counselling. (1) Lay counsellors, within churches, have usually received some training, while some are just members of the parish who think they can help. What comparisons have been made, however, have found that they are just as successful as trained professionals, though they usually work only with mild or moderately disturbed individuals. (2) The clergy deal with many mentally disturbed parishioners, indeed 39 per cent of those Americans who seek help go to clergy about it, and their problems are no less severe than those dealt with by the professionals. (3) Spiritual direction is done mainly by the clergy; the intention is to increase spirituality rather than deal with mental health, but it is found that 75 per cent of the clients have problems for which psychotherapy would be suitable (Worthington et al., 1996).

The therapeutic techniques used in religious counselling are different from those used in other varieties. Jones et al. (1992) surveyed 640 American religious counsellors and found the frequency of using various methods shown in Table 12.1.

The use of biblical concepts is almost universal. This makes religious therapy similar to cognitive therapy, but with a different terminology

TABLE 12.1 Percentages of religious counsellors using different methods

Method	%
Taught biblical concepts implicitly	68
Prayed outside sessions	61
Instructed in forgiveness	42
Confronted over sinful life-patterns	28
Used biblical concepts explicitly	28
Instructed in confession	22
Prayed with	18
Used guided religious imagery	12
Taught religious meditation	12

Source Jones et al., 1992

and set of concepts. It would present different models for behaviour, a different plan for life.

Encouraging forgiveness is also used by secular therapists, especially for marital and family problems, and has been found to lead to reduced depression and anxiety (Hebl and Enright, 1993). This can be done by exercises in imagining another person's point of view. Forgiveness leads to improved social relationships. It has been found to be produced by apology, via the arousal of empathy, in the same way that altruism is produced by empathy (McCullough et al., 1997).

Confession has been studied experimentally, though in a non-religious setting, by Pennebaker (1989). He found that if people had experienced stressful events, and they made a 5-minute 'confession', even into a tape-recorder, this produced better health as shown by reduced visits to the doctor.

Praying with patients is common. It has been found that the use of prayer in general has positive outcomes, for example, in 'religious coping', which is described in Chapter 11, but there is no research yet on the use of prayer in the context of therapy. Clients may be encouraged to pray for others, such as those with whom they have difficulties.

Confronting people with their sins has the strongest moral implications. Susan Howatch in her book *Glamorous Powers* (1988) describes such cases, in the setting of spiritual counselling, including dealing with 'evil forces' and the use of exorcism rituals. Non-religious therapists usually take a more accepting and non-judgemental attitude to the behaviour of their clients. Prayer and confession play an important part here, together with attention to the effect of behaviour on others, and the management of relationships. This kind of counselling would be likely to improve the ability to deal with complex moral issues, which we shall discuss in the next chapter.

Comparisons have been made of the effectiveness of religious counselling and cognitive therapy. Propst et al. (1992) compared eighteen hours of cognitive-behavioural therapy with similar treatment but having 25 per cent religious content for religious patients suffering from depression. The religious version was a little more effective, especially when given by non-religious therapists. One outcome of religious counselling can be conversion, or elevation to a different level of religiosity. This is not the purpose of most counselling, but when it happens the results are very beneficial.

Conclusions

1 Historically religion has been the origin of moral rules and principles in nearly all cultures, and provided sanctions for keeping them. Different societies and religions have arrived at very similar moral ideas. Religious prophets and leaders have discovered them, and religion has provided one of the main sanctions for keeping them. However, a more developed view is that moral principles should be followed because they are right, not for rewards or punishment. It is part of human nature to realise that it is wrong to cause others to suffer, and it is part of the nature of human society to need the basic rules of conduct.

China has managed without religious sanctions, and religion was not the main basis of moral rules in Greece or Rome. The moral rules that were developed, or discovered, have been very similar – not stealing, killing, etc., but with some variations. However, the authority for morals today is more in education and public opinion than in religion, which is only one source among others (Nowell-Smith, 1967).

Are moral rules invented or are they discovered, like the principles of mathematics, as Penrose (1994) has argued? The moral argument for the existence of God is that these commands must exist somewhere, indeed, must come from some authority. An alternative view is that they are the solutions to human problems, like the rule of the road, which are found to work, and are then enforced by society. Nevertheless, as we saw in Chapter 4, the experience of God is partly experience of his moral demands, so morality is a central feature of religion. Religion may reinforce natural moral tendencies, and motivate people to follow them, or it may lead to a higher standard of moral behaviour or insight in some ways.

2 Morals develop up to a point without religion, since there is some biological basis for moral behaviour, through the concern for kin – a very limited aspect of morals – and through an unlearnt tendency to empathise with those in distress.

3 Social learning, from parents and others, is more important, and also gives rise to guilt feelings. There are moral norms, in groups and the wider society, partly of historical religious origins, but groups suffer from in-group bias.

4 Religion can affect moral behaviour via fear of punishment; it can provide a guide to life from following religious models, thus giving

purpose in life, and following religious models, but religious education has weak effects. Religious counselling adds the use of prayer and confession, and biblical concepts can lead to a higher level of moral thinking.

5 Sin and guilt: we have seen in this chapter that awareness of sinfulness and the need for forgiveness are central to much religion. Religious individuals may feel that God is watching them, and will punish them. Guilt feelings can be relieved by conversion, confession and regular religious rituals based on sacrifice and atonement. We have seen how evangelical revivals used to play on sexual guilt feelings. However, guilt feelings seem to be a very inaccurate indicator of actual sinfulness. Psychopaths often inflict great suffering on other people but have no feelings of guilt at all. Neurotic introverts have much stronger guilt feelings, especially if they are female, middle-class, were strictly brought up, or belong to fundamentalist Protestant churches.

13

THE EFFECT OF RELIGION ON BEHAVIOUR

Introduction

There seems to be clear historical evidence of the role of religion as the origin of moral ideas. But how far does religion affect people's behaviour in the world today? Churches certainly tell their members what they ought to do, but do they do it? This can be investigated by comparing the behaviour of those who go to church, or to different churches, and those who don't, or who differ on other measures of religiosity. There are several areas of behaviour that are clearly the object of such moral instructions.

Charity

All religions have clear demands for charitable giving. This was particularly important in the ancient world before social security had been invented, but there are still many poor people at home and abroad. 'It is more blessed to give than to receive' (Acts of the Apostles 20.35), and there are similar requirements for Jews and Muslims. How far is this moral rule obeyed?

In Britain, people give away on average 1.4 per cent of income, including church and other donations. In 1993 those who said that religion was 'very important' gave £23.75 a month, about half of this to churches, while those for whom it was not important gave £7.94. In similar American surveys weekly attenders reported giving away 3.8 per cent of income, occasional attenders 1.5 per cent and non-attenders 0.8 per cent (Myers, 1992). Americans give a little more than 1 per cent to churches, and about 1 per cent to non-religious causes as well. There are strong correlations, of the order of .40, between donations to churches, frequency of church attendance and frequency of prayer.

The amount people give increases with income, but in American data the *proportion* that people give declines (Hoge and Yang, 1994), though in some surveys both the top and bottom gave more than the middle. A survey by Schverisch and Havens (1995) clearly shows this curvilinear effect for church giving – a higher percentage is given at top and bottom (Figure 13.1). The explanation of the high rate at the lower end is probably that American sects which the poor attend are very demanding, while the rich simply have extra cash to spare, and their donations are tax-deductible. There is a lot of variability in what people give, particularly at the top end: the most generous quarter of American millionaires gave an average of $136,000 p.a. The top 5 per cent of givers donated over 10 per cent of their incomes to churches and another 4 per cent to other causes – they were 'tithing'.

People give quite a lot to churches, but this is not all 'charity', a lot of it can be better regarded as 'club fees', to support the church and pay for it to provide services, in both senses of the word. It has been estimated that about 70 per cent of what is given to churches is like this. This is consistent with the strong correlation found between church giving and the amount of participation in church activities (Hoge and Yang, 1994). However, the wealthier members are contributing a lot more than their 'club fees'. If we apply the 70 per cent estimate to the British and American data given above, the amounts given to genuine charity by church members is still about twice as great as for other people in both countries. A lot of giving is to a wider in-group. Black American churches give a lot to charities outside their church, but these are mainly to Black organisations. American Jews give much more to Jewish than to non-Jewish charities (Furnham and Argyle, 1998).

Members of some denominations give more than others. In recent American surveys the Mormons gave most (5.5 per cent of income), followed by members of the Assembly of God (3.3 per cent) and Southern Baptists (2.6 per cent), while the Catholics gave 0.9 per cent,

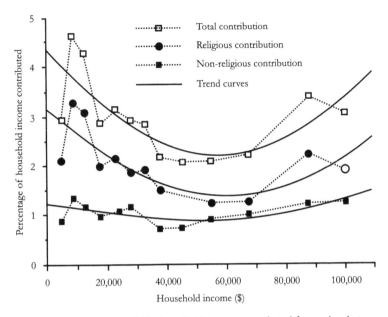

FIGURE 13.1 Percentage of US household income contributed for total, religious and non-religious causes

Note: The upper curve is the trend for the total contribution as a percentage of income for households who reported non-zero contributions. The middle and lower curves are the trends for the percentage of income contributed to religious and to non-religious organisations, respectively, by these same households.

Source Schverisch and Havens, 1995

Episcopalians 0.8 per cent and Methodists 1.1 per cent. Muslims think it is important to give to beggars, and two student studies have confirmed this, one in London and one in Kuala Lumpur.

Church members give less when the congregation is large, if it has other sources of income, and if there are a lot of rich members. People give more when they have a positive attitude to their church and their clergy.

The differences in giving between denominations can be explained in terms of these variables. So Catholics give much less than Protestants, but this is because (1) on average Catholics are poorer, (2) Catholic parishes are larger, and (3) they tend to have less positive attitudes to their Church, especially about participation in decisions (Hoge and Yang, 1994). The differences in giving between different Protestant Churches can similarly be explained: Episcopalians and Methodists in America give a smaller percentage of income because they have lower rates of prayer and participation in church activities, compared with members of the Assemblies of God or Baptists. The Mormons give the most, and this difference cannot be explained in this way, and must be due to other features of Mormonism.

Crime and deviance

It would be expected that religious individuals would be more law-abiding, because they are told to love their neighbours, religion encourages social cohesion, and because religion is widely believed to form part of the system of social control. But how well does it work?

A classic study was by Jensen and Erickson (1979) of 3,268 high school students in Arizona. With social class held constant, there were small negative correlations for eighteen kinds of crime and deviance and four kinds of religiosity. Church attendance was the strongest predictor, and the effect was greatest for alcohol and marijuana, with correlations of −.25; theft and violence were affected less. These findings have been widely replicated, in the USA and in other countries. It would be expected that religion would lead to less violent crime, both because of the content of teaching, and because of rituals like sacrifice which seem designed to reduce aggression (p. 118).

Drink and drugs are the crimes most affected by religion, or rather by church, together with promiscuous sexuality – which have been interpreted as 'hedonistic acts'. More serious forms of crime, violence and theft, have sometimes been found to be related to church attendance or membership, sometimes not. Stark et al. (1982) found that there was no effect on the West Coast of the USA, and thought that this might be because of the lower rate of church membership. Later research has confirmed this 'Stark effect', that religion affects serious crime and delinquency only in communities where organised religion is strong.

The apparent effect of church may really be due to the family. Benda and Corwyn (1997) studied 724 high school adolescents in Arkansas. They found as usual that church membership affected drink and drugs but not serious crime; however, if family variables like attachment to parents were taken into account the effect of church vanished. But, even after these family effects had been taken into account, an 'evangelism' factor correlated with a lower level of serious crime. This factor included items such as trying to convert someone else, and discussing religion with family and friends. The authors argue that it is only serious religious commitment which affects crime.

There are also denominational differences in the effect of church on crime. The strongest effect of religion on crime is for Mormons, which may partly be explained by the Stark effect. The lowest rates of crime are for Mormons and Jews, the highest for Catholics, with class held constant, though this may be due to the effects of Irish and Italian culture. Catholics have high rates for all kinds of theft.

There are denominational differences in forms of crime, and this helps to explain the general findings. For Mormons there are very high correlations between religious participation and drinking (−.77) and smoking (−.54). This clearly reflects the strong and unusual prohibitions of the Mormons. Members of fundamentalist groups also do not drink, and Jews have a tradition of very moderate drinking.

Some of these results are surprising. The Bible does not include alcoholism, smoking, or marijuana in its prohibitions. It is certainly against violence and theft, but here the effects of religion are weaker. It may be against promiscuous sex, and we turn to that next.

A milder form of crime is cheating and related forms of dishonesty. Harteshorne and May (1928) gave a number of tests of dishonesty to 11,000 Chicago schoolchildren. These included dishonest self-marking of tests and stealing coins used in problems. There was no relationship between religion or Sunday school attendance and cheating. Later studies with American college students found that a surprisingly large percentage of religious students admitted to having cheated, and there was no effect of religion, except that among Catholics the religious ones cheated more (Faulkner and De Jong, 1968) – perhaps they were more honest in reporting it.

The effect of religion on crime and deviance is quite weak, compared with religion's other effects. The effect has almost certainly declined in America, and this may be part of a process of desecularisation there (p. 219). The effect still survives, however, for Mormons and members of other strict churches, and especially in areas with a high rate of church membership – the 'Stark effect'. And the effect may be small because the victims are unlikely to be other members of the church community.

Sexual behaviour

Most religions in human history have had rules restraining sex, especially extra-marital sex. Sex was often believed to be for procreation only. This is certainly found in the Christian, Jewish and Muslim religions, and within Christianity there was a lot of early asceticism, and later the Puritans and now the fundamentalists have been active in trying to restrain sex. Sometimes clergy and always monks have had to be celibate. For the Shakers all were supposed to be celibate, with the inevitable result that this sect disappeared.

Extra-marital intercourse (EMI)

Extra-marital intercourse has always been the most strongly proscribed, probably because religious groups have always been in favour of family values. Janus and Janus (1993) carried out a survey of 2,765 Americans and found that 31 per cent of those who described themselves as 'very religious' reported at least one extra-marital affair, compared with 44 per cent of the non-religious (see Table 13.1).

Cochran and Beeghley (1991) used thirteen NORC surveys between 1971 and 1989, making a sample of 15,000 in all. They found that for

TABLE 13.1 Religion and sex in the USA

	Very religious %	Religious %	Slightly religious %	Not religious %
I have had an abortion.	18	21	27	32
I do use contraception.	61	66	65	66
I have had extra-marital affairs (at least once).	31	26	36	44
I have had sexual experience before marriage.	71	85	98	93
Oral sex is very normal or all right.	77	84	89	94
I consider myself to be sexually below average or inactive.	25	22	16	16
	Protestants	Catholics	Jews	None
I have had an abortion.	32	29	11	22
I do use contractption.	64.5	66.5	69	74

Source Janus and Janus, 1993

their whole sample there was a strong correlation (.51) between commitment to religion and believing that extra-marital intercourse was always wrong. The correlation with church attendance was weaker (.21). The percentages of different churches who thought that EMI is wrong varied from 44 per cent for sect members to 13 per cent for Episcopalians and Jews and 7 per cent for those with no religion. Cochran and Beeghley found that the correlation with thinking EMI wrong and religious commitment was very high for sect members (.67), and quite low for Episcopalians (.14), while for the other mainstream Protestant Churches and Catholics it was about .50.

Premarital intercourse (PMI)

The pattern with pre-marital intercourse is similar to EMI, except that there is much more PMI, 71 per cent for the very religious as Table 13.1 shows. The overall effect of religious commitment is similar to that for EMI, but the effect for sect members is greater (.72), as shown in Table 13.2. Other studies have found similar effects for Mormons. British surveys have found the same; for example, Wellings et al. (1994) in a survey with 19,000 subjects found that 20 per cent of men in mainstream churches and 22 per cent of women were opposed to PMI, compared with only 2.6 per cent and 3.8 per cent of the non-religious.

Sect members tend to marry earlier than others, and this may be a way of avoiding the temptations of PMI. PMI is behaviour that is not mentioned in the Bible, and about which there are no clear secular rules. Drugs and alcohol are similar, yet it is behaviour like this that religion seems to affect most.

TABLE 13.2 Attitudes to sexual acts

	No affil. %	Jews %	RC %	Episc. %	Baptists %	Other Protestant %	Total %
PMI always wrong	7	13	25	13	39	44	30
EMI always wrong	44	50	72	60	80	81	73
Homosexuality always wrong	42	37	71	57	86	82	74

Source Cochran and Beeghley, 1991

Homosexuality

Again, many religious people, and especially sect members and Baptists, are opposed to the homosexual form of behaviour.

Contraception and abortion

As Table 13.1 shows, contraception is widely practised, by Catholics as much as by members of other churches, despite the clear Catholic proscription of it. However, the American General Social Survey found in 1990 that Catholics were less in favour of abortions than the mainline Protestant Churches, but that Protestant sects were more opposed to abortion than Catholics were, especially when there were no extenuating circumstances, e.g. when 'The woman wants it for any reason' (Bainbridge, 1997). And Catholics have been very active in 'pro-life' organisations.

Total sexual activity

Kinsey et al. (1953) found that the devout had less sex of all kinds, about two thirds of the rate of orgasms of the non-devout for males; there was less effect for women, and as Table 13.1 shows there are more sexually inactive individuals among the religious. Although Kinsey found less marital sex among the devout, other studies have found that the devout have more sexual satisfaction in marriage. It has been suggested that religion and sex may meet the same needs, of attachment or of emotional expression, so that religion in some way is a substitute for sex.

Conclusion

There is a greater amount of restraint for Baptists and sect members, and these are the churches with the strongest views on sex. It has been suggested that there is a 'Protestant continuum' of degrees of proscription of sex (Hughes and Hughes, 1987). On the other hand the prohibition of contraception and abortion for Catholics has had very little effect.

Prejudice

Most religions exhort their members to behave well towards other people, to love their neighbours, even their enemies. It was very surprising to find that church members are usually more racially prejudiced towards Jews and Blacks than non-members were. This was first found in the authoritarian studies in California (Adorno et al., 1950), and has been widely replicated since. Batson et al. (1993) analysed forty-seven American studies, some with population samples, and found that in thirty-seven of them there was a clear relationship between church attendance or other measures of religiosity and racial prejudice; in eight studies the results were unclear, and in two, both with adolescents, the opposite result was found. The relationship is not strong, typically r = .30 – but it is in the opposite direction to what might be expected. And the least prejudiced people are non-church members. It is not always found: Jacobson (1998) studied samples of American sociology students from several northern states, and found no relation with prejudice for most groups, but for Mormons there was a strong effect in the opposite direction – the more religious ones were less prejudiced.

In some studies the pattern is curvilinear, as was found by Struening (1963), shown in Figure 13.2. It can be seen that the most and least religious are less prejudiced, but the reversal only happens to a small group at the top level of religiosity, those going to church more than once a week, 2.4 per cent of the population in this study.

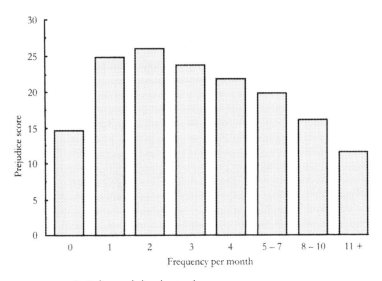

FIGURE 13.2 Prejudice and church attendance

Source Struening, 1963

The curvilinear pattern shown in Figure 13.2 was also found by Perkins (1985) in a survey of 1,197 British and American students. Humanitarian and egalitarian attitudes were lowest for those with weak religious attitudes, racist attitudes the strongest for those with moderate religious attitudes. The strongly religious scored as most liberal on all three dimensions. Clergy are often more liberal in these matters than their congregations, and several American studies have investigated the conditions under which they come out in public with their views. C. B. Thomas (1985) found that clergy came out in support of desegregation of Boston schools when they were under 40, Protestant, and had good support from other clergy or from national or regional church bodies.

Prejudice is greater for those with high extrinsic religiosity than for intrinsic religiosity, dimensions which we described in Chapter 3, and there is only a correlation with prejudice for the extrinsic dimension.

Batson et al. (1993) argued that intrinsics accept minority groups when prejudice against them has been proscribed by their church, but they can be prejudiced towards other groups. These authors found that intrinsics were not prejudiced towards Jews or Blacks but were towards homosexuals and communists, and amongst West Indians towards Rastafarians. Those high in Quest were unprejudiced to these groups, but this may reflect the views of the radical young. There have been exceptions to this finding.

Some denominations are more prejudiced than others. In America the most prejudiced are Southern Baptists and other fundamentalist churches, and they are also prejudiced towards members of other churches – they say they would not marry one or be friends with one (Rokeach, 1960). High correlations, sometimes as high as .70, have been found between prejudice and measures of fundamentalism, not only for populations of Christians but also for Jews, Muslims and Hindus (Hood et al., 1996).

Church was found to have a *positive* effect on racial attitudes in Holland. Billiet (1995) surveyed 1,500 Dutch Catholics, and found that church membership led to less prejudice towards immigrants, mainly via a factor of 'individualism', which was lower for church members. He thought this was due to the humanistic values of the church there, which promotes social solidarity and charity and opposes fundamentalism.

Batson's Quest dimension has been found to be almost the opposite of fundamentalism, and Batson et al. (1993) report a series of studies in which Quest has a negative correlation with prejudice. Another attempt to find a mature kind of religiosity was by Leak and Randall (1995). Their Global Faith Developmental Scale, which is rather like Fowler's higher stages, and like Symbolic Realism, correlated negatively with authoritarianism, and almost certainly with lack of prejudice.

However, overall religious people are *more* prejudiced than the non-religious; this is a disturbing finding from the religious point of view, but what is the psychological reason for it? There are several possible explanations.

1 Religious groups are very cohesive and supportive, and this can lead to rejection of those who are not members of the in-group, which explains why members of other churches are rejected as well as other races. There is a high level of intimacy between church members, and prejudice is heightened for intimate situations. We discussed earlier the research on 'terror management theory', which found that arousing fear of death made people avoid the company of those who did not share their opinions, thus heightening prejudice.

2 Fundamentalists tend also to be right-wing authoritarians – because fundamentalism encourages obedience to authority, conventionalism, self-righteousness and feelings of superiority (Altemeyer and Hunsberger, 1992).

3 Religious teaching can encourage prejudice. American anti-Semitism may be due to this: Glock and Stark (1965) found that 86 per cent of Southern Baptists thought 'The Jews can never be forgiven for crucifying Jesus'. But this cannot explain other kinds of prejudice.

Helping and altruism

It is a central part of Christianity and of other religions to care for the poor, the weak, the sick, and the outcasts of society, to show love, charity and compassion to them. How far is this done? Religious bodies and individuals made major contributions to social welfare before the state took it over.

Early studies used questionnaires, from which it was found that church members said that they did more to help other people. A recent version is Johnson et al.'s 56-item altruism scale (Chau, Johnson et al., 1990), mainly on reported help to strangers, which was found to correlate up to .42 for different samples with intrinsic religiosity; this scale had no correlation with the Lie scale, but psychologists are suspicious that such results may reflect what people think they ought to do rather than what they actually do. A little better are measures of 'empathy', which are regarded as an indicator of concern for others; these are found to correlate positively with intrinsic religiosity, negatively with extrinsic (Watson et al., 1984). And we saw in Chapter 4 that after strong religious experiences people say they have an enhanced concern for the welfare of others. The greater helpfulness of church members may be genuine, as it is also found in reports by others: Clark and Warner (1955) found this for seventy-two community members who were rated by fourteen others.

However, psychologists always think that behavioural measures are the most convincing. The first such study was the famous 'Good Samaritan' experiment by Darley and Batson (1973), which re-created that parable, but did not find that the more religious theological students helped any more than others. Later behavioural studies have obtained more positive results, with readiness to read to blind students, help a lonely girl, etc. In all these studies intrinsically religious subjects helped more, extrinsics did not, and quests helped somewhat more.

Batson obtained some evidence that intrinsics help in order to look good, while quests are more concerned with the other's needs. They found, for example, that intrinsics carried on helping after the victims had said he or she didn't need it, and in one study word associations found that high intrinsics produced words like 'praise' and 'merit', and low intrinsics about looking bad (Batson et al. 1993) – but the intrinsics still had the highest rate of helping.

A more serious kind of help is doing voluntary work. In a British survey voluntary workers were asked about the benefits of doing it and 44 per cent said: 'It's part of my religion or philosophy of life to give help' (Lynn and Smith, 1991). In the USA a Gallup poll found that 46 per cent of the 'highly spiritually committed' did such work among the poor, infirm or elderly, compared with 22 per cent of the non-religious (Myers, 1992).

Hoge and Yang (1994) found that American church attenders put in more time on church-centred voluntary work; if they were sect members, those who went to church once a week did 6.1 hours a month, mainline Protestants did 3.9 and Catholics 1.9 hours. The individuals who did more of this work also gave more money to their churches and were more active in the community in other ways. They tended to be between 50 and 69, more educated and in the middle range of incomes.

In addition to this activity on the part of individuals, whole congregations have sometimes been active in doing good works. In the nineteenth century middle-class congregations in Britain did a lot for working-class children, teaching them to read in Sunday schools. In the USA such middle-class charity activity has been important because of the limited provision of government welfare. Some religious orders have been active in this way, and have produced a number of saintly individuals like Mother Teresa of Calcutta.

Moral ideas and judgement

Moral knowledge includes knowing what is right and wrong, and being able to make moral decisions when different considerations conflict. Does religion improve such moral competence? It is usually measured by setting people moral problems and seeing how they solve them. Piaget (1932) started this line of work by proposing that at ages 4–7 children judge the rightness or wrongness of acts by their consequences and by how far they conform to parental rules, while after age 10 they take account of intentions as well as consequences, and know that some rules can be negotiated. Typical question: Which was worse, a boy who broke one cup while helping himself to the jam when his mother was out, and a boy who broke fifteen cups by accident?

The most influential scheme of moral development is that of Kohlberg (1969) which proposed that children may go through up to six stages, in a set order:

A The first two stages are based on conforming to external rules, and the consequences for oneself of behaviour:

  1 based on obedience and punishment;
  2 following rules because they are believed to be in one's own interest.

B The next two are based on internalised rules, and concern for others and society:

  3 be a nice person to gain approval of others;
  4 follow the rules and do your duty to society.

C   The last two stages go further to universal principles and values:

5   rules and laws are part of a social contract and can be changed, provided that life and liberty are intact;
6   follow universal ethical principles, of justice, equality of rights, etc.

The test consists of presenting three stories containing moral dilemmas to subjects and asking questions about what should be done. One concerned a man who stole a drug to save his wife's life, since he couldn't afford to buy it. There is a somewhat subjective scoring procedure; a more objective version was the Defining Issues Test, where twelve items about the stories are rated and ranked (Rest, 1979).

It might be expected that those who score higher on this measure would also behave more morally. Blasi (1980) analysed seventy-five studies of this issue, and found that the scale predicted moral behaviour in some areas but not in others. It was fairly successful for delinquency and for pro-social behaviour. The findings were mixed for honesty and cheating, and the scale did not predict disobedience in the Milgram obedience situation – i.e. refusing to give large electric shocks to another subject. The reason for these rather weak effects may be that social situations have particular demands and may pull people to another level from their usual one. Krebs et al. (1991) found that judgements of real-life conflicts produced scores one stage lower than Kohlberg's scale. One of the various criticisms of Kohlberg is that it focuses too much on principles and justice, and not enough on caring and responsibility. Gilligan (1982) observed that women tend to get lower scores, putting them at stage 3, below that of men, and suggested that this is because they are concerned with caring for others rather than with rights and justice. However, a meta-analysis of eighty studies, with 152 samples, by Walker (1991) did not support this idea – he found that the overall sex difference was very small and not significant.

Samples from other cultures often have lower scores on the Kohlberg scale, and this is particularly the case for people from folk or 'collectivist' cultures. The basis of morality is different here, being concerned with social harmony, co-operation, reciprocity and close personal ties, whereas urban western children are trained to be competitive and have many relationships, and obligations are based on contracts and payments (Argyle, 1991). The result is that the moral dilemmas are approached quite differently (Snarey and Keljo, 1991).

How is moral development in the Kohlberg sense related to religious development? Kohlberg came later (1981) to think that moral reasoning is not enough; why should one be moral in an unjust world? He thought that some religious basis for morals may be needed, and he approved of the scheme of faith development devised by Fowler (1981), which was described in Chapter 2. Kohlberg believed that faith development depended on moral development, while Fowler thought the opposite. Some studies have found little relation between the two variables, but Snarey et al. (1985) and Snary and Keljo (1991) with a sample of sixty Kibbutz members, found a correlation of .60 between the scales, and that 42 per cent of their subjects were at the same level in each. At the highest levels faith development was necessary for moral development. So there is some evidence here that religious judgement is necessary for moral judgement.

Conclusions

Church membership and commitment have been found to affect behaviour in a number of areas.

1 Church members give about twice as much money to charity, and some tithe. However, a lot of what is given is to the church itself or to a wider in-group.
2 There is little general effect on law-breaking, except for drinking and drugs, little effect on theft or violence, but there is a stronger effect for certain groups, like the Mormons especially, and any deviance is likely to be directed to those outside the religious community. We saw earlier that there is quite a strong effect of religion in making suicide less likely.
3 There is less extra-marital and premarital sex, especially for sect members, but there is little effect on contraception or abortions for Catholics. Churches value the integrity of the family, and we have seen that the divorce rate for church members is lower than for others, but high for religious mixed marriages, which may be due to the social cohesion created by shared beliefs and practices, and the loss of it when these are different.
4 Church members are overall more prejudiced than others, contrary to the teaching of churches. This is not true of those most religiously active, except for fundamentalists. There is also prejudice towards

members of other churches. This is consistent with the idea that religion is a social phenomenon, which creates bonds between members but sets them off from non-members, who do not share their beliefs.

5 Religious people engage in more good works such as doing social work, over twice as much as the non-religious. This would be expected from the contents of religious teaching.

6 Moral judgements of religious people are at a higher level of competence for those who are also at a high level of religious development; however, these moral judgements have only a weak effect on behaviour.

14

SECULARISATION AND THE PRESENT STATE OF RELIGION

Introduction

It is often said that religion is declining, in Britain and elsewhere, that it will eventually disappear, that there is 'secularisation' in which religion ceases to be important. It is well known that in Britain church attendance at any rate has declined; this may have given a misleading idea that the same thing is happening in the rest of the world. In this chapter we will first look carefully to see exactly what has happened to religion in Britain. Then the very different state of affairs in the USA will be examined. And in the next chapter we will look at some parts of the world where there has been expansion of religion rather than decline – such as Africa, Brazil and Korea. Sociologists, thinking about Europe, used to think that industrialisation was the cause of secularisation, but in some countries we shall see that over the last century industrialisation has been accompanied by more religion, not less. And while some churches have declined, other new churches have been born.

Religion in Britain in the twentieth century

There has long been a myth in Britain that there was more religious devotion in the past. However, going back to 1600 Keith Thomas reports that behaviour in church was often far from devotional.

'Members of the congregation jostled for pews, nudged their neighbours, hawked or spat, knitted, made coarse remarks, told jokes, fell asleep, and even let off guns' (1971: 161). During the first half of the nineteenth century there had been a massive growth in British churches, followed by a decline in the second half (Gill, 1993). But we turn to the present century: what is the present state of religion and has it declined or not?

Davie (1994) coined the phrase 'believing without belonging' to describe the state of religion in Britain today. She is right: attendance is low, but many more than this are religious in other ways. Table 14.1 summarises some of them.

We have to look at different measures of religious activity.

Church attendance

Church attendance is the measure which researchers like best – it is based on behaviour (or reported behaviour) and, as we have seen, correlates with the major causes and effects of religion. If we think that the social side of religion is important – belonging to a community and taking part in rituals – then church attendance is the most valid measure. Church

TABLE 14.1 The state of religion in Britain

Attendance	weekly 12–19% monthly 7% sometimes 24% belong to house group 22% watch *Songs of Praise* 4.1 million, c.10%
Pray	weekly 27% regularly feel the need for prayer, meditation or contemplation 53%

Beliefs	God 68%
	    God concerned personally 37%
	    feel close to God 46%
	 Jesus is Son of God 49%
	    Jesus can save us from our sins 30%
	 after-life 43%
	 miracles 54%
	 the Devil 30%
	 hell 25%

Feelings	Describe self as a religious person 54% Draw comfort or strength from religion 44%

Sources Davie, 1994; Greeley, 1992; Gill et al., 1998

attendance in Britain has fallen during this century, from about 24 per cent in 1900 to about 15 per cent now. It is here that there appears to have been a decline of religion. But although only about 15 per cent go to church every week, nearly 50 per cent go 'sometimes', which often means Christmas and Easter for Christians. And attendance says nothing about beliefs or inner commitment.

Church membership

Church membership has declined from 20.4 per cent of the population in 1901 to 14.4 per cent in the 1990s, adding up reported members of all churches. This is a very unsatisfactory measure, because all churches count their members in different ways, and because these methods can change over time. If a church or a government decides to levy a contribution from member churches based on their size, the number of members mysteriously shrinks. Some American churches do not count children or even women for this reason.

Beliefs

Surveys of beliefs in Britain have been carried out since the 1940s by Gallup and others. Gill et al. (1998) averaged 100 of these by decades, and here are their main findings. Belief in God has fallen from 79 per cent to 68 per cent. Belief in God as a Person fell from 43 per cent to 31 per cent, with a small increase in those who believed in God as a spirit or life-force (from 38 per cent to 40 per cent). Belief in Jesus as Son of God fell from 68 per cent to 49 per cent. Belief in life after death fell from 49 per cent to 43 per cent, and a lot more disbelieved in it (from 21 per cent to 41 per cent). Fewer now believe that the miracles in the Bible really happened (from 70 per cent down to 54 per cent). There was no real change in belief in God as a spirit or life-force, or in heaven, or the Devil, though more disbelieved in the Devil (from 54 per cent to 64 per cent). There was some increase in occult beliefs, such as believing it is possible to exchange messages with the dead (from 15 per cent to 31 per cent), and foretelling the future (from 41 per cent to 46 per cent). Many believed in ghosts (about 63 per cent) and in reincarnation (26 per cent) but with no change over time for either (Gill et al., 1998).

Sunday schools

In 1901, 22 per cent of children went to Sunday schools, but this figure fell to 10 per cent by 1961. Of those now over 65, i.e. born before 1933, most were brought up religiously, now about a third are. In 1950, 67 per cent of children received Anglican baptisms; this has now fallen to 27.5 per cent.

Private devotions

There are 53 per cent who say they regularly feel the need for prayer or meditation, and 27 per cent claim to pray weekly. For 44 per cent religion is a source from which they say they draw comfort or strength.

Changes in different denominations

Different Christian denominations have fared differently. Some churches have expanded their membership – Catholics from 4.6 per cent to 8.3 per cent of the population, the Church of Scotland from 22.4 per cent in Scotland in 1901 to 31.9 per cent in 1967. There have also been very large percentage increases in the Jehovah's Witnesses, the Seventh Day Adventists and others, though the numbers involved are small.

A common theory in the sociology of religion is that churches rise and fall, and when they fall they are replaced by other, more charismatic, more fundamentalist or simply stricter ones. This has happened to some extent in Britain. Methodism is a clear example, as shown in Figure 14.1. This shows the percentage of the British population aged 15 or over who were members of the Methodist Church. The Methodist Church increased in numbers until about 1840 and then declined. The Church of England and the total for Protestant Churches showed a rise to 1930 (Figure 14.2) followed by decline. We have seen the sharp fall in Anglican baptisms. The Roman Catholics have continued to expand, levelling off in 1970. Figure 14.2 shows some of this.

During the period since 1979 membership of the Methodist Church has declined most, and there has been a growth in pentecostal, charismatic, evangelical and Baptist Churches (Brierley, 1991). The fundamentalist sects have risen very rapidly, as shown in Figure 14.3. The Baptists are the nearest to a fundamentalist sect among mainstream churches, and they have continued to grow. Non-denominational house churches have also grown rapidly, as have Black churches, which are often

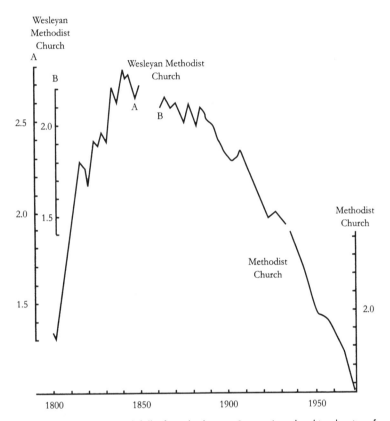

FIGURE 14.1 The rise and fall of Methodism in Britain (membership density of the Wesleyan Methodist Church and the Methodist Church at annual intervals, 1800–50, 1860–1932 and 1933–68 [per cent])

Source Currie et al., 1977

centres of their communities. However, Barker (1995) estimated that of the half million members lost by the established churches between 1975 and 1980 only 4 per cent joined small Protestant churches.

The pattern of religiosity is different in different social classes. Gerard (1985) devised a measure of religious commitment, based on questions about acceptance of traditional Christian beliefs, reported perception of oneself as a religious person, needing prayer and contemplation, and drawing strength and comfort from religion. Table 14.2 shows the class

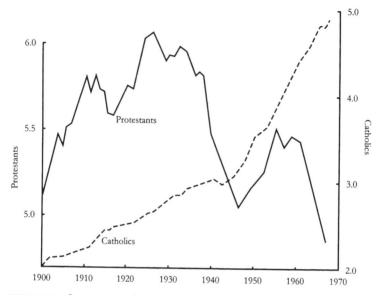

FIGURE 14.2 Protestants and Catholics in Britain, 1900–70 (membership of the major Protestant Churches and estimated Catholic population in Great Britain at annual intervals, 1900–68 [millions])

Source Currie et al., 1977

differences in this index in Britain. This table also shows class differences in weekly church attendance. It can be seen that while middle-class people are about twice as likely to go to church weekly as working-class ones, the opposite trend is found for Gerard's religious commitment index, based on feeling and beliefs. This could be because middle-class people find church services very congenial – good music, a short lecture, a coffee party – but their beliefs have been weakened by education. Working-class individuals on the other hand find church less congenial, don't like the music, but still hold traditional beliefs. They may pursue their religion in other ways – such as private prayer and Bible reading, radio and TV services. Perhaps, being under more economic and other stress, they need religion more. We have seen that certain stresses can be helped by religion (p. 159), and we shall see in the next chapter that sects and cults appeal to individuals under stress. Radio and TV services are the ultimate form of believing without belonging, and they compete with going to church.

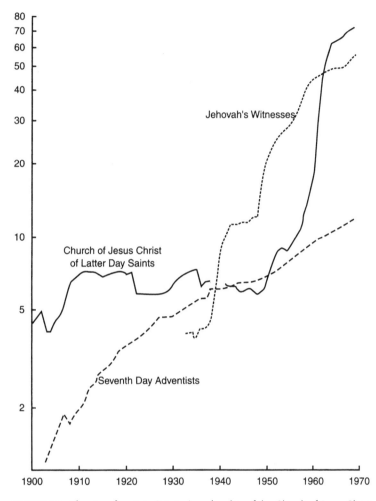

FIGURE 14.3 The rise of sects in Britain (membership of the Church of Jesus Christ of Latter Day Saints, Jehovah's Witnesses and Seventh Day Adventists at annual intervals, 1900–70 [thousands: semi-log])

Source Kelley, 1972

TABLE 14.2 Social class and two measures of religiosity in Britain: (a) religious commitment; (b) weekly church attendance

	Under £3,840	£3,840– £7,199	£7,200 and over (in 1981)
	%	%	%
(a) High score	26	21	15
Medium-high score	25	17	13
Low score	15	19	28

Source Gerard, 1985

(b)	AB	C1	C2	DE
	17%	11%	8%	9%

Source Reid, 1989

Working-class individuals are more likely to join small charismatic and fundamentalist sects, which are more expressive and less formal than the mainstream churches. However, charismatic renewal in mainstream churches has been more middle-class. Those who join these groups clearly have religious needs which cannot be met by the traditional services of what we have just seen are the declining mainstream churches.

Religion in Britain today consists of a minority of about 15 per cent who go to church regularly, together with a larger group who go monthly or 'sometimes', and who are religious in a weaker sense, but who say that they hold the basic beliefs, that draw strength and comfort from religion, and that God is important in their lives. The traditional churches are declining in membership, but newer religious movements, which are more charismatic, more evangelical, stricter, perhaps closer, are rising rapidly.

Religion in the USA during the twentieth century

The religious scene in the USA is very different from that in Britain. To begin with, many more people go to church, about 43 per cent compared with 15 per cent in Britain, and more hold beliefs and engage in other kinds of religious behaviour (see Table 14.3)

There has never been a state church, and this seems to have led to free competition especially between the many Protestant churches, whose

TABLE 14.3 The state of religion in the USA (percentages of Americans over 15 in 1990; figures for Britain in brackets)

Religious behaviour	%
Membership	church members 62 (14.4)
Behaviour	weekly attendance 43 (15) pray weekly 58 (27)
Beliefs	God 94 (68) after-life 78 (43) hell 71 (28) the Devil 47 (28) the Second Coming 20 religious miracles 73 (54)
Feelings	close to God 85 (46) describe self as religious 73 (43) have had a conversion experience 46 (17)

Source Greeley, 1992

numbers have been increased by schisms, as well as by the founding of new churches. According to theories of secularisation the effects of industrialisation, urbanisation, economic prosperity and other aspects of modernity would be expected to be a decline in religion, as has happened in Europe, but in the USA there has been a continuous increase in church membership and other measures of religious activity since 1800. Something similar has happened in South Korea more recently (p. 235). However, there has been a downturn for most churches since about 1965 (Roozen and Carroll, 1979).

Church membership
Church membership has been increasing from 17 per cent of the population in 1776 to about 62 per cent in the 1990s (Finke and Stark, 1992). Membership figures show a revival after 1945, the end of the Second World War, followed by a decline after 1965. If different indices are compared, the fall was first in baptisms, next in church school attendance and then in membership – these form a sequence where each affects the next (Doyle and Kelly, 1979).

Church attendance

The rate of attendance has been fairly constant since before the Second World War, at 42–44 per cent, again with a revival in 1952–60, as shown in Gallup polls; see Figure 14.4.

Beliefs

The level of beliefs has continued high since surveys started; about 95 per cent believe in God, 73 per cent in an after-life. However, Hoge (1979b) has found that in the period 1906–68 later generations of students held more liberal beliefs. The level of beliefs in recent surveys is shown in Table 14.3, with the corresponding figures for Britain alongside. The greatest differences are for hell (71 per cent v. 28 per cent) and the Devil (47 per cent v. 28 per cent), reflecting the strength of fundamentalist churches in the USA.

Feelings

It can be seen that as many as 85 per cent said they felt close to God, and 73 per cent described themselves as religious.

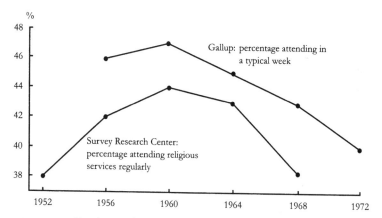

FIGURE 14.4 Church attendance in the USA, 1952–72 (comparison of church attendance trends as measured by the Gallup poll and the Survey Research Center, University of Michigan)

Source Roozen and Carroll, 1979

Other indices

Donations to churches continued at a high level with an increase starting in 1943–4. As we found in Chapter 7, church members gave away 3.8 per cent of their income, about half of this to churches, and many gave away 10 per cent of their incomes. Hymns on traditional dogmas fell in popularity, but hymns on love and gratitude and on the humanity of Jesus were more popular. Hoffman (1998) analysed successive surveys about confidence in organised religion; he found a continuous decline since those born in 1900, from 2.3 on a 3-point scale to 2.0. The decline was greater for the young, less for Blacks. There was an equal decline in confidence in financial institutions.

Denominational changes

As in Britain some churches declined while others rose. Stricter churches, and stricter branches within churches, rose, while liberal churches, and liberal branches within churches, fell (Kelley, 1972). This is shown in Figure 14.5.

The Methodists rose from 3 per cent of the population in 1776 to 34 per cent in 1850, after which membership declined and was overtaken by Catholics and Baptists. Methodism became a prosperous and middle-class church, but some of its members split off to form the Holiness bodies. The Baptists expanded and in the north they became a middle-class church, but not in the south. The largest church to continue to increase over this period in the USA was the Southern Baptists. Most of the members of this church live in the southern states; their churches are mostly small and rural, though there has been some shift to the cities, and members are white but low in education and income (Finke and Stark, 1992). Membership of the Catholic Church in America has fallen since 1965, but less than membership of most Protestant Churches.

The mainstream churches gradually changed in the direction of becoming more worldly, less in conflict with society, making fewer demands, and perhaps as a result offering fewer rewards. As their membership fell it was more evangelical churches which rose, and above all the Protestant sects, as in Britain.

This increase in 'new religious movements' in America occurred particularly in the late 1960s and early 1970s. Why did it happen then? Bryan Wilson (1976) thought that the rise of these movements is a response to secularisation, to the loss of religion in society. This would not explain this precise date, however, and we suggest below that this may have been a response to the counter-culture.

The explanation of American religiosity

Why do so many Americans belong to and go to churches? Here are three possible theories.

(1) Stark (1997) and others have proposed the idea of the 'religious market'. In the USA, it is argued, there is no one dominant or state church, and all churches are in open competition. As a result they have all engaged in aggressive marketing of their product and brought in many new members. Stark supported this by comparing first-, second- and third-generation German immigrants. He found that the later generations had progressively higher levels of church attendance and beliefs, and he gave examples of approaches from active clergy. However, Verwelj et al. (1997) did not find that this theory worked in a comparison of sixteen European countries. Absence of state regulation of churches and presence of religious pluralism were associated with more members but with less attendance. Part of the theory was confirmed by Hoge (1979a) who found more growth in churches which emphasised evangelism.

(2) We have already seen that in the USA it has been the 'strict' churches which have expanded: Southern Baptists, strict branches of other churches, small sects and charismatic churches. 'Strict' also means 'certain', and giving clear direction for how life should be lived; this may be a very attractive feature of a church for many people. Kelley suggested several other reasons why strict churches should prosper. Hoge (1979) tested these ideas in a study of sixteen Protestant Churches over the period 1955–75. Several of Kelley's ideas were confirmed: growth was greatest for churches which had a distinctive life-style and morality, disallowed individualism and pluralism in belief, and were against ecumenism and liberal theology. He did not find which of these was most important. Iannacone (1996a, 1996b) confirmed Kelley's hypothesis that strict churches expand faster, but he offered a different explanation – that strict churches demand more commitment, producing more resources for outreach and evangelism.

The recent history of American religion has been the rise of strict Protestant Churches, and this may be the main reason for the high level of religiosity. However, Perrin and Mauss (1993) found two factors of

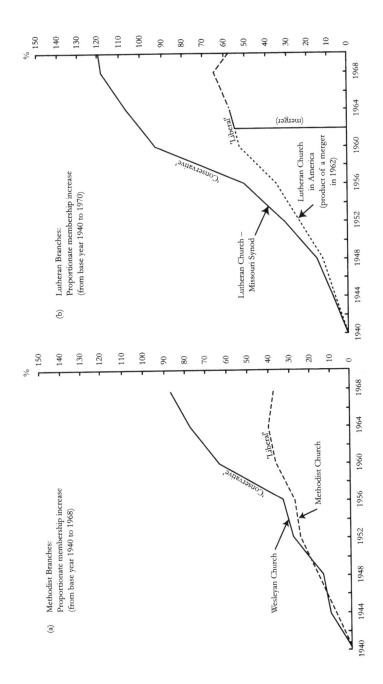

(a) Methodist Branches:
Proportionate membership increase
(from base year 1940 to 1968)

(b) Lutheran Branches:
Proportionate membership increase
(from base year 1940 to 1970)

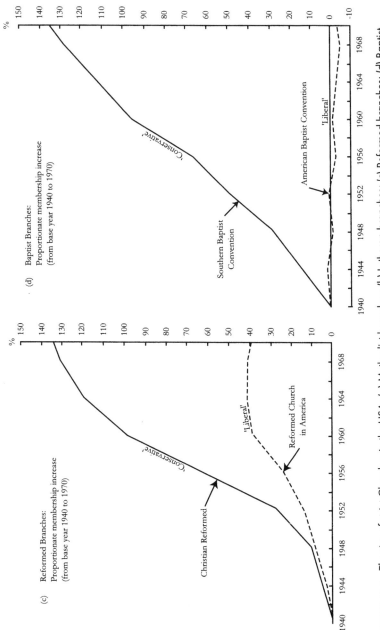

FIGURE 14.5 The rise of strict Churches in the USA: (a) Methodist branches; (b) Lutheran branches; (c) Reformed branches; (d) Baptist branches

Source Kelly, 1972

strictness: one was certainty, dogmatism and conformity, the second commitment, discipline and evangelical outreach. In this study the Vineyard Church was found to be high on commitment but low on strictness. Tamney and Johnson (1998) studied strict churches in 'Middletown', USA. They asked 576 individuals to rate the properties of their ideal church. Strictness seemed less popular than before, but was most popular among those who were less educated, older and female. Authoritative preaching was favoured by fundamentalists, and by Black, female, less educated and more authoritarian individuals.

Finke and Stark (1992) proposed another explanation of the rise of strict churches. They argued that joining a church is a rational act where great rewards are hoped for and great sacrifices thought reasonable, in the form of giving things up, and engaging in strange and socially stigmatising religious behaviour like glossolalia. The high costs keep out 'free riders' so that all members are committed, which increases the rewards of belonging to the fellowship.

A third theory about American churches is that church in the USA is much more a part of the normal culture, most people belong to one, and it is a major source of identity and place in society. Many American churches had roots in Europe with particular national groups, so that belonging to one of these churches is a way of keeping that national identity. Herberg (1955) thought that this was important for third-generation immigrants, in the period which he was studying, when there had been a massive influx of European immigrants, many of them refugees, who wanted to maintain their original national identity. In addition, belonging to churches is part of the middle-class life-style, and conveys social status. This may explain the existence in the USA of 'extrinsic religiosity', which we described earlier, where people go to church for non-religious reasons.

In addition the American culture seems to support religious values, which are endorsed by presidents and other politicians, and play a part in ceremonials, so that there has been said to be a 'civil religion'. As the churches have become secularised and adapted to society's values, the gap between church and society is small. Reimer (1995), who compared the USA and Canada, found that there was less difference between church attenders and others in the USA, and concluded that the non-religious had much the same outlook as the religious, which must be rather low in conviction for both.

This theory has been used to explain the decline in church membership since the 1960s. The decline was particularly strong among those who were then under 30. It was this group which had been influenced by the counter-culture, and experienced a major change of attitudes and values in the direction of greater tolerance and freedom, in relation to sex, drugs and civil liberties. These were attitudes and behaviours to which the churches were opposed, and the result was that those so affected moved away from the churches (Hoge, 1979).

Secularisation

The great sociologists of the past, Durkheim, Weber and Marx, all predicted that industrialisation, urbanisation and prosperity would lead to the decline, perhaps the disappearance, of religion. This was described as 'secularisation', though this term has been used to mean different things. The simplest meaning is that there will be less religious activity in terms of church membership and attendance. Another meaning is that religion will have less influence on people's behaviour. Another is that society will become 'desacralised', that is, supernatural forces will no longer be thought to be important. I shall consider how far secularisation in each of these three senses has in fact taken place.

Is there less religious activity?

We have seen that in Britain there was an increase in religious activity during the nineteenth century, a period when there was a great increase in industrialisation and urbanisation and other aspects of modernity, so evidently modernity did not produce secularisation then. In the present century membership of the main Protestant Churches has fallen, though the numbers of Catholics continued to rise for most of the century, partly because of their higher birth rate, and the numbers of Baptists and members of Protestant sects have increased. The main decline has been in church attendance, but there is no evidence that the level of beliefs has fallen, and 45–50 per cent still endorse the main Christian beliefs and say that they feel close to God. The condition of religion in Britain has been described as 'believing without belonging'.

In the USA, as we have seen, the picture is totally different. Far more people belong to and attend churches than in Britain: about 43 per cent compared with 15 per cent go to church on a typical Sunday. There has been a continuous increase in religious activity for at least two hundred years, during the period of modernisation, up to about 1965 when most churches started to decline. This took place first among the under-30s and is thought to be due to a value shift towards more liberal attitudes in this age group, rather than to industrialisation. As in Britain the mainstream Protestant Churches have declined most, though very slowly, while the Baptists, sects and new religious movements have continued to grow. This has been seen as a cycle between churches and sects – as churches accommodate to the surrounding culture their religious attraction falls and members leave to join stricter churches, which make greater demands and promise greater rewards.

If we look around the world there is certainly no evidence that religion is fading away. We shall look at some examples of spectacular growth in the next chapter – the rise of sects and cults in America and Britain, of cults in the Third World, and of 'mega-churches' in South Korea. Another area where religion is very important is in South America where the Catholic Church has played an important part in the political scene, through 'liberation theology', and where more recently Protestant Churches have become very active, and there has been a growth of charismatic churches. There has been an increase in Islamic fundamentalism throughout the Middle East and Asia; this is a reaction to modernisation, and is the opposite of secularisation. On the other hand there are other countries where religion is much less important, the most obvious being China.

Does religion now have less influence on people's lives?

In Chapter 13 we showed that religion affects sexual behaviour, health and several other aspects of behaviour. But is this influence now less than it was?

Suicide
Bainbridge (1997) examined the relation between suicide rates and church membership rates in different American cities. In 1926 there was a much lower suicide rate for cities where there were large numbers of church members. In 1980 the effect was still there, but was weaker; for forty city areas with low church membership it was 13.9 per 100,000, for

forty with high membership it was 11.4. This is a very elegant research design, and I shall try to find similar figures for other areas of behaviour. It so happens that I have been involved in three editions of a book on the psychology of religion since the first edition in 1958, and so have looked at the effects of religion in three successive periods.

In the nineteenth century Protestants had a suicide rate two or three times as great as that of Catholics, but the difference in Europe and the USA is now very small (Beit-Hallahmi and Argyle, 1997).

Fertility

Several churches encourage large families. In the USA in 1969–70 Catholic women had on average 4.1 children, non-Catholic women 3.2, but by 1973–5 there was no difference, both averaged 2.1. However, in Canada the Hutterites still had 5.3 children, Mennonites 3.3 and Mormons 3.04. In Europe most Catholic countries had a low birth rate, Spain 1.2, Italy 1.3 and France 1.7. So Catholics no longer have large families, but members of some of the smaller, stricter bodies do (Beit-Hallahmi and Argyle, 1997).

Sexual behaviour

In 1948 Kinsey found that the religious devout in the USA were much less likely to have had pre-marital intercourse than the non-religious; while 47 per cent of the non-religious had done it, only 8.4 per cent of Mormons, 9.3 per cent of church-attending Catholics and 14.2 per cent of fundamentalists had, and it made a big difference how often they went to church. In 1993 Janus and Janus found that 93 per cent of the non-religious had done it, and so had 71 per cent of those who rated themselves 'very religious' – though possibly before they had been converted in some cases. Furthermore 66.5 per cent of Catholics used contraception (74 per cent of non-religious), 29 per cent of Catholic women had had an abortion (22 per cent of non-religious), and 31 per cent of the very religious reported at least one extra-marital affair (44 per cent for non-religious). It looks as if the influence of religion on sexual behaviour in the USA is still there but is now much reduced.

Divorce

We saw in Chapter 10 that regular church attenders have a much lower divorce rate than non-attenders, and that Catholics and Mormons have much lower rates than Protestants. Similar or greater differences were reported in earlier studies, but this may be because they were less well controlled. However, this seems to be an area where religion still has a strong effect.

Law-breaking

Early studies found that juvenile delinquents had lower rates of church attendance than control groups of non-delinquents (39 per cent v. 67 per cent for the Gluecks, 1950), though this does not show the direction of causation. More recent American studies have found very little effect of religion on crime or delinquency, except for drugs and alcoholism, and not for more serious offences, though this may be because these recent studies were very well controlled for variables like social class and race (Beit–Hallahmi and Argyle, op. cit.). The effect of religion appears to be very small here.

Health

We saw in Chapter 11 that church members have better health than non-members, and that this effect is greater for members of strict churches like the Mormons, who live on average four years longer. The main cause is the better health behaviour which is enforced in these churches. There is no evidence of historical trends, but we can note the strength of the effect which remains. The clergy used to live longer than other professions but now live above average years but no longer than teachers. Mental health was damaged by attending very noisy revivals in the nineteenth century (see p. 162), and there are still hazards for a smaller group from joining suicidal sects. On the other hand some of the new sects have been successful in rescuing drug addicts.

Work ethic

Weber (1904–5) observed that Protestantism and capitalism were related, and that Protestants worked harder and made more money than Catholics. In the modern world there are still differences between Protestant and Catholic countries in measures of work ethic, and in economic prosperity. Within the USA members of most Protestant groups have on average more years of education, better jobs and larger incomes than Catholics, though Baptists are lower than Catholics, as are sect members, while Jews are higher than Protestants. The direction of causation may be the other way round – that the deprived are attracted by other-worldly churches. So the Protestant work ethic is still alive, though not all Protestants share in it, while Jews, and probably Chinese, work even harder.

Inter-group relations

Unfortunately the most compelling evidence that religion still affects the world is its role in major social conflicts and wars. However, the conflicts between Catholics and Protestants in Ireland, between Jews and Arabs in the Middle East, between Hindus and Muslims in India and Pakistan, and between the different factions in former Yugoslavia are not entirely caused by religion. Religious differences contribute to the tensions between the opposing sides, and give them distinctive identities. Religious rhetoric is evident in some cases, as with Muslim fundamentalists. We have seen that inter-group prejudice is partly due to the rejection of those who hold different beliefs – the opposite side of the strong positive attitudes towards those with the same ones. It is not the case that religion has ceased to have an influence on these affairs.

Has society become 'desacralised'?

This is the third sense of secularisation that we shall consider. Weber thought that industrialisation was leading to rational ways of thinking in which mystery, magic and the supernatural have no part. We quoted Keith Thomas (1971) earlier making fun of the unruly and not very devotional behaviour of some church-goers in the sixteenth century in England. However, he reports that religion at that time was believed to be able to work miracles, and that people had great faith in the powers of saints and sacraments. The magical aspects of religion were removed by the Protestant reformers, who rejected such supernatural powers. Berger (1973) thought that the church planted the seeds of its own destruction by the Protestant promotion of rationality at the expense of medieval mystery and faith in miracles, and Catholic ritual and sacraments. Berger also argued that the appearance of Methodism and then many other denominations led to devaluation of the authority of a single church, to a situation where one could choose any church or none. Bryan Wilson (1966) added the further theme that the rise of science and of empirical ways of thinking has led to a decline in religious styles of thought.

It is difficult to assemble hard evidence to test these ideas. We have seen that the mainstream churches have in various ways accommodated to the outside society, while at the same time stricter churches have grown up which are not desacralised at all; they hold literal beliefs in miracles and the rest of religion, and appear to have no difficulty in holding beliefs that are contradicted by scientists. It is not the case that everyone now thinks empirically. Sciences themselves, especially physics and astronomy, have become fields of great mystery, which is perhaps why such scientists have no difficulty in holding religious beliefs (see p. 85). There are more problems for biologists and psychologists, who are less likely to be religious, though here, too, there are areas of mystery like consciousness and free will, which show no signs of ever being solved in material terms. Those whose interests are in the humanities do not share these problems, since history and literature take them into realms of symbolism and the subjective meaning of life, which are very similar to religion.

Conclusions

1 In Britain there has been a decline in church attendance and member-ship during the twentieth century, and some fall in beliefs, especially in God as a person, Jesus as the son of God, and biblical miracles; the present state can, however, be described as 'believing without belong-ing'. Mainstream churches have been falling slightly in membership, but evangelical, charismatic and pentecostal churches have increased, in some cases rapidly. The explanation of the general decline may be the rise of secular values and thinking, or may be the rise and later fall of established churches; several churches, such as the Methodists, now being in the later stage.

2 In the USA church attendance is at a much higher level, having con-tinued to increase until quite recently; there is a high level of traditional fundamentalist beliefs. There has been a recent rapid rise in strict Prot-estant churches and sects. The high level of church activity in the USA may be due to open competition in the absence of a state or dominant church, the attractions of strict churches, or the role of the churches in giving a place in society, and the role of religious values in American society.

3 In some sense there has been secularisation in the Western world during this century, though sects have partly replaced churches. Religion still

affects people's lives, though less than before, for example, in suicide rates, marriage, and health. It also continues to affect inter-group conflicts. Many continue to believe that there is more than a material world.

4 When we look outside Britain, Europe and North America, the religious scene is totally different. In the next chapter we look at the rise of religion in the East and the Third World. Outside the Christian regions the rise of Muslim fundamentalism makes talk of secularisation irrelevant.

15

THE GROWTH OF NEW RELIGIOUS MOVEMENTS

Introduction

Sociologists assume that religion will fade away as the result of industrial-isation and other aspects of modernity. On the other hand, in several parts of the world, some of them industrialised, there has been rapid and spectacular growth of new churches. Psychologists sometimes assume that religion is simply passed on to the next generation. This does not happen with the leaders or the followers of new religious movements. These bodies are of great interest for another reason – they can be seen as a model for how all religions started: as small groups led by a charismatic leader.

Protestant sects

Protestant sects have been of great interest to social scientists, because a number of very active new ones have appeared since the 1960s, and because this is the form of religion which has shown the most rapid increase in membership. They can also be seen as a model for how all religions started as a small group under charismatic leadership. There is a great variety of new sects, though there are some common themes: their central feature is that they have split off from existing churches, to form smaller and often more ecstatic and demanding religious bodies. There are also a large number of them; it is estimated that there are about 500 in Britain, 1500–2,000 in the USA and 10,000 in Africa (Barker, 1989). It is thought that about one million people in Britain have had some connection with sects, many of them with TM and Scientology, which we describe later as cults, that is, groups whose origins do not lie in Christian churches. Many recruits do not stay longer than the initial workshop or whatever, and very few for more than two years (Barker, 1989).

The older ones date from the nineteenth century or before. Early Methodism had the characteristics of a sect, as did the Mormons and the Jehovah's Witnesses and Seventh Day Adventists; the last two are 'adventist' groups, i.e. they expect the Second Coming of Christ. Figure 14.3 shows their spectacular increase of membership in Britain.

The Nazarenes and Pentecostalists emerged in the USA early in the twentieth century; these are known as 'Holiness' sects, since they seek a purer, holier way of life. In the 1960s there was a rapid growth of 'New Religious Movements', such as the Unification Church or 'Moonies', the Black Muslims, Hare Krishna, and the Rajneesh movement led by the Bhagwan; some of these we shall discuss under 'cults'. There have been a number of smaller, commune-based groups, such as the Shakers, the Branch Davidians and the followers of Jim Jones. Others live in normal parts of the community, though they may be waiting for the Second Coming. Some are mainly concerned with physical or mental healing, as in Scientology.

There is as yet no agreed way of classifying sects. Wallis (1984) distinguished between (1) world-rejecting sects which are in total opposition to society, and live apart in special enclaves or communes, like the Moonies, and the followers of Jim Jones, (2) world-accepting sects which are less opposed to society, but are in conflict with the churches, in seeking a purer and older form of religion, as with the Pentecostalists and Holiness sects, and (3) cults, which are scarcely religious at all, but offer similar benefits.

Sects were contrasted with churches by Troeltsch (1931). He used the term sects to refer to religious groups which were smaller than churches, were more committed, rejected society's values, sought a purer way of life, and expected their members to be strongly committed and accept the discipline; if they failed to keep the rules they were liable to be expelled.

Members see themselves as an exclusive elite, seeking a purer life, and they have to be converted to be admitted; there is no concern with the wider society, as churches have. Sects are groups which have rebelled against existing churches and formed schismatic sub-groups; they are in a state of tension with the wider society. New religious groups are different from established bodies in that all their members are first-generation converts, they are young and fervent, and more demands are made of them, though the beliefs are fairly simple.

A number of common features can be found in most of these groups.

The leaders

The leaders are often seen by the outside world as mad, dangerous, sometimes evil, but there is more to it than that. They are 'charismatic', that is, they have a personality and behave in a way which makes their followers believe that they have religious authority (are filled with the Holy Spirit, in the case of Christian sects). However, these properties may reside not only in the leaders, for these speak on behalf of their followers, and can express the latter's needs and find a way of solving their problems. Charisma may be recognised in various ways, by 'miracles' of healing, by great asceticism or by great care for others. David Koresh was certainly regarded as mad by the American authorities, and so was Jim Jones; both made their followers commit mass suicide. However, their followers believed in their authority, and these leaders had made a serious effort to solve their followers' problems in religious terms. Jim Jones, for example, appealed to the needs of poor American Blacks and had a vision of an ideal, non-racist community.

Sect leaders can also be authoritarian, control their group of followers by demanding obedience, sometimes by physical punishment, and impose considerable restrictions on their behaviour, up to demanding in rare cases that they commit suicide. At a later stage, when the original leader has gone, a more normal and less inspirational leadership takes over. Wilson (1990) concludes that sects with democratic leaders have often failed. On the other hand there is usually objection to the establishment of a clerical elite; all of the members want to belong to the same spiritual elite.

We saw earlier that aspects of mental disorder are common in religious leaders (p. 160), even primitive shamans had experienced and overcome a period of 'chaos' (p. 134). However, there are also clear differences from the occupants of mental hospitals. Religious leaders with some signs of insanity are different in being able to discover a religious message with wide appeal to their followers, and to organise and lead this group. We discussed the concept of 'schizotypy' in connection with religious experience (p. 67). This describes individuals with incipient schizophrenia, who also have a capacity for religious experience and creativity. This is a possible way of explaining the connection between holiness and madness. Manic depression is another possible link, it is often found in creative individuals. Sect leadership is usually charismatic and authoritarian, and by one person, such as the Reverend Moon and the Bhagwan, but there are no regular clergy.

The members

(1) Most members are young, in their early twenties, usually single, often former students and other rebellious young people. (2) Members of the traditional sects are drawn mostly from the poor, members of ethnic minority groups, unemployed, underprivileged, or otherwise 'marginal' members of society, and the same is true of some new ones, like the Black Muslims, which were aimed at the poorest American Blacks. Most of the recent NRMs are more middle class, such as Hare Krishna and the Jesus Movement. (3) Members of sects are often alienated in other ways, have dropped out of college, taken to drugs, been in conflict with the law over radical politics, quarrelled with their families. Some have been in previous psychological trouble; Galanter (1982) found that 30 per cent of members of the Divine Light Mission had received psychological help, and 6 per cent had been in hospital for it. Joining a sect can be a kind of stepping-stone back to normal society. (4) They are all people who are seeking an improvement in their life, a changed identity, to be achieved by accepting a more disciplined way of life, and helped by a supportive group, some seeking a more ideal, co-operative community. (5) Many sect members were brought up as members of mainstream liberal churches; the majority are first-generation sect members. Perrin et al. (1997) found that 28 per cent of a sample of sect members had started as liberal Protestants, 32 per cent as Catholics and 26 per cent as members of conservative Protestant Churches. (6) Bader and Demaris (1996) found that sect members had less education, had been married more often and had more jobs, and therefore had less stake in the community, than church members. (7) Sect members are not suffering from above-average mental

disturbance, and the effect of belonging is to improve their mental health, since many had previously been on drugs (Richardson, 1985).

Recruitment

Some sects have highly organised and carefully planned methods of acquiring new members. A sect may target a particular kind of person. The Moonies, for example, would spot likely candidates looking alienated and lost and would invite them to a meal, later to a workshop, where they would be in a totally controlled environment and would be subjected to 'love bombing'. Some are brought in by subterfuge in which the nature of the organisation is concealed (Galanter, 1989). The Children of God used 'flirty fishing' to bring in new members. Some sects play on guilt feelings, use subliminal forms of influence, or extract confessions, which gives them a hold over members, or there may be deception in which some features of the sect are concealed. These and similar procedures have been described by the outside world as 'coercion' or 'brain-washing', though they are in fact very different from what has been done by the Russians and Chinese under that name in the past. Wright (1987) studied forty-five defectors from three cults and found that 9 per cent felt that they had been 'duped or brain-washed' and 7 per cent felt 'angry'.

Services

The services are usually highly emotional, even ecstatic, and may include healing and speaking in tongues. The services may be so intense that members experience altered states of consciousness, such as seeing haloes round others, having a distorted sense of the passage of time, and under-going other aspects of intense religious experience (Galanter, 1989). They are also very informal, though this changes as the body becomes more established, more like a church, less like a sect.

Practices

Practices may be unusual, even illegal, such as handling poisonous snakes, burning wives (*sati* in India), not recognising normal medicine, as with Christian Science, and committing suicide, as with the People's Temple at Jonesville, though it is now known that many of these were in fact murdered. Practices may be directed to various forms of healing. Sex may not be allowed at all, or only with the leader, or it may be actively encour-aged, and marriages of members may be controlled, as by the Moonies.

Sometimes there is unscrupulous extraction of money, and violence such as the beating of children may be encouraged. These practices can only be understood from the point of view of the other-worldly ideas of the sect.

Cohesion and commitment
Cohesion and commitment are high; the latter may have to be demonstrated by speaking in tongues or other public displays, as with Pentecostalists. In most sects a conversion experience is required before joining.

A purer life
There may be demands for a high standard of behaviour, including sexual conduct, there may be control over who members may marry, or of health behaviour and diet, as with the Mormons. Often an abstemious and ascetic life is demanded.

Negative image
Sects often have a negative image, and are believed to use brain-washing or coercion to bring in members and to prevent them from leaving. It is widely believed that it is difficult to leave some of these sects, but in fact the majority do leave, and over a period of time as many leave as join, there is a rotating membership. Barker (1984) studied 1,000 participants in Moonie workshops and found that less than 1 per cent who had joined still belonged two years later. Others have found the same: belonging to a sect is a short-term affair for the great majority.

Separation from family and society
Often sects keep apart from normal society, and members have to live in a commune, as with the People's Temple. Members may be forbidden to see friends or family and lose touch with them. This may place a great strain on parents and siblings, who feel bereaved. Sect members may have to use some degree of a private language, which further isolates them (Barker, 1989).

Beliefs
Beliefs include some that are in conflict with those of other churches as well as those of the wider society, e.g. that the world is shortly coming to an end, as with Adventist groups. The beliefs may be clearly compensatory, such as believing that only members of this particular group will

survive the end of the world, or be rewarded in heaven; some of these groups are very poor and believe that rich people will not go to heaven. A feature of sects, a very attractive feature to many, is the certainty of the beliefs of members, in contrast to the more abstract, less literal, more symbolic beliefs of members of liberal churches. Beliefs are simple, with no obscure doctrines.

Stark and Bainbridge (1987) found that sect members held very different beliefs and followed different practices from members of mainstream Protestant churches – on sex before marriage, drugs, abortion, pornography, and beliefs in the Second Coming, the Devil and miracles. The holding of such beliefs and the following of such practices place sect members in conflict with the surrounding society, as well as with other churches.

Sects and cults seem to appear most frequently during times of rapid social change, and they attract people who are 'marginal' in some way, such as belonging to ethnic minority groups, or who have been rejected for some other reason. Methodism grew fastest in areas of Britain occupied by the new industrial working class, whose life had been dislocated by the Industrial Revolution. Severe economic or other frustration can lead to millennial cults which anticipate the end of the world passively. In Britain and the USA the great increase in sects and cults in the 1960s was a little different. Many young people had become alienated or dropped out, joined the counter-culture, taken to drugs and become social misfits and isolates. Some of the new sects and cults held great attraction for such individuals.

Some sects develop over time into something else. The classical theory due to Weber and others is that they change first into denominations and then into churches. There is 'routinisation' as services become more formal, less emotional. A denomination is larger than a sect and is less demanding and exclusive, less in conflict with society, but does not have a universal appeal, or claim a monopoly of religious truth as does a church.

Stark and Bainbridge (1987) put forward a general theory of religion, including an analysis of sect formation. They propose that humans seek an exchange of rewards with the gods. When a religious body is socially stratified the more deprived group sees advantages in forming a schism, with more compensatory beliefs, such as social acceptance, good health and a good future for the poor in heaven, in exchange for more demanding rules, creating more tension with society. The rich on the other hand want to reduce the amount of conflict with society and their group accommodates more to it. Of course these changes cannot be achieved unless there are suitable leaders; a leader of the more deprived group may decide that it would be better to be the bishop of a new sect rather than an assistant curate in the old one.

As sects become bigger, the traditional theory goes, there are pressures to abandon the more extreme beliefs and practices in order to be more acceptable to new members and to command greater influence in the world. As the members follow ascetic practices and a more disciplined way of life they become prosperous and socially mobile and their religious needs change, they want more formal and less expressive services (Pope, 1942). This has certainly happened in some cases, and perhaps the Methodists fit the model best. In some other cases prosperous sect members have left to join another religious body which fits their new social position. Bainbridge (1997) found that many of those who joined sects were of low social class, income and education, but that those who left to join mainline Protestant bodies were at that time of higher social status. They had achieved social mobility through belonging to the sect. In other cases sects have become permanent sects and have not accommodated to the world, as with the Jehovah's Witnesses, the Seventh Day Adventists and the Mormons. Some denominations began without ever being sects, as with Presbyterians and the original Baptists. Some sects simply died out, often when the original leader died (Hamilton, 1995).

Wilson (1990) believed that the universal motivation behind sect membership is the search for salvation, by a more rapid route than the mainstream churches can provide. This may be seen as overcoming various forms of evil – illness, deprivation, racial problems, a life of misery, or punishment after death. Since sect members tend to be drawn from the socially deprived, joining them may be seen as a response to deprivation. However, it may be experienced in a more positive way, as 'life-enhancing', as will be clear when we look at the more specific motivations which seem to be involved.

We can have a good guess which are the human needs that are better met by joining sects rather than churches. (1) The intense social support of a very cohesive group can be a great source of happiness and well-being. Residential communes in particular are envisaged as ideal communities, 'heavens on earth'. (2) The highly emotional services have an appeal for the socially and economically deprived and those with health or mental health problems; they may be willing to accept the rules and asceticism in exchange for the promised rewards. (3) The authoritarian leadership and dogmatic certainty of beliefs give a clear sense of the meaning of life, and optimism for the future. Accepting such leadership gives members a sense of purpose, identity and belonging. (4) There are many benefits from belonging to these groups, including material help, a disciplined way of life, freedom from drugs, and social recognition as a member of an elite.

If sects offer all these advantages, why doesn't everybody join? The answer is that there are also costs, financial costs for a start, and in the case of commune sects membership may mean abandoning for the time at least job and career, undergoing separation from family and friends, in some cases giving up sex, or having an arranged marriage, acceptance of strict and sometimes tyrannical discipline, being compelled to do menial work like selling flowers.

Cults

Cults are usually distinguished from sects. While sects are the result of schisms from existing churches, cults have no connection with such churches, they are new groups, which are not Christian, though they may use ideas from Eastern religions. Examples are Transcendental Meditation, Scientology, the Rajneesh community, Hare Krishna, EST, Exegesis, and the Divine Light Mission; perhaps the Moonies should be included here; there are other groups advocating the use of hallucinogenic drugs or meditation to produce altered states of consciousness. These movements appeared in the USA and Britain at much the same time as the recent crop of sects were started by charismatic gurus, and can be seen as part of the counter-culture of the time. However, they appealed to a different social group: their members were more middle-class, and a little older than sect members, many with professional jobs. The appeal seems to have been self-improvement and better jobs, better psychological and physical health. There was also a direct appeal to hedonism. Bainbridge (1997) showed that in cities with low church membership in the USA there is a high rate of membership of TM, Scientology and other cults.

The most successful of these movements numerically is TM. This uses ideas from Hinduism but presents them as scientific, and uses a quasi-religious initiation ceremony. Claims are made of the benefits for physical and psychological health. There was a rapid peak of membership in the

USA in 1975, after the Beatles joined, followed by an equally rapid fall, possibly because Americans had discovered jogging, which was cheaper (Bainbridge and Jackson, 1981). This was followed by the invention of a more intense version, the 'sidhi' movement, which involved what was described as flying followed by the more dedicated members. It was claimed that if a sufficiently large number of people meditate, crime and other human ills, such as wars and traffic accidents, will disappear, a magical, millennial belief similar to those found in Third World sects.

Another cult which was very successful for a time was the Rajneeshees, the followers of the Bhagwan, who established a community first in Poona, then in Oregon, and now in Poona again after members of the first two ashrams had been expelled from India and America. He used ideas from psychology, such as discouraging repression, hence the emphasis on sex, and ideas from Buddhism, such as egolessness, which can be helped by giving away all worldly possessions, preferably to the ashram. The members were mainly those European and American youth who could afford it. The Bhagwan was famous in the Poona period for his many Rolls-Royces (paid for by the followers). Many studies have been made of members during the Oregon period: they were older, average age 34, 64 per cent were graduates, and they had previously held good jobs. They had high self-esteem and life-satisfaction, they scored above average on femininity and there was unusual gender equality, there was a strong supporting community with 'an open and loving life style' (Richardson, 1995). In some ways this was a new kind of utopian community, though other reports suggest that it was run in a very authoritarian way. The leaders in Oregon were arrested for illegal activities such as poisoning the water supply in an attempt to rig the local elections, and the ashram had to leave the USA.

New religions in the Third World

There have been hundreds of new religions during this century in Africa, in the Pacific Islands, among American Indians, and also in some more developed areas like South America and Korea. These movements have much in common with the sects which we have just been discussing, in the USA and Britain. Some have split off from other churches, in this case missionary churches. In some cases they are the same churches somewhat modified, such as pentecostal churches. While the other sects appealed to the economically and socially deprived, these appeal to peoples who feel under stress from colonial occupation in one way or another. They too are seeking an ideal world, free of the evils of this world, but the evils they wish to avoid are different.

There is no agreed way of classifying these movements, but here are some of the main varieties. I shall follow the classification introduced by Bryan Wilson in his book *Magic and the Millennium* (1973).

Millennialism and cargo cults

By millennial movements are meant those which believe in the coming of a transformed world, perhaps the end of the world. These were common in Europe in the Middle Ages, and are now common in the Third World. The transformed world may consist of regaining one which was lost, or which provides all material needs, has an ideal social order, or which simply gets rid of an oppressive group, such as white colonialists. This new world is to be brought about primarily by magic. Throughout Melanesia there have been many 'cargo cults', where it is believed that a ship or aeroplane will arrive, bringing quantities of food and the white man's material goods. The methods to bring this about were the construction of airstrips or wharves, or imitation aerials and telegraph posts, which it was hoped would deliver the goods by magical symbolism. The Marching Rule movement in the Solomon Islands appeared when the American troops left at the end of the Second World War. The magical method here was imitation military drill and organisation. While this was partly an independence movement it also produced real economic co-operation. Like other millennial movements it was religious only in the dependence on magical means (Worsley, 1968).

Revolutionary and military movements

Throughout Africa, especially southern and East Africa, there have been revolutionary religious movements, some of them engaging in warfare, in the hope of gaining independence from colonial powers. One of the best-known and the most aggressive was the Mau Mau, in the Kikuyu tribe in Kenya, which began in the 1930s. It was directed against the British authorities, and was precipitated by evictions and other disputes over land. It was also against the missionaries, who had forbidden female circumcision and polygamy. It was led by prophets who claimed to be able to heal the sick and communicate with the dead, and who invented rituals said to include drinking human blood, and oaths to put people under obligation, as well as traditional religious practices such as hymn-singing.

A similar revolutionary and aggressive sect appeared in New Zealand among the Maori, the Hau Hau, in the 1860s. Again there were disputes about land, there was a leader called Te Ua who said he had spoken to the Angel Gabriel, but is thought to have been mentally defective, and who claimed to have wrecked a British ship and led a small war against the whites. However, this was also a religious sect, with ecstasy, glossolalia and adventist beliefs, like a small Protestant sect.

Revitalisation by magic: the Ghost Dance

In the 1880s the American Indian tribe the Pawnee were under great stress; the loss of the buffaloes and the end of inter-tribal war had meant the end of much of their culture and its rituals. Sitting Bull had visions of the dead and invented the Ghost Dance, in which trances and visions occurred of the return of the buffaloes and of the dead, and the departure of the white man. This made possible the revival of hand games, rituals and ceremonies. This movement spread to many other Indian tribes. The Sioux had been fighting the white man, and leaders like Kicking Bear used the Ghost Dance as part of their aggressive defiance of the Americans. The movement lasted for a number of years but then died, to be replaced by the Peyote cult.

The Peyote cult

The Peyote cult came to a number of American tribes who had been moved on to reservations in the 1870s, and had lost their buffaloes and warfare. The cult consisted of chewing the cactus plant Peyote, now known to contain mescaline, in the course of an elaborate religious ritual. Those attending sat in a circle round a fire, and engaged in singing and prayer; a meeting might be held for the purpose of healing. People experienced visions, which were believed to give them divine power. There was a strong ethical system, based on love, honesty, charity and avoidance of alcohol. There were several variations, in one of which Albert Hensley introduced the Bible and a number of Christian beliefs. The cult persisted among many American Indian tribes (La Barre, 1938).

Witchcraft

In Africa, especially West Africa, there is much witchcraft – on the part of sorcerers who are believed to be able to cause accidents and illness at a distance. There are numerous anti-witchcraft shrines and cults, started by local prophets, priests and priestesses, who offer protection, by means of animal sacrifices, and can give explanations of accidents and illness; they make some use of Christian as well as more ancient pagan symbols and rituals. These activities have all grown since the Second World War, probably due to social disruption and envy of European achievements.

Pentecostalism in Brazil

Pentecostalism has been successfully exported to Africa and other Third World countries, but has been particularly successful in Brazil. Congregations are large, some churches holding 8,000, and services frequent. However, Pentecostalism has been 'vigorously re-interpreted' to enhance the magical elements and leave others out. There is great emphasis on physical healing, on exorcism and also on dancing, singing and trances, believed to give spiritual powers. Services are very noisy, rather frightening, the congregations shouting at devils, with little liturgy but much symbolism (Lehmann, 1996). Chestnut (1997) concluded from interviews that the main appeal of these churches is to the health problems of the poor. The Bible is carried as an object of spiritual power, but not actually read, since most members are illiterate, nor do they interrupt the dancing to listen to the sermon (B. R. Wilson, 1973). The members are mostly Black, poor, migrants or widowed. It has been suggested that the popularity of speaking in tongues is due to this being a symbolic protest on the part of the illiterate, a way of getting attention, against the hierarchy of those oppressing them (Cox, 1996).

African Pentecostalism

There are now at least 5,000 independent Christian churches in Africa south of the Sahara. This is part of the common culture of Central Africa (De Craimer, 1976). Whether these are called pentecostal or not, that is basically what they are – with glossolalia, healing, exorcism, dancing and clapping. There is free expression of emotion, there is no hierarchy, and there are often themes of liberation. This is the form Christianity has taken in Africa, and these churches are expanding rapidly – faster than Islam, for example (Cox, 1996).

Many of these churches have split off from missionary churches, in being more 'spiritual', and offering healing and protection against witches. They are started by a leader who has a vision of a better society for his people; each body may last twenty to thirty years, when it is replaced by another. These churches are African versions of older churches; description of a healing service at one was given on p. 137.

Korean mega-churches

Christianity has grown rapidly in Korea since the end of the war with Japan in 1945, and now makes up 25 per cent of the population, 12 million people. Many are members of 'mega-churches', a term which has been used to refer to churches with more than 10,000 adults attending services in the main church; there are now thirteen such churches, mainly in Seoul. The largest is the Yoido Full Gospel Church. There are also about 130 churches with over 1,000 members, as well as a lot of smaller churches. Mega-churches have a large building which will seat 7,000 in one case, and have up to seven services each Sunday, together with 'sanctuaries' where the service can be followed on TV. Services are also held in the many house groups or 'cells'.

Up to the end of the Second World War the main religions in Korea were Confucianism, Buddhism and Shamanism, together with some missionary churches. The first mega-churches appeared after 1945, the end of the Second World War, and 1963, the end of the Korean War. There had been several kinds of Christianity in Korea, which had been suppressed by the Japanese, but it was the Presbyterian, Methodist and the American Assemblies of God and pentecostal churches that developed into mega-churches. At the end of the two wars there was much social dislocation and stress in Korea: many people had been refugees or prisoners, and there was rapid urbanisation and industrialisation.

Hong (1999) distinguishes three kinds of mega-church in Korea. (1) Traditional mega-churches are the oldest, originally part of the independence movement, and came from the Presbyterian Church. (2) 'Enthusiastic' mega-churches are Holiness or Full Gospel type churches, and emerged later, growing fast between 1970 and 1990. The Yoido Church is one of these. (3) Middle-class mega-churches emerged in parts of Seoul with many graduates living there, and display rather less 'enthusiasm'.

The style of these churches is similar to pentecostal and Holiness churches. They are fundamentalist, 'Full Gospel', closely based on the Bible, with inspirational preaching, very rousing services, glossolalia, healing and exorcism. There is 'triple salvation' from spiritual death, physical sickness and death, and from environmental poverty. Much use is made of women leaders, 70 per cent of the assistant pastors and 90 per cent of cell group leaders being women, though none of the head pastors are. The latter have great power and seem to run the churches in an authoritarian way, with little consultation.

The rate of growth of these churches has been remarkable. The Yoido Church began in a tent with 5 members in 1958, and now has 745,999 members including satellite churches, 1,042 pastors, 716 assistant pastors and 58,000 house groups. It still has the original head pastor, the Rev. Young Gi Cho. What is the explanation of this phenomenon? Why did it happen in this country at this time? We have already mentioned the social dislocation of the time, due to the wars and rapid urbanisation and industrialisation. Protestant Christianity played an important part in independence; it was seen as part of Western culture and modernity, and Protestant missionaries had used indirect methods through providing schools and hospitals. The fact that these are 'strict' churches suggests that the reasons we gave for the expansion of similar American churches may apply. There has been a great emphasis on evangelism and outreach, a desire to become very large, on the part of pastors, who had visions of growth, gave out a message of the importance of church growth, and set targets for it; they saw it as a sign of success. The general cultural background is also relevant. Shamanism valued large size and patriarchal leadership; Buddhism had conservative beliefs; Confucianism encouraged reverence for the pastor; and there is a cultural value in Korea for sheer size, big is beautiful.

Hong (1999) suggests that a key factor has been the charismatic leadership provided by the founders of these churches, and has found that the leaders of mega-churches are seen in this way by their followers. This idea was originally proposed by the sociologist Max Weber, but had not previously been followed up in connection with church growth. The leaders of these mega-churches have clearly been remarkable men, and continued as head pastors for many years (thirty-nine years in the case of Cho). Hong carried out case studies of several of these leaders and concluded that they had acquired their charisma in different ways, by carrying out what were seen as miracles of healing, by holiness of life, by inspirational preaching, or some combination of these. But as with other forms of leadership the followers also play a role; there would not be charismatic leaders unless their followers were willing to be obedient to a strong leader, and there would not be large churches unless many people liked this kind of church (Ro and Nelson, 1995). Another theory about the growth of these churches is that it is due to the great emphasis on healing and healing miracles (Cox, 1996).

Conclusions

1 Large numbers of Protestant sects have appeared in the modern world, during times of rapid social change, mostly by schisms from older churches. The leaders, who have often had a period of mental disturbance, have a vision of a better life, the followers are found by aggressive recruiting and are drawn from the young and alienated, or the poor and marginal. The members seek salvation of various kinds, especially health and social acceptance, and are prepared to pay the costs in terms of strict discipline, authoritarian leadership, sometimes leaving their families.

2 Cults, like TM and Scientology, are based on Eastern religions, the use of drugs, or psychology. They too have leaders with visions, but appeal to older and better-educated followers than the sects, and offer improved mental and physical health, and worldly success.

3 New religions in the Third World are similar to American Protestant sects, in appealing to peoples who have experienced social upheaval, and who feel deprived in comparison to the colonial occupiers. They are also similar in that each is started by a single charismatic leader, who has ideas that appeal to his followers. These ideas are similar to those of some Protestant sects, in that they have a vision of an ideal society, in this case one where there are no white men. They are different, however, in that there is often a more political, even a military, side to these sects; they are seeking land, material goods, power or independence, sometimes by magical methods, sometimes by political or aggressive action, and some have become independence movements; their worldly aspirations are expressed in religious terms. They are also different in making more use of magical methods, perhaps because their members are less educated, and less aware of the failure of facts to fit beliefs.

4 Korean mega-churches have had remarkable expansion since the

Korean War, probably due to the social dislocation of two wars, rapid industrialisation, and the constructive work of Protestant missionaries. It may also have been due to the charismatic leadership of the original pastors.

16

CONCLUSIONS FOR RELIGION

Psychology v. religion

Freud assumed that religion was an illusion, something that psychology could explain. Although later psychologists have not said this in these words, they too have assumed that religion is an illusion which they should be able to explain. In some ways this is a new kind of conflict between science and religion. The traditional solution to the science v. religion problem was to say that science deals with the material world and religion with the subjective world; but psychology claims to deal with the inner world too. In a parallel field there have been limited attempts to explain the effects of music on emotion, and it can be partly understood in terms of the physics of music, but this tells us little about our experience of the beauty and meaning of music. What seems to be wrong with all this is a failure to take seriously the experiences of those concerned, to recognise the power of metaphors and symbolic behaviour, which are felt to express some kind of truth, as in what we called 'symbolic realism'. In contrast, psychologists have not tried to 'explain' mathematics, which is recognised as having an independent existence. Nor have they tried to explain physics, chemistry and the rest. At any rate psychology now recognises the existence of consciousness – immediate evidence for a non-material sphere. And the physical sciences have become far more abstract and mysterious than before – it is not far from cosmology to theology.

If we treat religion seriously, what are the experiences or phenomena we need to take into account? (1) Religious experience is the most obvious, and we have seen that this has been studied systematically, and that there are universal features. These experiences have a quality and power which gives them their own validity for those who have them. (2) Worship and sacrifice are pervasive aspects of religious behaviour throughout the ages, and here the evidence comes from comparative religion and church history rather than psychology; psychology has had no success in explaining them. However, psychological theory can make no sense of either of them. Perhaps the nearest is a version of exchange theory – if you want salvation or some other benefit you expect to pay for it in some way, though what God gets out of worship or sacrifice is not clear. Freud and Jung produced stories about the possible innate effects of pre-history, neither of them generally accepted. Explaining them in psychological terms may be no more possible than explaining chemistry. (3) Beliefs about religion are unlike beliefs about the physical world: they are not verifiable in the same way, they are couched in symbols and myth, they represent commitment and relationship, and they need to be measured and studied in a different way from other kinds of beliefs.

Psychology can certainly tell us a great deal about religion. Psychology looks at and understands human beings by the use of various models or metaphors – early models said we were like telephone systems or hydraulic systems, later ones that we are like computers, or like animals. None of these models seems to fit the human experiences of love and joy, despair and guilt, or religious experiences of awe and reverence, sacrifice and being saved. The psychology of religion is in an awkward position, since by using the methods of psychology it seems to lead inevitably to a reductionist, materialist interpretation of religion, in which all is explained in terms of childhood experiences, social deprivation, fear of death or cognitive needs. But we have seen that these explanations are only partly successful. And some of the best-known psychologists of religion have not taken this route; William James (1902), for example, thought that religion was something outside man, and that religious experiences could not be explained by psychology. Jung's views were more mysterious, but he, too, thought that his archetypes are more than human projections. The study of the psychology of religion does not necessarily lead to explaining religion away.

Religious experience

The occurrence of religious experiences is one of the main roots of religion, the sense of some transcendent realm of being or meaning outside our normal lives, of something of importance outside the physical world. In primitive society it took the form of awe and taboos, the sense of the 'holy'. William James studied religious experiences through the rare and intense experiences of famous religious persons of the past. Then it was discovered by Alister Hardy and others that these experiences are not so rare, and social surveys found that about 34 per cent of the population have had some intense religious experience, usually once or twice. However, there is a milder kind of religious experience which is much more common, which has some of the same features, and which many have in church on Sundays, for example.

Religious experiences, intense or mild, although varied, contain certain 'core' features, a sense of the Transcendent (awe, reverence, contact with a divine being), as well as of the Mystical or Immanent (loss of self, timelessness, etc.). Some traditions emphasise the first, some the second. These experiences also contain a social component, a sense of social fusion, positive attitudes towards others, and sensory aspects, e.g. of light or warmth, or a sense of 'presence'. Cultural traditions and the build-up and passing on of religious traditions affect the nature of the experiences.

The 'argument from religious experience' was never very convincing to sceptics, since these experiences are not in the public realm of objective verifiability. But to those who have them they are totally convincing, and carry their own validity, give a feeling of contact with ultimate reality. They have long-lasting positive effects, for positive moods and happiness, for altruistic urges to help others, and for the integration of the self.

Ritual and other religious behaviour

Worship in groups, under the direction of a priest, in a sacred place, with singing, is central to religion, from primitive religions onwards. Rituals are forms of behaviour which are symbolic, express beliefs, and are intended to influence the deity or produce some worldly results like healing. They are an important way of expressing beliefs, by symbolic behaviour, and of generating religious experiences. The psychological motivation for worship is not clear but it has clear effects of positive moods and enhanced social cohesion. A common feature of religious rituals is sacrifice, usually of animals, though this is now usually symbolic; the psychological interpretation of sacrifice is still obscure, though it may be a case of exchange intended to lead to salvation, the avoidance of punishment or the neutralisation of aggression in society. One benefit of ritual is often healing, and this is one of the main goals of religion.

Much use is made of non-verbal symbols in these rituals, and they work in a complex way. They refer to bodily parts and actions, such as wine for blood, washing with water for purification. They also refer to social groups, as totem animals refer to tribal groups. The first way charges symbols with emotion, the second relates them to group values.

Prayer is usually performed alone, and is frequently resorted to by those who are ill or in danger or despair. There are several kinds of prayer; one of the rarer kinds, meditative prayer, gives the greatest subjective benefits in the form of peace and subjective well-being.

Some religious rituals are rites of passage, where individuals pass from one state to another, as in weddings, funerals, marriages and initiation rites. The second or 'liminal' phase of these rites is of interest since it has been observed that it generates a special religious state of 'communitas', an ideal state of love, equality and harmony.

The nature of religious beliefs

Beliefs are often thought to be central to an individual's religiosity; they are what students argue about, and what get bishops into trouble for being 'unsound'. We have seen, however, that religious beliefs are quite different from other beliefs, such as the belief that Julius Caesar once invaded Britain. It might be better to call them something else. They are really attitudes which are expressed by images, using certain metaphors and accompanied by certain emotions. We have seen that most people do not consider that 'faith' consists of a set of beliefs, it is more a relationship with God.

Beliefs include the holding of certain images: for example, of God as a father, king, ruler, friend, etc., of the Holy Spirit as a wind or fire. There is also an emotional component to beliefs; they are more than cognitions:

awe, reverence, love and hope are part of religious faith. For many people, especially those who are more educated, older and not fundamentalist, religious beliefs are held metaphorically, with different degrees of demythologising. Metaphors are for expressing difficult or abstract ideas by using more familiar models. These models may be earthly entities, like one's own father, as in Freud's theory, or something more other-worldly like the universal concept of the father in Jung's theory. The growth of religious understanding may consist of finding the right symbols to express religious experiences. It is not only religion which uses metaphors to express inner life, literature does it too, and so in a different way does music. Both have been used to express religion. The statement of a verbal proposition gives very little idea of what is in the mind of the person asserting it, and may amount to a lot or very little.

There is an element of commitment in believing, a leap of faith in conversion. Both can be likened to human love. Fundamentalist and other strict churches are very dogmatic in matters of belief, and insist that their members hold the correct ones. We have seen that such churches are expanding, partly because their certainty is attractive to many. However, our analysis suggests that beliefs are far more than assent to verbal propositions, but the other components, the images and emotions, are not mentioned in creeds.

Beliefs may turn out to be refuted by facts; for example, when the Second Coming doesn't come, or the cargo for a cargo cult fails to arrive. This is usually dealt with by revising the date, or by constructing a more abstract and less verifiable version of the belief. Some scientists feel that their science and their faith are in conflict; they deal with it by moving to a more metaphorical kind of belief. For psychologists and other biological scientists the problem is worse, since the 'scholarly distance' is less; they are less likely to be believers.

The benefits of religion

The pragmatic 'argument' for the existence of God is that this belief 'works'. Well, does it? In terms of twentieth-century society at least we now know.

Church members are somewhat happier than non-church members, and the effect is stronger for the old, and for members of churches that are very certain of their beliefs. There is some effect on health, especially for Mormons and members of other churches with strict rules about health behaviour, who as a result live longer on average. Religious healing services have a strong effect on subjective (that is, reported) health but no immediate effect on actual physical health, though this may be improved, too, as a result in the long run.

There is some relation with good mental health, for the seriously religious, and for them religion can buffer the effects of uncontrollable stressful events, by 'religious coping'. Catholics no longer commit suicide less than Protestants, but members of all churches now have a much lower rate than non-members. Fear of death is widespread, but is very low among the religious.

Religion has some success in generating good behaviour. In modern society church members give more money to charity; indeed, some give 10 per cent of their incomes. There is not much effect on crime, though there is an effect on drink and drugs. Most religions have tried to restrain sexual behaviour, and church members now engage in somewhat less extra-marital and premarital sex. Mormons, Baptists and members of fundamentalist Protestant Churches are more influenced in all these ways than members of mainstream churches. There is clear evidence that church members engage in more helping behaviour; for example, they do more voluntary work. Religion produces benefits for society – via social cohesion and social support, and the moral effects for care and altruism cited above.

Overall there are many positive effects of religion, some of them strong. And we can see, from a human point of view, how this happens. Part of the explanation of the benefits of religion is that church communities are very socially supportive. The relation with God may be experienced in a similar way. Certainty of beliefs, religious experiences, talking to God, and the whole outlook of religion have a very positive effect. Disciplined behaviour is good for health, marriage and occupational success.

Religion is a social phenomenon

We have seen in every chapter that, in several different ways, religion is a social phenomenon. From primitive religion onwards, religious rituals have been conducted in groups, and they are found to generate positive feelings within the group. Marriages are more successful for church members, who have a lower divorce rate and greater marital happiness. But marriage between two people who belong to different churches is a recipe for disaster.

The leaders of new sects and cults have visions of a better society, which appeal to their followers, and may bring about improved social arrangements. The services or group meetings usually have high levels of emotional excitement. Sects develop over time, and in order to appeal to a wider section of society have to accommodate to it, some becoming denominations or churches. There is a build-up of religious traditions, which are passed on to later generations via religious education.

Religious experiences may occur in the course of church services, but also alone, as in the intense classical kind of experience. There is a social aspect of the solitary kind too, since those involved have often been monks or have been trained to meditate. And the contents of religious experiences, mild or intense, include a strong pro-social impulse, to help other people. Moral experience is part of the experience.

There has always been a close relation between religion and morals, that is, good behaviour to other people. Christianity introduced some new moral ideas – it stressed the importance of forgiveness and repentance, and it valued every individual, including outcasts, the poor and weak, as well as some more theological ideas such as the need for God's grace to help us to carry out this behaviour. We have seen that religion does have an effect on moral behaviour: for example, more given to charity, more voluntary work. This cannot be explained by biological processes such as the selfish gene, since such good behaviour is not restricted to kin.

While religion has often emphasised the need to repent and be forgiven for sins, a common index of sinfulness is guilt feelings. This is a very inaccurate index, however, since psychopaths engage in antisocial behaviour and have no guilt feelings, while neurotic introverts and members of strict Protestant churches often have strong guilt feelings.

Can psychology explain religion?

There are a lot of empirical findings about religious behaviour, belief and experience, about their causes and effects. And some theories have received some confirmation. Some examples follow.

(1) Socialisation, the social learning of religious beliefs and attitudes: the effects of parents, peer groups and education are just as important here

as in the acquisition of any other attitudes. Socialisation can also explain why there are individual differences in religiosity, which cannot be accounted for by differences in personality. However, religion is not just due to learning it, since there is constant rebirth of churches, initiated by gurus who have found a new religious vision, and joined by followers who were not brought up to it.

(2) The theory of God as a projected father-figure: a modified version of Freud's theory, including mothers as well as fathers, has received some confirmation: the image of God is similar to the images of parents. This fits the transcendent aspect of religious experience well, but there are other religious objects which are not at all parent-like, such as the Holy Spirit in Christianity, and the numinous spiritual realm in Eastern religions.

(3) Religion as compensation for social deprivation: this is a popular line of thinking which has been put forward in several versions, from Karl Marx onwards. It fits those religious groups which appeal to the poor and ethnic minorities, but it does not fit those churches which are full of prosperous middle-class individuals. It would be tautological to speculate about some other forms of deprivation from which they might be suffering.

(4) Fear of death: belief in an after-life does reduce fear of death, and could have been invented to do so. This is supported by the findings that very old people believe in it more, and those who do so are less worried about death than those who do not. This does not, however, explain why so many people believe in hell, 71 per cent in the USA – this might give them a lot more to worry about.

(5) We have seen that religion conveys considerable benefits for happiness and health, and that this can be explained via the social support of the church, the relationship with God, and better health behaviour. It does not, however, explain why church communities are so very supportive, or why the relation with God is experienced as another supportive relationship.

Even when some kind of psychological explanation has been found, it does not follow that the beliefs in question are false. And we have already located several areas where psychology has so far failed to provide a useful explanation.

Is religion fading away?

This was predicted by Freud and by nineteenth-century sociologists. The latter thought that industrialisation and other aspects of modernity would have this result. And during the twentieth century church attendance in the main churches has indeed fallen off in Europe, though it started by increasing for most of them. In the USA, on the other hand, where there has been plenty of industrialisation and modernity, church attendance continued to rise until recently, and attained a level far above that in Europe. There is evidently no simple connection between modernity and not going to church. The American phenomenon may be due to the vigorous competition between churches, or to the popularity of 'strict' churches, because of their certainty and cohesiveness, or because church in the USA is more a part of the normal culture and a source of identity, particularly important for immigrant groups. And in several other parts of the world religion is growing rather than shrinking – there has been a massive expansion of churches in Korea and South America, for example.

Meanwhile other, smaller, more ecstatic and newer churches continued to grow, and proliferated after the Second World War. Some sects have developed historically into denominations or churches; this is how churches start. At the same time there has been a proliferation of cults, which are not really religious; some of these have been good for their members, others disastrous. In the mainstream churches there has been charismatic revival. And in Britain although church attendance has declined, as have some beliefs, many people still regard themselves as religious, claim that they hold the basic beliefs and say their prayers – what has been described as 'believing without belonging'; this is particularly true of working-class people – it is the middle classes who enjoy church more.

Does religion have any negative effects?

(1) The most serious negative effect which we have found is the prejudice which many church members have, not only towards ethnic minority groups, but also to members of other religions, including other churches. Religious differences have added force to nearly all wars, though religion itself was not usually the main source of conflict. The most prejudiced are members of fundamentalist groups, not only in Christianity but in other

faiths too. The main reason for this prejudice seems to be that members of religious groups form very close relations with each other, as a result of their shared rituals and beliefs, and this has the effect of distancing them from other groups. Fear of death, 'terror management', also creates a need to keep to the company of those who share the same beliefs and to avoid others who do not.

(2) Batson et al. (1993) were concerned at the loss of freedom to think on the part of church members, what they called 'cognitive bondage'. This is especially strong for members of strict Protestant churches. However, research shows that irrational commitment and a leap of faith are central aspects of the religious life, and should not be regarded as a loss. The trouble may be that this dogmatism and rigidity may be part of the reason that members of these same churches are unwilling to accept members of other churches or no church.

(3) There are problems with some sects and cults. They provide great benefits for many of their members; for example, curing addiction to drugs, by a regime of discipline and social support. The costs may be considerable, however – financial, separation from family, control of marriages, punitive discipline, and in several cases mass suicide. The reason for this is that sects arise from the vision of the original leader or guru. While these visions may contain inspired insights, or the design of a better kind of community, they may also contain insane ideas. This is because there is something in common between the personalities of gurus and certain kinds of mental patient, for example, incipient schizophrenia or manic depression. The main difference is that a successful religious leader's ideas have a wide appeal and can solve the problems of a number of followers; but if the followers are uninformed and uncritical they may be willing to accept insane ideas.

(4) We have seen the world-wide growth of charismatic and pentecostal churches. Their appeal is partly through the claim to be able to heal people through a process of exorcism, casting out of devils. Some sociologists have been critical of this concern with evil. The psychological concern is with what kind of healing can be achieved by these methods. Follow-up studies have repeatedly found that religious healing makes people feel better, partly because they define 'health' in a broader way; however, there is no evidence of any immediate medical change.

(5) The success of strict churches is due partly to their cohesiveness, partly to the certainty of their dogmatic beliefs, partly to their ecstatic

services, but why do people seek churches with strict rules and prohibitions? Members of mainstream churches sometimes leave these because they are not 'spiritual' enough. When new sects are started they are always strict and ecstatic, as if this is a central aspect of religion.

Implications for theology

Some would say that the empirical study of psychology can have no implications for theology. That was Jung's view. However, a number of points have emerged in this book which appear to be legitimate conclusions for theology.

1 The argument from religious experience is strengthened by the finding that such experiences are very widespread, and contain widely shared core components.

2 The nature of belief: we have seen that religious beliefs consist partly of images, and that the most common images of God are as a person in a relationship who can be known and related to, and who is like a father or king, but who is also a great transcendent power. Religious beliefs cannot be reduced to verbal propositions since they also contain reference to emotional religious experiences. They are not much affected by logical arguments or demands for consistency.

3 Ritual: religion consists partly of religious behaviour, such as worship and sacrifice; these are symbolic expressions of beliefs. The present state of world religion includes a rise in charismatic, behavioural forms of worship; such churches have expanded while liberal ones have declined.

4 It has been found that prayer works, but the impact is primarily on the person praying, and it can induce religious experiences and healing. As these experiences are partly other-directed, it is likely that prayer will motivate behaviour which cares for others.

5 It could be said that those who turn to religion are in search of 'salvation', but of several different kinds. Traditionally they were seeking relief from feelings of sin, i.e. guilt feelings. Others seek salvation from physical illness, or from oppression or from poverty. Others, however, have none of these needs, so that their religion has some other motivation or none.

6 Religion says that we are all sinners, sometimes that we are tainted by

original sin. A possible interpretation of the latter is to say that we are born with a selfish, greedy biological nature, like animals, and have to learn more pro-social attitudes to others. This learning owes a lot to social traditions of religious origins, and to the religious life and beliefs of individuals. Guilt feelings may reflect real harm to others, but can also be derived from early relations with parents or from having a certain kind of personality, and contact with Protestant religious training.

7 There is a paradox with strict churches. On the one hand they convey powerful benefits, as their members have a high level of certainty and optimism, and their social cohesion gives powerful social support. On the other hand these are the most dogmatic, authoritarian and prejudiced religious groups, more so than the non-religious, and this is a major source of social conflict.

REFERENCES

Aaronson, B. S. and Osmond, H. (eds), (1970). *Psychedelics: the Uses and Implications for Hallucinogenic Drugs*. Garden City, NY: Anchor Books.

Acklin, M. W. (1985). An ego developmental study of religious cognition. PhD dissertation, Georgia State University.

Adorno, T. W., Frenkel-Brunswik, E., Levinson, D. J. and Sanford, R. N. (1950). *The Authoritarian Personality*. New York: Harper & Row.

Allport, G. W. (1950). *The Individual and his Religion*. New York: Macmillan.

Allport, G. W. and Ross, J. M. (1967). Personal religious orientation and prejudice. *Journal of Personality and Social Psychology*, 5, 432–43.

Alston, W. P. (1967). Religious language. In: *The Encyclopedia of Philosophy*, Vol. 7, ed. P. Edwards (pp. 168–74). New York: Macmillan.

Altemeyer, B. (1988). *Enemies of Freedom: Understanding Right-Wing Authoritarianism*. San Francisco, Calif.: Jossey-Bass.

Altemeyer, B. and Hunsberger, B. (1992). Authoritarianism, religious fundamentalism, quest and prejudice. *International Journal for the Psychology of Religion*, 2, 113–33.

Anderson, R. M. (1979). *Vision of the Disinherited*. London: Oxford University Press.

Anderson, R. M. (1987). Pentecostal and charismatic Christianity. *Encyclopedia of Religion*, 11, 228–35.

Argyle, M. (1964). Introjection: a form of social learning. *British Journal of Psychology*, 55, 391–402.

Argyle, M. (1988). *Bodily Communication*, 2nd edn. London: Methuen.

Argyle, M. (1991). *Cooperation*. London: Routledge.

Argyle, M. (1994). *The Psychology of Social Class*. London: Routledge.

Argyle, M. (1996). *The Social Psychology of Leisure*. Harmondsworth: Penguin.

Argyle, M. and Beit-Hallahmi, B. (1975). *The Social Psychology of Religion*. London: Routledge & Kegan Paul.

Argyle, M. and Delin, P. (1965). Non-universal laws of socialization. *Human Relations*, 18, 77–86.

Argyle, M., and Henderson, M. (1985). *The Anatomy of Relationships*. Harmondsworth: Penguin Books.

Argyle, M. and Hills, P. (in press). Religious experiences and their relationships with happiness and personality. *International Journal for the Psychology of Religion*.

Argyle, M., Martin, M. M. and Lu, L. (1995). The measurement of happiness. In C. D. Spielberger and J. B. Brebner (eds), *Testing for Stress and Happiness* (pp. 178–87). New York: Taylor & Francis.

Asch, S. E. (1958). The metaphor: a psychological enquiry. In R. Tagiuri and L. Petrullo (eds), *Person Perception and Interpersonal Behavior* (pp. 86–94). Stanford, Calif.: Stanford University Press.

Badcock, C. R. (1980). *The Psychoanalysis of Culture.* Oxford: Blackwell.

Badcock, C. R. (1992). *Essential Freud.* Oxford: Blackwell.

Bader, C. and Demaris, A. (1996). A test of the Stark–Bainbridge theory of affiliation with religious cults and sects. *Journal for the Scientific Study of Religion, 35,* 285–303.

Bainbridge, W. S. (1997). *The Sociology of Religious Movements.* New York: Routledge.

Bainbridge, W. S. and Jackson, D. H. (1981). The rise and decline of transcendental meditation. In B. Wilson (ed.), *The Social Impact of New Religious Movements* (pp. 135–58). New York: Rose of Sharon Press.

Balch, R. W. (1980). Looking behind the scenes in a religious cult: implications for the study of conversion. *Sociological Analysis, 45,* 301–14.

Bandura, A. (1977). *Social Learning Theory.* Englewood Cliffs, NJ: Prentice-Hall.

Bandura, A. and Walters, R. H. (1963). *Social Learning and Personality Development.* New York: Holt, Rinehart & Winston.

Barbour, I. G. (1990). *Religion and Science,* revised edn. London: SCM Press.

Barbour, I. G. (1996). *Religion in an Age of Science.* San Francisco, Calif.: Harper & Row.

Barker, E. (1984). *The Making of a Moonie.* Oxford: Blackwell.

Barker, E. (1989). *New Religious Movements: A Practical Introduction.* London: HMSO.

Barker, E. (1995). The post-war generation and establishment religion in England. In W. C. Roof, J. W. Carroll and D. A. Roozen (eds), *The Post-War Generation and Established Religion* (pp. 1–25). Boulder, Colo.: Westview Press.

Barlow, H. (1987). The biological role of consciousness. In C. Blakemore and S. Greenfield (eds), *Mindwaves* (pp. 361–74). Oxford: Blackwell.

Barrett, J. L. and Keil, F. C. (1996). Conceptualizing a nonnatural entity: anthropomorphism in God concepts. *Cognitive Psychology, 31,* 219–47.

Barrow, J. and Tipler, F. (1986). *The Anthropic Cosmological Principle.* Oxford: Oxford University Press.

Barry, H., Bacon, M. K. and Child, I. L. (1957). A cross-cultural study of sex differences in socialization. *Journal of Abnormal and Social Psychology, 55,* 327–32.

Bartkowski, J. P. and Swearingen, W. S. (1997). God meets Gaia in Austin, Texas: a case study of environmentalism as implicit religion. *Review of Religious Research, 38,* 308–24.

Batson, C. D. (1991). *The Altruism Question.* Hillsdale, NJ: Erlbaum.

Batson, C. D. (1995). Prosocial motivation: why do we help others? In A. Tesser (ed.), *Advanced Social Psychology* (pp. 333–417). New York: McGraw-Hill.

Batson, C. D., Schoenrade, P. and Ventis, W. L. (1993). *Religion and the Individual.* New York: Oxford University Press.

Baumann, G. (1987). *National Integration and Local Integrity.* Oxford: Clarendon Press.

Beit-Hallahmi, B. (1996) Unpublished data on reported religious experiences. University of Haifa.

Beit-Hallahmi, B. and Argyle, M. (1997). *The Psychology of Religious Behaviour, Belief and Experience.* London: Routledge.

Beit-Hallahmi, B. and Nevo, B. (1987). 'Born-again' Jews in Israel: the dynamics of an identity change. *International Journal of Psychology, 22,* 75–81.

Bellah, R. N. (1964). Religious evolution. *American Sociological Review, 29,* 358–74.

Bellah, R. N. (1970). *Beyond Belief.* New York: Harper & Row.

Benda, B. B. and Corwyn, R. F. (1997). Religion and delinquency: the relationship after considering family and peer influences. *Journal for the Scientific Study of Religion, 36,* 81–92.

Berger, P. (1973). *The Social Reality of Religion.* Harmondsworth: Penguin.

Bianchi, U. (1987). Confession of sins. *Encyclopedia of Religion, 4,* 1–7.

Bibby, R. W. (1978). Gender differences in the effects of parental discord on pre-adolescent religiousness are growing: Kelley revisited. *Journal for the Scientific Study of Religion, 17,* 129–37.

Billiet, J. B. (1995). Church involvement, individualism, and ethnic prejudice among Flemish Roman Catholics: new evidence of a moderating effect. *Journal for the Scientific Study of Religion, 34,* 224–33.

Blasi, A. (1980). Bridging moral cognition and moral action: a critical review of the literature. *Psychological Bulletin, 88,* 593–637.

Bonta, B. D. (1997). Cooperation and competition in peaceful societies. *Psychological Bulletin, 121,* 299–320.

Boston, R. (1988). Holy terrors. *Church and State, 41,* 154–6.

Bowker, J. (1973). *The Sense of God: Sociological, Anthropological and*

Psychological Approaches to the Origin of the Sense of God. Oxford: Oxford University Press.

Braithwaite, R. (1955). *An Empiricist's View of the Nature of Religious Belief.* Cambridge: Cambridge University Press.

Brasher, B. E. (1997). My beloved is all radical: two case studies of congregational-based Christian fundamentalist female enclaves and the religious experiences they cultivate among women. *Review of Religious Research, 38,* 231–46.

Brierley, P. (1991). 'Christian' England. London: Marc Europe.

Brooke, J. H. (1991). *Science and Religion: Some Historical Perspectives.* Cambridge: Cambridge University Press.

Brown, D. R. and Gary, L. E. (1991). Religious socialization and educational attainment among African Americans: an empirical assessment. *Journal of Negro Education, 60,* 411–26.

Brown, L. B. (1987). *The Psychology of Religious Belief.* London: Academic Press.

Brown, L. B. (1988). *The Psychology of Religion: an Introduction.* London: SPCK.

Brown, R. (1995). *Prejudice.* Oxford: Blackwell.

Bryant, C. (1983). *Jung and the Christian Way.* London: Darton, Longman & Todd.

Bucke, R. M. (1901). *Cosmic Consciousness.* New York: Dutton.

Burris, C. T. (1994). Curvilinearity and religious types: a second look at Intrinsic, Extrinsic, Quest relations. *International Journal for the Psychology of Religion, 4,* 245–60.

Byrd, R. C. (1988). Positive therapeutic effects of intercessory prayer in a coronary care unit population. *Southern Medical Journal, 81,* 826–9.

Campbell, D. T. (1975). On the conflicts between biological and social evolution and between psychology and moral tradition. *American Psychologist, 30,* 1103–26.

Carroll, M. P. (1983). Visions of the Virgin Mary: the effects of family structures on Marian appearances. *Journal for the Scientific Study of Religion, 22,* 205–21.

Carter, M., Kay, W. K. and Francis, L. J. (1996). Personality and attitude toward Christianity among committed adult Christians. *Personality and Individual Differences, 20,* 265–6.

Cattell, R. B. and Pawlik, K. (1964). Third-order factors in objective personality tests. *British Journal of Psychology, 55,* 1–18.

Cavalli-Sforza, L. L., Feldman, M. W., Chen, K.-H. and Dornbusch, S. N. (1982). Theory and observation in cultural transmission. *Science, 218,* 19–27.

Cavan, R. S., Burgess, E. W., Havighurst, R .J. and Goldhamer, H. (1949). *Personal Adjustment in Old Age.* Chicago, Ill: Science Research Associates.

Chamberlain, K. and Zika, S. (1988). Religiosity, life meaning and well-being: some relationships in a sample of women. *Journal for the Scientific Study of Religion, 27,* 411–20.

Charlton, J. (1987). Women in seminary. *Review of Religious Research, 28,* 305–18.

Chau, L. L., Johnson, R. C., Bowers, J. K. and Darvill, T. J. (1990). Intrinsic and extrinsic religiosity as related to conscience, adjustment and altruism. *Personality and Individual Differences, 11,* 397–400.

Chestnut, R. A. (1997). *Born Again in Brazil: The Pentecostal boom and the pathogens of poverty.* New Brunswick, NJ: Rutgers University Press.

Claridge, G. (1997). *Schizotypy.* Oxford: Oxford University Press.

Clark, E. T. (1929). *The Psychology of Religious Awakening.* New York: Macmillan.

Clark, W. H. and Warner, C. M. (1955). The relation of church attendance to honesty and kindness in a small community. *Religious Education, 50,* 340–2.

Clarke, P. B. (1993). *Women as Teachers and Disciples in Traditional and New Religions.* Lewiston NY: Edwin Mellen Press.

Cobb, W. F. (1913). Forgiveness (NT and Christian). *Hastings Encyclopedia of Religion and Ethics, 6,* 78–82.

Cochran, J. K. and Beeghley, L. (1991). The influence of religion on attitudes toward nonmarital sexuality: a preliminary assessment of reference group theory. *Journal for the Scientific Study of Religion, 30,* 45–62.

Coe, G. A. (1916). *The Psychology of Religion.* Chicago, Ill: University of Chicago Press.

Comstock, G. W. and Partridge, K. B. (1972). Church attendance and health, *Journal of Chronic Diseases, 25,* 665–72.

Cox, H. (1996). *Fire from Heaven.* London: Cassell.

Crandall, J. E. and Rasmussen, R. D. (1975). Purpose of life as related to specific values. *Journal of Clinical Psychology, 31,* 483–5.

Crumbaugh, J. C. and Maholick, L. T. (1964). An experimental study in existentialism: the psychometric approach to Frankl's concept of 'noogenic' neurosis. *Journal of Clinical Psychology, 20,* 200–7.

Cupitt, D. (1980). *Taking Leave of God.* London: SCM Press.

Curran, C. E. (1987). Christian ethics. *Encyclopedia of Religion, 3,* 340–8.

Currie, R., Gilbert, A. and Horsley, L. (1977). *Churches and Church-Goers: Patterns of Church Growth in the British Isles.* Oxford: Clarendon Press.

Danso, H., Hunsberger, B. and Pratt, M. (1997). The role of parental fundamentalism and right-wing authoritarianism in child-rearing goals and practices. *Journal for the Scientific Study of Religion, 36,* 496–511.

Darley, J. and Batson, C. D. (1973). From Jerusalem to Jericho: a study of situational and dispositional variables in helping behavior. *Journal of Personality and Social Psychology, 27,* 100–8.

Darley, J. M. and Schultz, T. R. (1990). Moral rules: their content and acquisition. *Annual Review of Psychology, 41,* 525–56.

Davie, G. (1994). *Religion in Britain since 1945.* Oxford: Blackwell.

Davis, J. A. and Smith, T. W. (1994). *General Social Surveys 1972–1994.* Chicago, Ill.: National Opinion Research Center.

Dawkins, R. (1967). *The Selfish Gene.* Oxford: Oxford University Press.

Dawkins, R. (1991). *The Blind Watchmaker.* Harmondsworth: Penguin.

De Craimer, W., Vansima, S. and Fox, R. (1976). Religious movements in central Africa. *Comparative Studies in Society and History 18,* 458–75.

De Jong, G. F. and Faulkner, J. F. (1972). Religion and intellectuals: findings from a sample of university faculty. *Review of Religious Research, 14,* 15–24.

de Vaus, D. A. (1984). Workforce participation and sex differences in church attendance. *Review of Religious Research, 25,* 247–56.

Deikman, A. J. (1963). Experimental meditation. *Journal of Nervous and Mental Disease, 136,* 329–73.

Downing, J. J. and Wygant, W. (1964). Psychedelic experience and religious belief. In R. Blum (ed.), *Utopiates: the Uses and Abuses of LSD* (pp. 187–98). New York: Atherton.

Doyle, R. T. and Kelly, S. M. (1979). Comparison of trends in ten denominations. In D. R. Hoge and D. A. Roozen (eds), *Understanding Church Growth and Decline, 1950–1978* (pp. 179–97). New York: Pilgrim Press.

Drevenstadt, G. L. (1998). Race and ethnic differences in the effects of religious attendance on subjective health. *Review of Religious Research, 39,* 245–63.

Duff, R. W. and Hong, L. K. (1995). Age density, religiosity and death anxiety in retirement communities. *Review of Religious Research, 37,* 19–32.

Dulaney, S. and Fiske, A. P. (1994). Cultural rituals and obsessive-compulsive disorder: is there a common psychological mechanism? *Ethos, 22,* 243–83.

Durkheim, E. (1897). *Suicide.* London: Routledge & Kegan Paul.

Eagly, A. H. (1995). The science and politics of comparing men and women. *American Psychologist, 50,* 145–58.

Earle, J. B. B. (1981). Cerebral laterality and meditation: a review of the literature. *Journal of Transpersonal Psychology, 13*, 155–73.

Eisenberg, N. and Strayer, J. (eds) (1987). *Empathy and its Development.* Cambridge: Cambridge University Press.

Eliade, M. (ed.), (1987). *The Encyclopedia of Religion* (16 vols). New York: Macmillan.

Ellison, C. G. (1991). Religious involvement and subjective well-being. *Journal of Health and Social Behavior, 32*, 80–99.

Ellison, C. G. (1995). Race, religious involvement and depressive symptomatology. *Social Science and Medicine, 40*, 1561–72.

Ellison, C. G., Gay, D. A. and Glass, T. A. (1989). Does religious commitment contribute to individual life satisfaction? *Social Forces, 68*, 100–23.

Ellison, C. G. and Sherkat, D. E. (1983). Conservative Protestantism and support for corporal punishment. *American Sociological Review, 58*, 131–44.

Ellison, C. G. and Sherkat, D. E. (1993). Obedience and autonomy: religion and parental values reconsidered. *Journal for the Scientific Study of Religion, 32*, 313–29.

Ellison, C. G. and Taylor, R. J. (1996). Turning to prayer: social and situational antecedents of religious coping among African Americans. *Review of Religious Research, 38*, 111–36.

Erickson, J. A. (1992). Adolescent religious development and commitment: a structural equation model of the role of family, peer group, and educational influences. *Journal for the Scientific Study of Religion, 31*, 131–52.

Erikson, E. H. (1958). *Young Man Luther: A Study in Psychoanalysis and History.* New York: Norton.

Evans-Pritchard, E. E. (1956). *Nuer Religion.* Oxford: Oxford University Press.

Eysenck, H. J. (1976). *The Measurement of Personality.* Lancaster: MTP Press.

Eysenck, H. J. and Eysenck, S. B. G. (1975). *Manual of the Eysenck Personality Questionnaire.* London: Hodder & Stoughton.

Faulkner, J. E. and De Jong, G. F. (1968). A note on religiosity and moral behavior of a sample of college students. *Social Compass, 15*, 37–44.

Feifel, H. (1974). Religious conviction and fear of death among the healthy and the terminally ill. *Journal for the Scientific Study of Religion, 13*, 353–60.

Fenwick, P. (1987). Meditation and the EEG. In M. A. West (ed.), *The Psychology of Meditation* (pp. 104–17). Oxford: Oxford University Press.

Festinger, L., Riecken, H. W. and Schachter, S. (1956). *When Prophecy Fails*. Minneapolis, Minn.: University of Minnesota Press.

Fichter, J. H. (1961). *Religion as an Occupation: A Study in the Sociology of Professions*. Notre Dame, Ind.: Notre Dame University Press.

Finke, R. and Stark, R. (1992). *The Churching of America, 1776–1990*. New Brunswick, NJ: Rutgers University Press.

Firth, R. (1973). *Symbols, Public and Private*. London: Allen & Unwin.

Fishbein, M. and Ajzen, I. (1975). *Belief, Attitude, Intention, Behavior: An Introduction to Theory and Research*. Reading, Mass.: Addison-Wesley.

Fletcher, B. (1990). *Clergy under Stress*. London: Mowbray.

Florian, V. and Mikulincer, M. (1993). The impact of death-risk experiences and religiosity on the fear of personal death: the case of Israeli soldiers in Lebanon. *Omega, 26*, 101–11.

Fortune, M. M. and Poling, J. N. (1994). *Sexual Abuse by Clergy: A Crisis for the Church*. Decatur, Ga: Journal of Pastoral Care.

Fowler, J. W. (1981). *Stages of Faith*. San Francisco, Calif.: Harper & Row.

Fowler, J. W., Nipkow, K. E. and Schweitzer, F. (eds), (1991). *Stages of Faith and Religious Development*. New York: Crossroad.

Fox, J. W. (1992). The structure, stability, and social antecedents of reported paranormal experiences. *Sociological Analysis, 53*, 417–31.

Francis, L. J. (1984). *Monitoring the Christian Development of the Child*. Abingdon: Culham College Institute.

Francis, L. J. (1987). Denominational schools and pupil attitudes towards Christianity. *British Educational Research Journal, 12*, 145–52.

Francis, L. J. (1991). The personality characteristics of Anglican ordinands: feminine men and masculine women? *Personality and Individual Differences, 12*, 1133–40.

Francis, L. J. (1992). Is psychoticism really a dimension of personality fundamental to religiosity? *Personality and Individual Differences, 13*, 645–52.

Francis, L. J. and Brown, L. B. (1991). The influence of home, church and school on prayer among sixteen-year-old adolescents in England. *Review of Religious Research, 33*, 112–22.

Frankel, B. G. and Hewitt, W. E. (1994). Religion and well-being among Canadian university students. *Journal for the Scientific Study of Religion, 33*, 62–73.

Frankl, V. (1962). *Man's Search for Meaning*. Boston, Mass.: Beacon Press.

Frankl, V. (1975). *The Unconscious God: Psychotherapy and Theology*. New York: Simon & Schuster.

Freud, S. (1907). Obsessive acts and religious practices. In *The Standard Edition of the Complete Psychological Works of Sigmund Freud*, ed. J. Strachey Vol. 9 (pp. 115–27). London: Hogarth Press.

Freud, S. (1910). Leonardo da Vinci and a memory of his childhood. In *The Standard Edition of the Complete Psychological Works of Sigmund Freud*, ed. J. Strachey, Vol. 11 (pp. 57–137) London: Hogarth Press.

Freud, S. (1913). *Totem and Taboo*. London: Hogarth Press.

Freud, S. (1927). *The Future of an Illusion*. London: Hogarth Press.

Fromm, E. (1950). *Psychoanalysis and Religion*, New Haven, Conn.: Yale University Press.

Fullerton, J. T. and Hunsberger, B. (1982). A unidimensional measure of Christian orthodoxy. *Journal for the Scientific Study of Religion, 21* 317–26.

Furnham, A. (1990). *The Protestant Work Ethic*. London: Routledge.

Furnham, A. and Argyle, M. (1998). *The Psychology of Money*. London: Routledge.

Galanter, M. (1982). Charismatic religious sects and psychiatry: an overview. *American Journal of Psychiatry, 139*, 1248–53.

Galanter, M. (1989). *Cults*. New York: Oxford University Press.

Gallup, G. and Castelli, J. (1989). *The People's Religion*. London: Collier Macmillan.

Gallup, G. and Proctor, W. (1982). *Adventures in Immortality*. New York: McGraw-Hill.

Garrison, C. E. (1976). The effect of participation in congregational structures on church attendance. *Review of Religious Research, 18*, 36–43.

Geertz, C. (1966). Religion as a cultural system. In M. Banton (ed.), *Anthropological Approaches to the Study of Religion* (pp. 1–46). London: Tavistock.

Genia, V. (1996). I, E, Quest, and fundamentalism as predictors of psychological and spiritual well-being. *Journal for the Scientific Study of Religion, 35*, 56–64.

Gerard, D. (1985). Religious attitudes and values. In M. Abrams, D. Gerrard and N. Timms (eds), *Values and Change in Britain* (pp. 50–92). Basingstoke: Macmillan.

Gergen, K. J. (1982). *Toward Transformation in Social Knowledge*. New York: Springer-Verlag.

Gibbons, D. and de Jarnette, J. (1972). Hypnotic susceptibility and religious experience. *Journal for the Scientific Study of Religion, 11*, 152–6.

Gill, R. (1993). *The Myth of the Empty Church*. London: SPCK.

Gill, R., Hadaway, C. K. and Marler, P. L. (1998). Is religious belief declining in Britain? *Journal for the Scientific Study of Religion, 37,* 507–16.

Gilligan, C. (1982). *In a Different Voice.* Cambridge, Mass.: Harvard University Press.

Giorgi, L. and Marsh, C. (1990). The Protestant Work Ethic as a cultural phenomenon. *European Journal of Social Psychology, 20,* 499–517.

Girard, R. (1972). *Violence and the Sacred.* Baltimore, Md: Johns Hopkins University Press.

Glik, D. C. (1986). Psychosocial wellness among spiritual healing participants. *Social Science and Medicine, 11,* 579–86.

Glock, C. Y and Stark, R. (1965). *Religion and Psychiatry in Tension.* Chicago, Ill.: Rand McNally.

Glueck, S . and Glueck, E. (1950). *Unraveling Juvenile Delinquency.* London: Oxford University Press.

Goldman, R. J. (1964). *Religious Thinking from Childhood to Adolescence.* London: Routledge & Kegan Paul.

Goodman, F. D. (1972). *Speaking in Tongues: A Cross-Cultural Study in Glossolalia.* Chicago, Ill.: Chicago University Press.

Gorer, G. (1955). *Exploring English Character.* London: Cresset.

Gorer, G. (1965). *Death, Grief and Mourning.* New York: Doubleday.

Granqvist, P. (1998). Religiousness and perceived childhood attachment: on the question of compensation. *Journal for the Scientific Study of Religion, 37,* 356–67.

Greeley, A. M. (1975). *The Sociology of the Paranormal.* London: Sage.

Greeley, A. M. (1992). Religion in Britain, Ireland and the USA. In G. Prior and B. Taylor (eds), *British Social Attitudes, the 9th report* (pp. 51–70). Aldershot: Dartmouth.

Green, R. M. (1987). Morality and religion. *Encyclopedia of Religion, 10,* 92–106.

Greenberg, J., Solomon, S. and Pyszczynski, T. (1997). Terror Management Theory of self-esteem and cultural worldviews: empirical assessments and conceptual refinements. *Advances in Experimental Social Psychology, 29,* 61–139.

Greyson, B. (1990). Near-death encounters with and without near-death experiences: comparative NDE scale profiles. *Journal of Near-Death Studies, 8,* 151–61.

Gustafsson, B. (1972). The cemetery as a place for meditation. *Lumen Vitae, 27,* 85–138.

Hall, G. S. (1882). The moral and religious training of children. *The Princeton Review, 9,* 26–48.

Hamilton, M. B. (1995). *The Sociology of Religion.* London: Routledge.

Hamilton, W. D. (1964). The evolution of social behavior. *Journal of Theoretical Biology, 7,* 1–52.

Hanson, A. and Hanson, A. (1981). *Reasonable Belief.* Oxford: Oxford University Press.

Hardy, A. (1979). *The Spiritual Nature of Man.* Oxford: Clarendon Press.

Harms, E. (1944). The development of religious experience in children. *American Journal of Sociology, 50,* 112–22.

Harre, R. and Secord, P. (1972). *The Explanation of Social Behaviour.* Oxford: Blackwell.

Harris, H. A. (1998). *Fundamentalism and Evangelicals.* Oxford: Oxford University Press.

Harris, P. L. (1989). *Children and Emotion.* Oxford: Blackwell.

Harteshorne, H. and May, M. A. (1928). *Studies in Deceit.* New York: Macmillan.

Hay, D. (1982). *Exploring Inner Space.* Harmondsworth: Penguin.

Hay, D. (1990). *Religious Experience Today.* London: Mowbray.

Hay, D. and Heald, G. (1987). Religion is good for you. *New Society, 8* (17 April): 20–2.

Hay, D. and Morisy, A. (1978). Reports of ecstatic, paranormal, or religious experience in Great Britain and the United States – a comparison of trends. *Journal for the Scientific Study of Religion, 17,* 255–68.

Hay, D. and Nye, R. (1998). *The Spirit of the Child.* London: Fount.

Hayden, B. (1987). Alliances and ritual ecstasy: human responses to resource stress. *Journal for the Scientific Study of Religion, 26,* 81–91.

Heaton, T. B. and Call, V. R. A. (1997). Modeling family dynamics with event history techniques. *Journal of Marriage and the Family, 57,* 1978–90.

Heaton, T. B. and Cornwall, M. (1989). Religious group variation in the socioeconomic status and family behavior of women. *Journal for the Scientific Study of Religion, 28,* 283–99.

Heaton, T. B. and Goodman, K. L. (1985). Religion and family formation. *Review of Religious Research, 26,* 343–59.

Hebl, J. and Enright, R. D. (1993). Forgiveness as a therapeutic goal with elderly females. *Psychotherapy, 30,* 658–67.

Heiler, F. (1932). *Prayer: A Study in the History and Psychology of Religion.* New York: Oxford University Press.

Henninger, J. (1987). Sacrifice. *Encyclopedia of Religion, 12,* 544–57.

Herberg, W. (1955). *Protestant, Catholic, Jew.* New York: Doubleday.

Hertel, B. R. and Donahue, M. J. (1995). Parental influences on God's images among children: testing Durkheim's metaphoric parallelism. *Journal for the Scientific Study of Religion, 34*, 186–99.

Hertel, B. R. and Hughes, M. (1987). Religious application, attendance, and support for 'pro-family' issues in the United States. *Social Forces, 65*, 835–82.

Hick, J. (1989). *An Interpretation of Religion*. Basingstoke: Macmillan.

Higgins, E. T. (1989). Self-discrepancy theory: what patterns of self-beliefs cause people to suffer. *Advances in Experimental Social Psychology, 22*, 93–136.

Highet, J. (1957). The churches in Glasgow. *British Weekly, 22* (29 August).

Hills, P. and Argyle, M. (1998). Musical and religious experiences and their relation to happiness. *Personality and Individual Differences, 25*, 91–102.

Hoffman, M. L. (1991). Empathy, social cognition, and moral action. In W. M. Kurtines and J. L. Gewirtz (eds), *Handbook of Moral Behavior and Development*, Vol. 1 (pp. 275–301). Hillsdale, NJ: Erlbaum.

Hoffman, M. L. and and Salzstein, H. C. (1967). Parent discipline and the child's moral development. *Journal of Personality and Social Psychology, 5*, 45–57.

Hoffmann, J. P. (1998). Confidence in religious institutions and secularisation: trends and implications. *Review of Religious Research, 39*, 321–43.

Hoge, D. R. (1979a). A test of theories of denominational growth and decline. In D. R. Hoge and D. A. Roozen (eds), *Understanding Church Growth and Decline 1959–1978* (pp. 179–97). New York: Pilgrim Press.

Hoge, D. R. (1979b). National contextual factors influencing church trends. In D. R. Hoge and D. A. Roozen (eds), *Understanding Church Growth and Decline 1959–1978* (pp. 94–122). New York: Pilgrim Press.

Hoge, D. R., Petrillo, G. H., and Smith, E. I. (1982). Transmission of religious and social values from parents to teenage children. *Journal of Marriage and the Family, 44*, 569–80.

Hoge, D. R. and Thompson, A. D. (1982). Different conceptualizations of goals of religious education and youth ministry in six denominations. *Review of Religious Research, 23*, 297–304.

Hoge, D. R. and Yang, F. (1994). Determinants of religious giving in religious denominations. *Review of Religious Research, 36*, 123–48.

Hogg, M. A. and Vaughan, G. M. (1998). *Social Psychology*, 2nd edn. London: Prentice Hall (Europe).

Holm, N. G. (1991). Pentecostalism: conversion and charismata. *International Journal for the Psychology of Religion, 1*, 135–51.

Holmes, D. S. (1987). The influence of meditation versus rest on physiological arousal: a second examination. In M. A. West (ed.), *The Psychology of Meditation* (pp. 81–103). Oxford: Clarendon Press.

Homola, M., Knudsen, D., and Marshall, H. (1987). Religion and socio-economic achievement. *Journal for the Scientific Study of Religion, 26*, 201–17.

Hong, Y.-G. (1999). Charismatic leadership in Korean mega-churches. PhD dissertation, University of Wales.

Hood, R. W. (1975). The construction and preliminary validation of a measure of reported mystical experience. *Journal for the Scientific Study of Religion, 14*, 29–41.

Hood, R. W., (1995). The facilitation of religious experience. In R. W. Hood (ed.), *Handbook of Religious Experience* (pp. 569–97). Birmingham, Ala.: Religious Education Press.

Hood, R. W. and Kimbrough, D. L. (1995). Serpent-handling holiness sects: theoretical considerations. *Journal for the Scientific Study of Religion, 34*, 311–22.

Hood, R. W. and Morris, J. (1983). Toward a theory of death transcendence. *Journal for the Scientific Study of Religion, 22*, 353–65.

Hood, R. W., Morris, R. J. and Watson, P. J. (1993). Further factor analysis of Hood's Mysticism Scale. *Psychological Reports, 3*, 1176–8.

Hood, R. W., Spilka, B., Hunsberger, B. and Gorsuch, R. (1996). *The Psychology of Religion: an Empirical Approach*, 2nd edn. New York: Guilford.

Hostie, R. (1957). *Religion and the Psychology of Jung*. London: Sheed & Ward.

Howatch, S. (1988). *Glamorous Powers*. London: HarperCollins.

Hummer, R. A., Rogers, R. G., Nam, C. B. and Ellison, C. G. (1999). Religious involvement and U.S. adult mortality. *Demography, 36*, 273–85.

Humphrey, N. K. (1983). *Consciousness Regained*. Oxford: Oxford University Press.

Hunsberger, B., Alisat, S., Pancer, S. M. and Pratt, M. (1996). Religious fundamentalism and religious doubts: content, connections and complexity of thinking. *International Journal for the Psychology of Religion, 6*, 201–20.

Hunsberger, B. and Brown, L. B. (1984). Religious socialization, apostasy, and the influence of family background. *Journal for the Scientific Study of Religion, 23*, 239–51.

Hunsberger, B., Pratt, M. and Pancer, S. M. (1994). Religious fundamentalism and integrative complexity of thought: a relationship for existential content only? *Journal for the Scientific Study of Religion, 33*, 335–46.

Hunt, R. A. (1972). Mythological–symbolic religious commitment: the LAM scales. *Journal for the Scientific Study of Religion, 11*, 49–52.

Hutsebaut, D. (1996). Post-critical belief: a new approach to the religious attitude problem. *Journal of Empirical Theology, 9*, 48–66.

Hutsebaut, D. and Verhoeven, D. (1995). Studying dimensions of God representation: choosing closed or open-ended research questions. *International Journal for the Psychology of Religion, 5*, 49–60.

Hyde, K. (1990). *Religion in Childhood and Adolescence*. Birmingham, Ala.: Religious Education Press.

Iannacone, L. R. (1996a). Rejoinder to Hoge, Hadaway, and Marler: pitfalls revisited. *Journal for the Scientific Study of Religion, 35*, 226–8.

Iannacone, L. R. (1996b). Reassessing church growth: statistical pitfalls and their consequences. *Journal for the Scientific Study of Religion, 35*, 197–216.

Idler, E. L. (1995). Religion, health, and non-physical sense of self. *Social Forces, 74*, 683–704.

Idler, E. L. (1987). Religious involvement and the health of the elderly. *Social Forces, 66*, 266–38.

Idler, E. L. and Benyamini, Y. (1997). Self-rated health and mortality: a review of twenty-seven community studies. *Journal of Health and Social Behavior, 38*, 21–37.

Idler, E. L. and Kasl, S. V. (1992). Religion, disability, depression and the timing of death. *American Journal of Sociology, 97*, 1052–79.

Inglehart, R. (1990). *Culture Shift in Advanced Industrial Society*. Princeton, NJ: Princeton University Press.

Jackson, M. (1997). Benign schizotypy? The case of spiritual experience. In G. Claridge (ed.), *Schizotypy* (pp. 227–50). Oxford: Oxford University Press.

Jackson, M. C. (1991). A study of the relationship between psychotic and religious experience. DPhil. thesis, Oxford University.

Jacobs, J. L. (1987). Deconversion from religious movements: an analysis of charismatic bonding and spiritual commitment. *Journal for the Scientific Study of Religion, 26*, 294–308.

Jacobs, J. L. (1989). *Divine Disenchantment: Deconverting from New Religions*. Bloomington, Ind.: Indiana University Press.

Jacobson, C. K. (1998). Religiosity and prejudice: an update and denominational analysis. *Review of Religious Research, 39*, 264–72.

Jakobsen, M. (1999). Negative Religious Experiences. Oxford: Alister Hardy Centre.

James, W. (1902). *The Varieties of Religious Experience*, 2nd edn. New York: Longman Green.

Janus, S. S. and Janus, C. L. (1993). *The Janus Report.* New York: Wiley.

Jarvis, G. K. and Northcott, H. C. (1987). Religion and differences in morbidity and mortality. *Social Science and Medicine, 25,* 813–24.

Jaynes, J. (1976). *The Origin of Consciousness in the Breakdown of the Bicameral Mind.* Boston, Mass.: Houghton Mifflin.

Jensen, A. E. (1963). *Myth and Cult among Primitive Peoples.* Chicago, Ill.: Chicago University Press.

Jensen, G. F. and Erickson, M. L. (1979). The religious factor and delinquency: another look at the hellfire hypothesis. In R. Wuthrow (ed.), *The Religious Dimension* (pp. 152–77). New York: Academic Press.

Jenson, A. E. (1963). *Myth and Cult among Primitive Peoples.* Chicago, Ill.: Chicago University Press.

Johnson, P. E. (1959). *The Psychology of Religion,* revised edn. New York: Abingdon Press.

Jolly, C. (1970). The seed-eaters: a new model of hominid differentiation. *Man, 5,* 5–26.

Jones, S. L., Watson, E. J., and Wolfram, T. J. (1992). Results of the Rech conference survey on religious faith and professional psychology. *Journal of Psychology and Theology, 20,* 147–58.

Judah, J. S. (1974). *Hare Krishna and the Counterculture.* New York: Wiley.

Jung, C. G. (1918). *Studies in Word Association.* London: Heinemann.

Jung, C. G. (1921). *Psychological Types.* London: Routledge & Kegan Paul.

Jung, C. G. (1933). *Modern Man in Search of a Soul.* London: Routledge & Kegan Paul.

Jung, C. G. (1936). The concept of the collective unconscious. In *The Collected Works of C. G. Jung,* Vol. 9 (pp. 42–53). The Bollingen Foundation.

Jung, C. G. (1938). *Psychology and Religion.* New Haven, Conn.: Yale University Press.

Jung, C. G. (1954). Transformation symbolism in the Mass. In *The Collected Works of C. G. Jung,* Vol. 11 (pp. 201–96). The Bollingen Foundation.

Jung, C. G. (1962). *Memories, Dreams, Reflections.* New York: Pantheon.

Jung, C. G. (1968). *Man and his Symbols.* London: Aldus Books.

Kahoe, R. D. (1974). Personality and achievement correlates of intrinsic and extrinsic religious orientations. *Journal of Personality and Social Psychology, 29,* 812–18.

Kahoe, R. D. (1977). Intrinsic religion and authoritarianism: a differentiated relationship. *Journal for the Scientific Study of Religion, 16,* 179–82.

Kaldor, P. (1994). *Winds of Change.* Homebush West, NSW: Anzea.

Kasamatsu, A. and Hirai, T. (1966). An electrocephalographic study on the Zen meditation (Zazen). *Folio, 20,* 315–36.

Kelley, D. M. (1972). *Why Conservative Churches are Growing.* New York: Harper & Row.

Kelley, M. W. (1958). The incidence of hospitalized mental illness among religious sisters in the United States. *American Journal of Psychiatry, 115,* 72–5.

Kinsey, A. C., Pomeroy, W. B. and Martin, C. E. (1953). *Sexual Behavior in the Human Male.* London: Saunders.

Kirk, G. S. (1970). *Myth: its Meaning and Functions in Ancient and Other Cultures.* Cambridge: Cambridge University Press.

Kirkpatrick, L. A. (1992). An attachment-theory approach to the psychology of religion. *International Journal for the Psychology of Religion, 2,* 3–28.

Kirkpatrick, L. A. and Shaver, P. R. (1990). Attachment theory and religion: childhood attachments, religious beliefs and conversion. *Journal for the Scientific Study of Religion, 29,* 315–34.

Kline, P. (1981). *Fact and Fantasy in Freudian Theory,* 2nd edn. London: Methuen.

Kohlberg, L. (1969). Stage and sequence: the cognitive-developmental approach to socialization. In D. A. Goslin (ed.), *Handbook of Socialization Theory and Research* (pp. 347–480). Chicago, Ill.: Rand McNally.

Kohlberg, L. (1981). *The Philosophy of Moral Development.* San Francisco, Calif.: Harper & Row.

Kohlberg, L. and Higgins, A. (1987). School democracy and social interaction. In W. N. Kurtines and J. L. Gewirtz (eds), *Moral Development through Social Interaction* (pp. 102–28). New York: Wiley.

Kose, A. (1996). Religious conversion: is it an adolescent phenomenon? The case of native British converts to Islam. *International Journal for the Psychology of Religion, 6,* 253–62.

Krebs, D. L., Vermeulen, S. C. A., Carpendale, J. I. and Denton, K. (1991). Structural and situational influences on moral judgment: the interaction between stage and dilemma. In W. N. Kurtines and J. L. Gewirtz (eds), *Handbook of Moral Behavior and Development,* Vol. 2 (pp. 139–69). New York: Erlbaum.

Kuhlen, R .G. and Arnold, M. (1944). Age differences in religious beliefs and problems during adolescence. *Journal of Genetic Psychology, 65,* 291–300.

Kuhn, T. (1970). *The Structure of Scientific Revolutions.* Chicago, Ill.: University of Chicago Press.

La Barre, W. (1938). *The Peyote Cult.* New Haven, Conn.: Yale University Press.

La Barre, W. (1962). *They Shall Take up Serpents.* Minneapolis, Minn.: University of Minnesota Press.

Lakatos, I. (1978). *The Methodology of Scientific Research.* Cambridge: Cambridge University Press.

Lambert, W. W., Triandis, L. M. and Wolf, M. (1959). Some correlates of beliefs in the malevolence and benevolence of supernatural beings: a cross-societal study. *Journal of Abnormal and Social Psychology, 58,* 162–9.

Langer, S. K. (1942). *Philosophy in a New Key.* Cambridge, Mass.: Harvard University Press.

Lans, J. M. van der (1987). The value of Sunden's role-theory demonstrated and tested with respect to religious experiences in meditation. *Journal for the Scientific Study of Religion, 26,* 401–12.

Lans, J. M. van der (1991). Interpretation of religious language and cognitive style: a pilot study with the LAM scale. *International Journal for the Psychology of Religion, 1,* 107–23.

Larsen, L. and Knapp, R. H. (1964). Sex differences in symbolic conceptions of the deity. *Journal of Projective Techniques and Personality Assessment, 28,* 303–6.

Lasagna, L., Mosteller, F., von Felsinger, J. M. and Beecher, H. K. (1954). A study of the placebo response. *American Journal of Medicine, 16,* 770–9.

Leak, G. K. and Randall, B. A. (1995). Clarification of the link between right-wing authoritarianism and religiousness: the role of religious maturity. *Journal for the Scientific Study of Religion, 34,* 245–52.

Lehman, E. C. and Shriver, D. W. (1968). Academic discipline as predictive of faculty religiosity. *Social Forces, 47,* 171–82.

Lehmann, D. (1996). *Struggle for the Spirit.* Cambridge: Polity Press.

Lehrer, E. L. and Chiswick, C. U. (1993). Religion as a determinant of marital stability. *Demography, 30,* 385–404.

Lenski, G. (1963). *The Religious Factor.* Garden City, NY: Doubleday.

Levin, J. S. (1993). Age differences in mystical experience. *Gerontology, 33,* 507–13.

Levin, J. S. (1994). Religion and health: is there an association, is it valid, and is it causal? *Social Science and Medicine, 38*, 1475–82.

Lewis, C. A. and Maltsby, J. (1995). Religiosity and personality among US adults. *Personality and Individual Differences, 18*, 529–31.

Lewis, I. M. (1989). *Ecstatic Religion*, 2nd edn. London: Routledge.

Lienhardt, G. (1961). *Divinity and Experience*. Oxford: Oxford University Press.

Loftus, J. A. and Camargo, R. J. (1993). Treating the clergy. *Annals of Sex Research, 6*, 287–303.

Lynn, P. and Smith, J. D. (1991). *Voluntary Action Research*. London: The Volunteer Centre.

McClelland, D. C. (1961). *The Achieving Society*. Princeton, NJ: Van Nostrand.

McClelland, D. C. (1987). *Human Motivation*. Cambridge: Cambridge University Press.

McClenon, J. (1997). Shamanic healing, human evolution, and the origin of religion. *Journal for the Scientific Study of Religion, 36*, 345–50.

McCrae, R. R. and Costa, P. T. (1985). Updating Norman's 'adequate taxonomy': intelligence and personality dimensions in natural language and in questionnaires. *Journal of Personality and Social Psychology, 49*, 710–21.

McCrae, R. R. and Costa, P. T. (1989). Reinterpreting the Myers–Briggs Type Indicator from the perspective of the five-factor model of personality. *Journal of Personality, 57*, 17–40.

McCreery, C. (1993). Schizotypy and out-of-the-body experiences. DPhil. thesis, Oxford University.

McCullough, M. E., Worthington, E. L. and Rachal, K. C. (1997). Interpersonal forgiving in close relationships. *Journal of Personality and Social Psychology, 73*, 321–36.

McFague, S. (1975). *Speaking in Parables*. Philadelphia, Pa: Fortress Press.

McGrath, A. E. (1997). *Christian Theology*, 2nd edn. Oxford: Blackwell.

McIntosh, D. N., Silver, R. C. and Wortman, C. B. (1993). Religion's role in adjusting to a negative life event: coping with the loss of a child. *Journal of Personality and Social Psychology, 65*, 812–21.

Malan, J. (1932). The possible origin of religion as a conditioned reflex. *American Mercury, 25*, 314–17.

Malinowski, B. (1927). *Sex and Repression in Savage Society*. London: Routledge & Kegan Paul.

Malinowski, B. (1936). *The Foundation of Faith and Morals*. London: Oxford University Press.

Malony, H. N. and Lovekin, A.A. (1985). *Glossolalia: Behavioral Science Perspectives on Speaking in Tongues.* New York: Oxford University Press.

Marcel, A. J. and Bisiach, E. (eds) (1988). *Consciousness in Contemporary Science.* Oxford: Clarendon Press.

Marrett, R. R. (1914). *The Threshold of Religion.* London: Methuen.

Maslow, A. H. (1970). *Motivation and Personality,* 2nd edn. New York: Harper & Row.

Masters, R. E. L. and Houston, J. (1966). *The Varieties of Psychedelic Experience.* London: Turnstone Books.

Mattlin, J. A., Wetherington, E. and Kessler, R. C. (1990). Situational determinants of coping and coping effectiveness. *Journal of Health and Social Behavior, 31,* 103–22.

Michael, C. P. and Norrisey, M. C. (1984). *Prayer and Temperament: Different Prayer Types for Different Personalities.* Charlottesville, Va: Open Door.

Moberg, D. O. and Taves, M. J. (1965). Church participation and adjustment in old age. In A. M. Rose and W. A. Peterson (eds), *Older People and their Social World* (pp. 113–24). Philadelphia, Pa: F.A. Davis.

Mosher, D. L. (1968). Measurement of guilt in females by self-report inventories. *Journal of Consulting and Clinical Psychology, 32,* 690–5.

Mussen, P. H., Conger, J. J., Kagan, J. and Huston, A. C. (1990). *Child Development and Personality,* 7th edn. New York: Harper & Row.

Myers, D. G. (1992). *The Pursuit of Happiness.* New York: William Morrow.

Myers, D. G. and McCaulley, M. H. (1985). *Manual: A Guide to the Development and Use of the Myers–Briggs Type Indicator.* Palo Alto, Calif.: Consulting Psychologists Press.

Nelson, T. J. (1997). He made a way out of no way: religious experience in an African-American congregation. *Review of Religious Research, 39,* 5–26.

Nowell-Smith, P. H. (1967). Religion and morality. In P. Edwards (ed.), *The Encyclopedia of Philosophy,* Vol. 7, (pp. 150–8). New York: Macmillan.

O'Connor, K. V. (1983). The Structure of Religion: a Repertory Grid Approach. Unpublished PhD dissertation, University of New South Wales, Sydney.

Osarchuk, M. and Tate, S. J. (1973). Effect of induced fear of death on belief in afterlife. *Journal of Personality and Social Psychology, 27,* 256–60.

Oswald, R. M. and Kroeger, O. (1988). *Personality Type and Religious Leadership.* Washington, DC: Alban Institute.

Otto, R. (1917). *The Idea of the Holy*. London: Oxford University Press.

Oxford Dictionary of the Christian Church (1997) 2nd edn. ed. F. L. Cross and E. A. Livingstone. Sacrifice (pp. 1437–8). Oxford: Oxford University Press.

Oxman, T. E., Rosenberg, S. D., Schnurr, P. P., Tucker, G. J. and Gala, G. G. (1988). The language of altered states. *Journal of Nervous and Mental Disease, 176*, 401–8.

Ozarak, E. W. (1989). Social and cognitive influences on the development of religious beliefs and commitment in adolescence. *Journal for the Scientific Study of Religion, 28*, 448–63.

Pahnke, W. H. (1966). Drugs and mysticism. *International Journal of Parapsychology, 8*, 295–314.

Pahnke, W. H. (1967). The mystical and/or religious element in the psychedelic experience. In D. H. Salman and R. H. Prince (eds), *Do Psychedelics have Religious Implications?* (pp. 41–56). Montreal: R. M. Bucke Memorial Society.

Palmer, M. (1997). *Freud and Jung on Religion*. London: Routledge.

Paloutzian, R. F. (1981). Purpose in life and value changes following conversion. *Journal of Personality and Social Psychology, 41*, 1153–60.

Pargament, K. I. (1997). *The Psychology of Religion and Coping*. New York: Guilford Press.

Park, C., Cohen, L. M. and Herb, L. (1990). Intrinsic religiousness and religious coping as life stress moderators for Catholics versus Protestants. *Journal of Personality and Social Psychology, 59*, 562–74.

Parker, R. (1986). Greek religion. In J. Boardman, J. Griffin and O. Murray (eds), *The Oxford History of the Classical World* (pp. 254–74). Oxford: Oxford University Press.

Pattison, E. M., Lapins, N. A. and Doerr, H. A. (1973). A study of personality and function. *Journal of Nervous and Mental Disease, 157*, 397–409.

Peacocke, A. (1993). *Theology for a Scientific Age*. London: SCM Press.

Penfield, W. (1975). *The Mystery of the Mind: A Critical Study of Consciousness and the Human Brain*. Princeton, NJ: Princeton University Press.

Pennebaker, J. W. (1989). Confession, inhibition and disease. *Advances in Experimental Social Psychology, 22*, 211–44.

Penrose, R. (1995). *Shadows of the Mind*. Oxford: Oxford University Press.

Perkins, H. W. (1985). A research note on religiosity as opiate or prophetic stimulant among students in England and the United States. *Review of Religious Research, 26*, 269–80.

Perrin, R. D., Kennedy, P. and Miller, D. E. (1997). Conservative church growth. *Journal for the Scientific Study of Religion, 36,* 71–80.

Perrin, R. D. and Mauss, A. L. (1993). Strictly speaking . . . Kelley's quandary and the Vineyard Christian Fellowship. *Journal for the Scientific Study of Religion, 32,* 125–35.

Persinger, M. A. (1987). *Neuropsychological Bases of God Beliefs.* New York: Praeger.

Pescosolido, B. A. and Georgianna, S. (1989). Durkheim, suicide and religion: toward a network theory of suicide. *American Sociological Review, 54,* 33–48.

Peterson, M., Hasker, W., Reichenbach, B. and Basinger, W. (1998). *Reason and Religious Belief.* New York: Oxford University Press.

Petrovic. O. (1988). An examination of Piaget's theory of childhood artificialism. DPhil. thesis, Oxford University.

Pfister, O. (1948). *Christianity and Fear.* New York: Macmillan.

Philbert, P. J. and O'Connor, J. P. (1982). Adolescent religious education. *Review of Religious Research, 23*(3).

Phillips, D. Z. (1966). *The Concept of Prayer.* London: Routledge & Kegan Paul.

Piaget, J. (1932). *The Moral Judgement of the Child.* London: Routledge & Kegan Paul.

Ploch, D. R. and Hastings, D. W. (1994). Graphic representations of church attendance using General Social Survey data. *Journal for the Scientific Study of Religion, 33,* 16–33.

Pollner, M. (1989). Divine relations, social relations, and well-being. *Journal of Health and Social Behavior, 30,* 92–104.

Poloma, M. (1982). *The Charismatic Movement.* Boston, Mass.: G. K. Hall.

Poloma, M. (1996). *The Toronto Report.* Bradford-on-Avon: Terra Nova.

Poloma, M. M. (1997). The 'Toronto Blessing': charisma, institutionalization, and revival. *Journal for the Scientific Study of Religion, 36,* 257–71.

Poloma, M. M. and Gallup, G. H. (1991). *Varieties of Prayer: A Survey Report.* Philadelphia, Pa: Trinity Press International.

Poloma, M. M. and Hoelter, L. F. (1998). The 'Toronto Blessing': a holistic model of healing. *Journal for the Scientific Study of Religion, 37,* 257–72.

Poloma, M. M. and Pendleton, B. F. (1989). Religious experiences, evangelism, and institutional growth within the Assemblies of God. *Journal for the Scientific Study of Religion, 28,* 415–31.

Poloma, M. M. and Pendleton, B. F. (1991). *Exploring Neglected Dimen-*

sions of Religion in Quality of Life Research. Lewiston, NY: Edwin Mellen Press.

Pope, L. (1942). *Millhands and Preachers.* New Haven, Conn.: Yale University Press.

Pratt, J. B. (1924). *The Religious Consciousness.* New York: Macmillan.

Pratt, J. B. (1950). *Eternal Values in Religion.* New York: Macmillan.

Pratt, M. W., Hunsberger, B., Pancer, S. M. and Roth, D. (1992). Reflections on religion: aging, belief orthodoxy, and interpersonal conflict in adult thinking about religious issues. *Journal for the Scientific Study of Religion, 31,* 514–22.

Propst, L. R., Ostrom, R., Watkins, P., Dean, T. and Washburn, D. (1992). Comparative efficacy of religious and nonreligious cognitive-behavioral therapy for the treatment of clinical depression in religious individuals. *Journal of Consulting and Clinical Psychology, 60,* 94–103.

Puhakka, K. (1995). Hinduism and religious experience. In R. W. Hood (ed.), *Handbook of Religious Experience.* Birmingham, Ala.: Religious Education Press.

Rasmussen, L. and Charman, T. (1995). Personality and religious beliefs: a test of Flugel's superego projection theory. *International Journal for the Psychology of Religion, 5,* 109–23.

Rees, D. G. (1967). Denominational concepts of God. MA thesis, University of Liverpool.

Reich, K. H. (1991). The role of complementarity reasoning in religious development. In F. W. Oser and W. G. Scarlett (eds), *Religious Development in Childhood and Adolescence* (pp. 77–89). San Francisco, Calif.: Jossey-Bass.

Reich, K. H. (1997). Do we need a theory for the religious development of women? *International Journal for the Psychology of Religion, 7,* 67–91.

Reid, I. (1989). *Social Class Differences in Britain,* 3rd edn. London: Fontana.

Reimer, S. H. (1995). A look at cultural effects on religiosity: a comparison between the United States and Canada. *Journal for the Scientific Study of Religion, 34,* 445–57.

Rest, J. and Narvaez, D. (1991). The college experience and moral development. In W. M. Kurtines and J. L. Gewirtz (eds), *Handbook of Moral Behavior and Development,* Vol. 2 (pp. 229–45). New York: Erlbaum.

Rest, J. R. (1979). *Development in Judging Moral Issues.* Minneapolis, Minn.: University of Minnesota Press.

Reynolds, V. and Turner, R. E. S. (1995). *The Social Ecology of Religion.* New York: Oxford University Press.

Richardson, J. T. (1985). Psychological and psychiatric studies of new religions. In L. B. Brown (ed.), *Advances in the Psychology of Religion* (pp. 209–23). Oxford: Pergamon.

Richardson, J. T. (1995). Clinical and personality assessment of participants in new religions. *International Journal for the Psychology of Religion, 5,* 145–70.

Richter, P. J. (1995). God is not a gentleman: the sociology of the Toronto Blessing. In S. E. Porter and P. J. Richter (eds), *The Toronto Blessing – or is it?* (pp. 5–37). London: Darton, Longman & Todd.

Ringer, A. L. (1987). Religious music in the West. *Encyclopedia of Religion, 10,* 209–16.

Ro, P. R. and Nelson, M. L. (1995) *Korean Church Growth Explosion.* Seoul: World of Life Press.

Robbins, M., Francis, L. and Rutledge, C. (1997). The personality characteristics of Anglican parochial clergy. *Personality and Individual Differences, 23,* 199–204.

Rokeach, M. (1960). *The Open and Closed Mind.* New York: Basic Books.

Rokeach, M. (1968). *Beliefs, Attitudes and Values.* San Francisco, Calif.: Jossey-Bass.

Rokeach, M. (1981). *The Three Christs of Ypsilanti.* New York: Columbia University Press.

Rokeach, M. and Mezei, L. (1966) Race and shared beliefs as factors in social choice. *Science, 151,* 167–72.

Rolls, E. T. (1997). Brain mechanisms of vision, memory, and consciousness. In M. Ito, Y. Miyashita and E. T. Rolls (eds), *Cognition, Computation and Consciousness* (pp. 81–120). Oxford: Oxford University Press.

Roof, C. W. and Roof, J. L. (1984). Review of the polls: images of God among Americans. *Journal for the Scientific Study of Religion, 23,* 201–5.

Roof, W. C. (1993). *A Generation of Seekers: The Spiritual Journeys of the Baby-Boom Generation.* San Francisco, Calif.: Harper.

Roozen, D. A. and Carroll, J. W. (1979). Recent trends in church membership and participation: an introduction. In D. R. Hoge and D. A. Roozen (eds), *Understanding Church Growth and Decline, 1950–1978* (pp. 21–41). New York: Pilgrim Press.

Ross, C. F. J., Wiess, D. and Jackson, L. (1996). Relationship of Jungian personality type to religious orientation and practices. *International Journal for the Psychology of Religion, 6,* 263–79.

Rubin, K. H. and Schneider, F. W. (1973). The relationship between moral judgment, egocentrism, and altruistic behavior. *Child Development, 44,* 661–5.

Ryan, R. M., Rigby, S. and King, K. (1993). Two types of religious internalization and their relations to religious orientations and mental health. *Journal of Personality and Social Psychology, 65,* 586–96.

Salzman, L. (1953). The psychology of religious and ideological conversion. *Psychiatry, 16,* 177–87.

Samarin, W. J. (1972). *The Tongues of Angels and of Men.* New York: Collier-Macmillan.

Sander, W. (1992). Catholicism and the economics of fertility. *Population Studies, 46,* 477–89.

Sarbin, T. R. (1997). The poetics of identity. *Theory and Psychology, 7,* 67–82.

Sargant, W. (1957). *Battle for the Mind.* London: Heinemann.

Schachter, S. (1964). The interaction of cognitive and physiological determinants of emotional state. *Advances in Experimental Social Psychology, 1,* 49–80.

Scherer, K. R. and Oshinsky, J. S. (1977). Cue utilization in emotion attribution from auditory stimuli. *Motivation and Emotion, 1,* 331–46.

Schoenherr, R. A. and Young, L. A. (1990). Quitting the clergy: resignations in the Roman Catholic priesthood. *Journal for the Scientific Study of Religion, 29,* 463–81.

Schverisch, P. G. and Havens, J. J. (1995). Explaining the curve in the U-shaped curve. *Voluntas, 6,* 203–25.

Searle, J. (1984). *Minds, Brains and Science.* London: BBC.

Sethi, S. and Seligman, M. E. (1993). Optimism and fundamentalism. *Psychological Science, 4,* 256–9.

Shand, J. D. (1990). A forty-year follow-up of the religious beliefs and attitudes of a sample of Amherst college grads. In M. L. Lynn and D. O. Moberg (eds), *Research in the Social Scientific Study of Religion,* Vol. 2 (pp. 117–36). Greenwich, Conn.: JAI Press.

Simpson, M. E. and Conklin, G. H. (1989). Socioeconomic development, suicide and religion: a test of Durkheim's theory of religion and suicide. *Social Forces, 67,* 945–64.

Singer, P. (1987). Ethics, *Encyclopedia Britannica, 18,* 627–48.

Slugoski, B. R., Marcia, J. E. and Koopman, R. F. (1984). Cognitive and social interactional characteristics of ego identity statuses in college males. *Journal of Personality and Social Psychology, 47,* 646–61.

Smart, N. (ed.), (1964). *Philosophers and Religious Truth.* New York: Macmillan.

Smetana, J. G. (1981). Preschool children's conception of moral and social rules. *Child Development, 52,* 1333–6.

Smith, J. M. and Ghose, S. (1989). Religious experience. *Encyclopedia Britannica, 26*, 624–37.

Smith, W. Robertson (1889). *Lectures on the Religion of the Semites.* London: Black.

Snarey, J. and Keljo, K. (1991). In a gemeinschaft voice: the cross-cultural expansion of moral development theory. In W. M. Kurtines and J. L. Gewirtz (eds), *Handbook of Moral Behavior and Development,* Vol. 1 (pp. 395–424). New York: Erlbaum.

Snarey, J., Reimer, J. and Kohlberg, L. (1985). The development of social–moral reasoning among kibbutz adolescents: a longitudinal and cross-cultural study. *Developmental Psychology, 20*, 3–17.

Soskice, J. M. (1985). *Metaphor and Religious Thought.* Oxford: Clarendon Press.

Spanos, N. P. and Hewitt, E. C. (1979). Glossolalia: a test of the 'trance' and psychopathology hypotheses. *Journal of Abnormal and Social Psychology, 88*, 427–34.

Spanos, N. P. and Moretti, P. (1988). Correlates of mystical and diabolical experiences in a sample of female university students. *Journal for the Scientific Study of Religion, 27*, 105–16.

Spickard, J. V. (1991). Experiencing religious rituals. *Sociological Analysis, 52*, 191–204.

Spilka, B., Brown, G. A. and Cassidy, S. A. (1992). The structure of religious mystical experience. *International Journal for the Psychology of Religion, 2*, 241–57.

Spilka, B., Hood, R. W. and Gorsuch, R. L. (1985). *The Psychology of Religion: An Empirical Approach.* Englewood Cliffs, NJ: Prentice-Hall.

Spilka, B., Ladd, K. L., McIntosh, D. N., Milrose, S. and Bickel, C. O. (1996). The content of religious experience: the role of expectancy and desirability. *International Journal for the Psychology of Religion, 6*, 95–105.

Spilka, B. and McIntosh, D. N. (1995). Attribution theory and religious experience. In R. W. Hood (ed.), *Handbook of Religious Experience* (pp. 421–45). Birmingham, Ala.: Religious Education Press.

Spiro, M. E. (1966). Religion: problems of definition and explanation. In M. Banton (ed.), *A.S.A. Monograph no.3. Anthropological Approaches to the Study of Religion* (pp. 85–126). London: Tavistock.

Stace, W. T. (1960). *Mysticism and Philosophy.* Philadelphia, Pa: J. B. Lippincott.

Stack, S. and Wasserman, I. (1992). The effect of religion on suicide ideology: analysis of the network perspective. *Journal for the Scientific Study of Religion, 31*, 457–66.

Stanley, G., Bartlett, W. K. and Moyle, T. (1978). Some characteristics of charismatic experience: glossolalia in Australia. *Journal for the Scientific Study of Religion, 33,* 269–77.

Starbuck, E. D. (1899). *The Psychology of Religion.* New York: Scribner.

Stark, R. (1971). Psychopathology and religious commitment. *Review of Religious Research, 12,* 165–76.

Stark, R. (1997). German and American religiousness: approximating a crucial experiment. *Journal for the Scientific Study of Religion, 36,* 182–93.

Stark, R. and Bainbridge, W. S. (1987). *A Theory of Religion.* New York: Lang.

Stark, R., Kent, L. and Doyle, D. P. (1982). The ecology of a 'lost' relationship. *Journal of Research in Crime and Delinquency, 19,* 4–24.

Steinitz, L. Y. (1980). Religiosity, well-being and Weltanschauung among the elderly. *Journal for the Scientific Study of Religion, 19,* 60–7.

Stone, S. (1934). The Miller delusion: a comparative study in mass psychology. *American Journal of Psychiatry, 91,* 593–623.

Strozier, C. B. (1994). *Apocalypse: On the Psychology of Fundamentalism in America.* Boston, Mass.: Beacon Press.

Struening, E. I. (1963). Anti-democratic attitudes in a Midwest university. In H. H. Remmers (ed.), *Anti-Democratic Attitudes in American Schools* (pp. 210–58). Evanston, Ill.: Northwestern University Press.

Sunden, H. (1959). *Die Religion und der Rollen. Eine Psychologische Untersuchung der Fromigheit.* Berlin: Alfred Topelmann.

Sunden, H. (1969). Die rollenpsychologie und die weisen des religions-erlebens. In C. Horgl, K. Krenn and F. Rauh (eds), *Wesen und Wiesen der Religion* (pp. 132–44). Munich: Max Hueber.

Swenson, W. M. (1961). Attitudes towards death in an aged population. *Journal of Gerontology, 16,* 49–52.

Tamminen, K. (1964). Religious experiences in childhood and adolescence: a viewpoint of religious development between the ages of 7 and 20. *International Journal for the Psychology of Religion, 4,* 61–85.

Tamney, J. B. and Johnson, S. D. (1998). The popularity of strict churches. *Review of Religious Research, 39,* 209–23.

Thapa, K. and Murphy, V. H. (1985). Experiential characteristics of certain altered states of consciousness. *Journal of Transpersonal Psychology, 17,* 77–86.

Thomas, C. B. (1985). Clergy in racial controversy: a replication of the Campbell and Pettigrew study. *Review of Religious Research, 26,* 269–80.

Thomas, K. (1971). *Religion and the Decline of Magic: Studies in Popular*

Beliefs in Sixteenth- and Seventeenth-Century England. London: Weidenfeld & Nicolson.

Thomas, L. E. and Cooper, R. E. (1978). Measurement and incidence of mystical experience: an exploratory study. *Journal for the Scientific Study of Religion, 17,* 433–7.

Thouless, R. H. (1935). The tendency to certainty in religious beliefs. *British Journal of Psychology, 26,* 16–31.

Thun, T. (1963). *Die Reliose Entscheidung der Jugend.* The Hague: Mouton.

Thurston, H. (1951). *The Physical Phenomena of Mysticism.* London: Burns & Oates.

Troeltsch, E. (1931). *The Social Teachings of the Christian Churches.* London: Allen & Unwin.

Truett, K. R., Eaves, L. J., Meyer, J. M. and Heath, A. C. (1992). Religion and education as mediators of attitudes: a multivariate analysis. *Behavior Genetics, 22,* 43–62.

Turner, V. W. (1967). *The Forest of Symbols.* Ithaca, NY: Cornell University Press.

Turner, V. W. (1969). *The Ritual Process.* London: Routledge & Kegan Paul.

Turner, V. W. (1977). Symbols in African religion. In J. I. Dolgin and D. S. Kemnitzer (eds), *Symbolic Anthropology: A Reader in the Study of Symbols* (pp. 183–94). New York: Columbia University Press.

Ullman, C. (1982). Cognitive and emotional antecedents of religious conversion. *Journal of Personality and Social Psychology, 43,* 183–92.

Valentine, C. W. (1962). *The Experimental Psychology of Beauty.* London: Methuen.

Van Gennep, A. (1908). *The Rites of Passage.* Chicago, Ill.: Chicago University Press.

Veenhoven, R. (1994). *Correlates of Happiness.* Rotterdam: RISBO.

Vergote, A. (1969). *The Religious Man.* Dublin: Gill & Macmillan.

Verwelj, J., Ester, P. and Nauta, R. (1997) Secularisation as an economic and cultural phenomenon: a cross-cultural analysis. *Journal for the Scientific Study of Religion, 36,* 309–24.

Vrcan, S. (1994). The war in ex-Yugoslavia and religion. *Social Compass, 41,* 413–22

Walker, L. J. (1991). Sex differences in moral reasoning. In W. M. Kurtines and J. L. Gewirtz (eds), *Handbook of Moral Behavior and Development,* Vol. 2 (pp. 333–64). New York: Erlbaum.

Wallis, R. (1984). *The Elementary Forms of the New Religious Life.* London: Routledge.

Ward, K. (1996). *God, Chance and Necessity.* Oxford: Oneworld.

Ward, S. and Kemp, S. (1991). Religious experiences, altered states of consciousness and suggestibility: cross-cultural and historical perspectives. In J. F. Schumaker (ed.), *Human Suggestibility* (pp. 159–92). New York: Routledge.

Watson, G. B. (1929). An approach to the study of worship. *Religious Education, 24,* 849–58.

Watson, P. J., Hood, R. W., Morris, R. J. and Hall, J. R. (1984). Empathy, religious orientation, and social desirability. *Journal of Psychology, 117,* 211–16.

Watson, P. J., Howard, R., Hood, R. W. and Morris, R. J. (1988). Age and religious orientation. *Review of Religious Research, 29,* 271–80.

Watson, P. J., Morris, R. J. and Hood, R. W. (1987). Antireligious humanistic values, guilt, and self-esteem. *Journal for the Scientific Study of Religion, 26,* 535–46.

Watts. F. N. (1996). Psychological and religious perspectives on emotion. *International Journal for the Psychology of Religion, 6,* 71–87.

Watts, F. and Williams, M. (1988). *The Psychology of Religious Knowing.* Cambridge: Cambridge University Press.

Weber, M. (1904–5). *The Protestant Ethic and the Spirit of Capitalism.* London: Allen & Unwin.

Weiskrantz, L. (1997). *Consciousness Lost and Found.* Oxford: Oxford University Press.

Wellings, K., Field, J., Johnson, A. M. and Wadsworth, J. (1994). *Sexual Behaviour in Britain.* Harmondsworth: Penguin.

West, M. A. (1987). *The Psychology of Meditation.* Oxford: Oxford University Press.

Whitam, F. L. (1968). Revivalism as institutionalized behavior. *Southwest. 49,* 115–27.

Whiting, J. W. M. and Child, I. L. (1953). *Child Training and Personality.* New Haven, Conn.: Yale University Press.

Whiting, J. W. M., Kluckhohn, R. and Anthony, A. A. (1958). The function of male initiation ceremonies at puberty. In E. E. Maccoby, T. M. Newcomb and E. L. Hartley (eds), *Readings in Social Psychology,* 3rd edn. (pp. 359–70). New York: Wiley.

Wilson, B. R. (1961). *Sects and Society.* London: Heinemann.

Wilson, B. R. (1966). *Religion in Secular Society.* London: Watts.

Wilson, B. R. (1970). *Religious Sects.* London: Weidenfeld & Nicolson.

Wilson, B. R. (1973). *Magic and the Millennium.* London: Heinemann.

Wilson, B. R. (1976). *Contemporary Transformations of Religion.* London: Oxford University Press.

Wilson, E. O. (1975). *Sociobiology: The New Synthesis*. Cambridge, Mass.: Harvard University Press.

Wilson, J. and Sherkat, D. E. (1994). Returning to the fold. *Journal for the Scientific Study of Religion, 33,* 148–61.

Witter, R. A., Stock, W. A., Okun, M. A. and Haring, M. J. (1985). Religion and subjective well-being in adulthood: a quantitative synthesis. *Review of Religious Research, 26,* 332–42.

Worsley, P. (1968). *The Trumpet Shall Sound: a Study of 'Cargo' Cults in Melanesia.* London: MacGibbon & Kee.

Worthington, E. L., Kuruso, T. A., McCullough, M. E. and Sandage, S. J. (1996). Empirical research on religion and psychotherapeutic processes and outcomes: a 10-year review and research perspective. *Psychological Bulletin, 119,* 448–87.

Wright, D. and Cox, E. (1967). A study of the relationship between moral judgement and religious belief in a sample of English adolescents. *Journal of Social Psychology, 72,* 135–44.

Wright, S. A. (1987). *Leaving Cults: the Dynamics of Defection.* Washington, DC: Society for the Scientific Study of Religion, Monograph no. 7.

Wulff, D. M. (1997). *Psychology of Religion,* 2nd edn. New York: Wiley.

Wuthnow, R. (1978). *Experimentation in American Religion.* Berkeley, Calif.: University of California Press.

Wuthnow, R. (1994). *God and Mammon in America.* New York: Free Press.

Yamane, D. and Polzer, M. (1994). Ways of seeing ecstasy in modern society: experimental–expressive and cultural–linguistic views. *Sociology of Religion, 55,* 1–25.

Yeaman, P. A. (1987). Prophetic voices: differences between men and women. *Review of Religious Research, 28,* 367–76.

Youniss, J. F. (1980). *Parents and Peers in Social Development.* Chicago, Ill.: University of Chicago Press.

Zock, H. (1997). The predominance of the feminine sexual mode in the psychology of religion: Erikson's contribution to the sex and gender debate in the psychology of religion. *International Journal for the Psychology of Religion, 7,* 187–98.

Zuesse, F. M. (1987). Ritual. *Encyclopedia of Religion, 12,* 405–22.

NAME INDEX

Allport, G.W. 31
Aquinas, T. 171
Argyle, M. 54–5, 61–2, 63, 128, 144
Augustine, St 2, 4, 171

Bach, J.S. 114
Bacon, F. 1
Bainbridge, W.S. 216–17, 228–9
Batson, C.D. 21–2, 31, 73, 79–82, 87–8, 153, 172–3, 192, 193, 195, 248
Beeghley, L. 189–90
Bellah, R.N. 127
Berger, P. 219
Bhagwan, the 231
Bohr, N. 5
Boyle, R. 1
Braithwaite, R. 95
Bryan, W.J. 3

Calvin, J. 2, 4
Campbell, D.T. 172
Cochran, J.K. 189–90
Comstock, G.W. 156
Copernicus, N. 1
Copleston, Bishop 2
Costa, P.T. 34

Darwin, C. 2, 99
Davie, G. 201
Dawkins, R. 4, 172
Durkheim, E. 91, 119, 164, 215

Eddington, A.S. 5
Einstein, A. 5
Erickson, M.L. 187

Fowler, J.W. 26, 28, 179, 198
Frankl, V. 38, 178
Freud, S. 9, 91, 97–104, 118–19, 132, 174–5, 239, 240, 243, 246, 247

Fullerton, J.T. 78–9

Galilei, Galileo 1–2
Gerard, D. 204–5, 207
Gill, R. 202
Girard, R. 100, 118–19
Goodman, K.L. 147–8
Graham, B. 21, 24, 114
Greeley, A.M. 54, 58, 60, 61, 77–8

Hamilton, W.D. 171–2
Hardy, A. 47, 53–4, 241
Havens, J.J. 185, 186
Hay, D. 48, 49, 57
Heald, G. 48, 49
Heaton, T.B. 147–8
Heisenberg, W.K. 5
Hensley, G. 129–31
Hills, P. 54–5, 61–2, 63, 144
Homola, M. 150, 151
Hong, Y.-G. 235, 236–7
Hood, R.W. 52, 53, 66, 73
Hunsberger, B. 78–9
Hunt, R.A. 87
Hutsebaut, D. 84, 88, 89–90
Huxley, T.H. 2–3

Jacobs, J.L. 24, 25
James, W. 21, 46, 52, 73, 161, 240, 241
Janus, C.L. 189
Janus, S.S. 189
Jensen, G.F. 187
Johnson, R.C. 194–5
Jones, J. 163, 224
Jones, S.L. 180
Jung, C.G. 9–10, 39–40, 91, 104–10, 119, 133, 240, 243

Keech, Mrs 86
Kelley, D.M. 82, 211, 212–13

SUBJECT INDEX

Printed in the USA/Agawam, MA
February 6, 2014